Foreword

If there is a nation of people that is dottier about dogs than ours, I haven't yet found it.

Possibly I am dottier than most. I met my wife Marina while out walking my dog Inca (she was walking her dog Maggi at the time). Now — seven years on — we have two young children added into the mix and are an ever-expanding inseparable unit.

Growing up, my whole family had the same obsession — not surprisingly as my father Bruce was a vet — and dogs were very much part of the family. Now with my own children I can see how dogs are managing to weave even extra magic into the dynamics of our family.

I spend so much time away filming that holidaying with my family brings special joy. And on British holidays it is lovely to be able to pile into the car en masse and set off together. It's so much more enjoyable to see the dogs full of excited anticipation rather than endure the sad expression of one left behind.

Finding a truly dog-friendly place to stay is a delight. And it's not that I'm grateful to discover people who will simply tolerate my dog — the richness goes far deeper. In my experience the people who are happy to house strangers' dogs are also the sort to be easy about children playing boisterously in the garden and sharing the breakfast table and about muddy boots in the hall.

I enjoy the eclecticism of Sawday's places and discovering the rich seams of individuality and friendliness in the owners as well as in the fabric of the places themselves. Making fresh discoveries in Britain gives me as much joy as travelling to far-flung corners. What better than to spend the day outdoors with the family, return to human warmth and deep comfort and then to all turn in for a stress-free, happy sleep — including the dog tucked up at the end of the bed.

Ben Fogle

www.benfogle.com
www.creatureclothes.com

First edition
Copyright © 2011
Alastair Sawday Publishing Co. Ltd
Published in November 2011
ISBN-13: 978-1-906136-60-4
Reprinted March 2013

Alastair Sawday Publishing Co. Ltd,
The Old Farmyard, Yanley Lane,
Long Ashton, Bristol BS41 9LR, UK
Tel: +44 (0)1275 395430
Email: info@sawdays.co.uk
Web: www.sawdays.co.uk

The Globe Pequot Press,
P. O. Box 480, Guilford,
Connecticut 06437, USA
Tel: +1 203 458 4500
Email: info@globepequot.com
Web: www.globepequot.com

Series Editor Alastair Sawday
Editorial Director Annie Shillito
Content & Publishing Manager
Jackie King
Copy Editor Jo Boissevain
Editorial Assistance Claire Wilson,
Lianka Varga
Photo processing Alec Studerus
Sales & Marketing
John Firth, 01275 395433

*We have made every effort to ensure the accuracy
of the information in this book at the time
of going to press. However, we cannot accept any
responsibility for any loss, injury or
inconvenience resulting from the use of
information contained therein.*

Maps: Maidenhead Cartographic Services
Printing: Graficas Cems, Navarra, Spain
UK distribution: Penguin UK, London
Production: Pagebypage Co. Ltd

Alastair Sawday's

Special Places
to Stay

Dog-friendly
Breaks in Britain

4 Contents

When we inhabited a tiny office and were looking for support from a bank manager, the office dog (we have always had them) jumped on his lap and spilt his tea all over him. We still got the loan! Maybe there is more to having a dog than just having a dog.

Our little whippet is buried below the office allotment, finally in one predictable place and not haring around Somerset in pursuit of the canine grail. We went, en childe masse, 'just to have a look at her' in the dogs' home; one simpering whippety stare and we were irretrievably committed – by the children. That night she bit through the fridge flex and hit the walls wailing. But she settled down to long days in the basket punctuated by hectic streaking

Photo: Mark Bolton

across the park and through distant woods. Several cars came close to extinction as they swerved to avoid her. I pretended not to belong.

Dogs, I understand now, take over. I was recently with my wife in a French B&B owned by a potty lady whose dog had legs the length of a zebra's. It would sit on Em's lap, each set of legs still firmly on the ground, stomach on her thighs – quite a feat. Drinking coffee was a challenge in that position, for Em anyway. The dog's owner was oblivious. We are all a bit mad, 'tis true, but dog owners invent new ways of being so, bless them. But it may be just that touch of madness than makes them so loveable. For they are; I am devoted to the idea. If I know I am going to a house of dogs I know I am going to be happy. There may be the odd hair on the sofa but the house won't be pompous and is very likely to be informal and, above all, very human.

I am always fascinated to learn how effective dogs (and other animals) are in raising spirits, tackling depression and improving patient 'outcomes' in hospital. I suspect that animals do an efficient job of cheering most people. If so then the impact on visitors will be doubly benign: happy owners AND happy visitors. A perfect solution. I am beginning to wonder if we should insist on every B&B having a pooch…

Alastair Sawday

It's simple. There are no rules, no boxes to tick. We choose places that we like and we are subjective in our choices. We look for comfort, originality, authenticity, and a genuine welcome. The way guests – and their pets! – are treated comes as high on our list as the setting, the atmosphere and the food.

Inspections

Our inspectors know their patch. They don't take a clipboard and they don't have a list of what is acceptable and what is not. Instead, they chat with the owner and look round – closely – and if the visit happens to be the last of the day, they stay the night. It's all very informal, but it gives us an excellent idea of who would enjoy staying there; our simple aim is to match places with guests. Once in the book, properties are re-inspected every four years so that we can keep things fresh and up to date.

What to expect

This long-awaited guide contains a wonderful mix of places that welcome you and your dog. (Or dogs – some allow two.) Not only that, each of these Special Places has a bedroom – in many cases, several bedrooms – set aside for those who come with dog in tow. (Note there are just a couple of self-catering exceptions, where dogs may sleep downstairs but not in the bedroom above; check before you book.) Dogs may NOT, however, anywhere, sleep on the bed!

There's a fascinating mix inside these pages of B&Bs, hotels, self-catering escapes, inns and glamping/camping

Photo: Paul Nattress (Kenji)

retreats. So, remote and simple or wrapped in luxury, there's something for every pooch and its owner here.

At the back of the England section and at the back of the Wales section, we also feature a number of pubs you can visit for a pint with dogs in tow – picked from our *Pubs & Inns of England & Wales* guide. All have bar areas that welcome dogs, and often gardens, too. Even, on occasion, juicy gravy bones to savour. You never know, you might like it so much that you stay on for a meal – and come back the next day for more.

Map

If you know which region you want to stay in, our maps are your best guide. Lozenges flag up properties in colours denoting whether they are catered, self-catering or pubs-for-a-pint. Eleven glamping/camping retreats are also listed, under self-catering. The maps are the perfect starting point for planning a stay – but please don't use them for navigation.

Types of places to stay

B&Bs

B&Bs, however grand, are people's homes, not hotels. You'll most probably have breakfast and dinner with your hosts and/or fellow guests, and the welcome will be personal. Some owners give you a front door key so you may come and go as you please; others like to have the house empty between, say, 10am and 4pm.

Do expect
• a personal welcome
• a willingness to go the extra mile
• a degree of informality, and a fascinating glimpse into someone else's way of life

Don't expect
• a lock on your bedroom door
• your room cleaned and your bed made every day
• a private table at breakfast and dinner
• an immediate response to your booking enquiry
• a TV in your room

Hotels

Those we choose generally have fewer than 50 rooms; most are family-run with friendly staff; many are in historic buildings – perhaps a castle or two; others have a boutique feel. All those in this book like dogs!

Inns

Our one-page inns entries vary from swish suites with plasma TVs to sweet simple rooms overlooking the sea. Staying in a pub – above the bar or in the converted barn behind – is often great value for money.

Photo above: Russell Wilkinson (Sassa)
Photo right: Winforton Court, entry 81

sitters so you can have a night out at a non-dog-friendly place.

Subscriptions

Owners pay to appear in this guide. Their fee goes towards the costs of inspecting, publishing, marketing, and maintaining our websites. It is not possible for anyone to buy their way onto these pages as we only include places that we like. Nor is it possible for owners to write their own description. We say if the bedrooms are small, the stairs are steep or if a main road is near. We aim not to mislead you!

Our websites

www.sawdays.co.uk and www.sawdays.co.uk/self-catering have online pages for all the Special Places to Stay featured here, and from our other books – around 5,000 places in total. There's a searchable database, the write-ups and two to ten photos per entry. For our glamping/camping entries, go to www.canopyandstars.co.uk

and you can also follow us on Facebook and Twitter.

Disclaimer

We make no claims to pure objectivity in choosing these places. They are here simply because we like them. Our opinions and tastes are ours alone and this book is a statement of them – we do hope you will share them. We have done our utmost to get our facts right but apologise unreservedly for any mistakes that may have crept in.

You should know that we don't check such things as fire regulations, swimming pool security or any other laws with which owners of properties receiving paying guests should comply. This is the responsibility of the owners.

We hope you enjoy our dog-friendly selection – we're almost 100% sure that you and your hound will have a brilliant holiday.

Photo above: Halzephron House, entry 22
Photo opposite: Paul Rowbottom (Maggie)

WINNER

When we wanted a handsome hound to star on the cover of this book we launched a competition, asking our newsletter readers to enter their dogs. Ten finalists' photos were posted on our Facebook page and Maggie Barker here was the dog that received the most positive feedback.

Maggie is the resident dog at the holiday cottages her owners run. She is responsible for meet and greet and is also their chief tour guide on walks up Glastonbury Tor.

Missy is an excitable six-month-old english cocker spaniel. She loves the countryside and travelling. She is happy, bubbly and always friendly towards other dogs and humans.

Ritchie is a four-year-old norfolk terrier who would like to be in the pub that his owners run far more often than he is allowed. He loves chasing cyclists but is very loyal and devoted.

Oscar is a one-and-a-half-year-old orange roan cocker spaniel. As well as walks with his brother Boris he loves going on holiday to dog-friendly B&Bs and hotels.

Eric is a border terrier. He is a great character, enjoys escaping and chasing rabbits, but most of all he loves swimming in the river Thames and making friends.

Jack is a friendly and happy 10-month-old Jack Russell. He loves everyone, other dogs, sticks, swimming and holidays in the camper van. He's a very good dog.

Jessie is a soft-coated wheaten terrier, perfectly charming to all new friends. She is a most valuable member of her family and they could not praise her enough!

Archie is a loving bearded collie and a real character. His exuberance can cause problems: he has knocked his owner over, once breaking her arm and the second time giving her two black eyes!

Poppy is a cockapoo, very friendly, intelligent and cheeky. She is just about to go with her family to her first dog-friendly hotel by the sea.

Cracker is a norfolk terrier crossed with a Jack Russell. He is a true character, one of life's great optimists, his glass is always half full!

At Sawday's you'll always find a dog under your desk, or under your feet, says Sarah Bolton (cat lover)

Now, this might strike some of you as odd but I'm a cat person. I know!! It's weird!! How could you like cats when there are dogs?? Well I do – I'm drawn to their free-spirited, haughty, lazy selves, intrigued by their slinky, nocturnal ramblings and cheered by their cleaning habits – both of themselves and their inevitable deposits. So, working at Sawday's was going to be a challenge for me, an office where it seemed quite a few workers brought their dogs to work. How would I cope? Would I be hounded out?

When I started here eleven years ago, there were three regular dog faces – Suki, an elegant whippet belonging to Alastair, Daisy the cocker/springer spaniel and Sam, the super-softy Alsatian who came in with Sheila, head of Accounts. Sam was the sort that liked to give you a bear hug and a

Photos: Annie Shillito (Daisy); Alastair Sawday (Suki); Sheila Clifton (Sam)

sloppy kiss – well, that's okay if it's George Clooney or Jose Mourinho but not so hot when you're confronted by a six-foot (on hind legs) muscular beast with big paws pinning you to a door frame, a not insignificant amount of drool swinging from his lips.

Daisy was of the 'butter wouldn't melt in her mouth' variety; in fact, nothing would melt in her mouth because it wouldn't have time, wolfed down as it was before you could bellow "nooooo, that's my luuuuuuuunch". Daisy enjoyed many lunches pilfered from unwitting newbies who had left their food in a bag under their desks – always popular when the nearest shop is a twenty-minute walk away. I can't count the number of times I would hear the words "Daisy!! Get out!" and then a shamefaced spaniel would slink past licking her chops. Perhaps one of her finest hours was when she managed to devour a whole pâté destined for an office lunch for some visitors; she had cleverly bided her time as people ferried food back and forth.

Suki was more of a nervous type – I well remember having to bring her into work in my car as she spent the whole journey with her front legs on the dashboard, quivering uncontrollably. As she became an old lady, less spry and with a whiskery grey nose, she lost the inclination to use the outside facilities and preferred to just go where she wanted: a desk leg, the carpet, a laptop bag – all were fair game.

From time to time a dog called George would pop in to wow the ladies – there was something about his quiet demeanour that endeared him to everyone (me included). His owner, Jenny, used to treat him with slight disdain – "Oh George, he's okay I suppose but he's not really mine, I've just got to look after him now the children have left home" – but we knew she didn't mean it; she too was smitten by his gentle, brown eyes and smooth, tan coat.

Then on to the scene came Dora – a doe-eyed dear of a bichon frisé. If she could have talked (I'm sure you know that all dogs CAN talk) she would have been least likely to say, "let's go and chase some rabbits" and most likely to say, "what time is my appointment at the pooch parlour?" She was a city dog and unused to the rough ways of the country types she had to mix with at the office. Known as the walking pyjama case, she was very much the lap dog, resting alongside various members of

Photo: Paul Groom (Jo Boissevain's Dora)

staff as they tapped away. Usually extraordinarily docile, she once ran amok and, to everyone's horror, made off with the draught excluder (a sausage dog), which she ran around with and tossed from side to side through barred pearly whites, snarling as we tried to extricate it. She finally bit its head off and retired under a desk to savour it. Fortunately, Dora's owner Jo is a dab hand with a needle and Old Brown Velvety lived to exclude many more draughts, before being auctioned off for charity.

Dora was soon joined by Bobbie – a Tibetan terrier – the dog with special needs. Apparently this breed suffers separation anxiety if left for more than roughly three seconds. It had previously been decided that any more dogs and we'd have a full on pack roaming about the office; Bobbie, however, was given an exemption. So we all thrilled to the sound of her howling as Nicola, then our British B&B editor, nipped to the loo or sprinted to the photocopier. After years of therapy, Bobbie was finally sent to the home of a retired couple where she's now very happy and never left alone.

So now Sawday's has fewer office dogs. Sam left for a new life in France (probably Alsace) and George departed for Cornwall. Very sadly, Suki and Daisy are no more – Suki was buried with her little bowl and familiar basket nearby while Daisy passed away two years ago leaving owner Annie bereft. Dora still potters in, but how much longer she can manage, no

one knows. She has lost a little sparkle – her nose has turned from glistening black to murky brown, her eyes are rheumy and she's hard of hearing. She still finds the occasional burst of energy for a little race around the office – surprising new recruits who thought she was a stuffed toy – but, like a former Hollywood star, her glory days are over.

There seems little chance that their like will be seen again around Sawday's. New MD Toby Sawday was not that impressed when Dora had a wee under his desk, or when she chewed through someone's computer cable. There's less appetite now

Photo above: Nicola Crosse (Bobbie)
Photo right: Jenny Purdy (George)

for a dog's birthday lunch (this went one step too far when a couple of employees cooked up a string of organic sausages to celebrate Suki's). So the dog days at Sawday's are all but over. No more will employees have to muffle the phone call to a smart hotel owner as four canine tearaways race through barking in unison. Never again will staff witness the phenomenon of a dog coming to work without its owner (a surprisingly regular occurrence at Sawday's HQ).

But wait, who's this streaking through the office pursued by Annie? What is that flash of black fur moving at lightning speed towards the kitchen? It's Elsie, much-loved successor to Daisy, just as pretty but not quite so greedy. She's sweet and she likes to play with the farm dog next door – an identical spaniel called Todd. I spot them out of the corner of my eye rolling crazily in the garden, a wild ball of black furry ears and paws.

I find myself cheered by the sight because, despite my cat leanings, I've grown accustomed to the doggy presence here. I like the way they come around for an occasional pat – and that you can borrow one at lunchtime and yomp across the fields. To be honest, you can't say that about a cat; they're not that keen on walkies, or indeed on going into the office at all.

If you're reading this, you're presumably planning on holidaying with your dog, so why not make a commitment to working with your dog, too? Productivity rises, happiness levels soar and they are a great talking point for visitors and interviewees. If you train them properly, you can draft them in to do small tasks such as handing out the post or rounding people up for meetings. So I do recommend having a dog or six at work. They are ideal for combatting stress, and your boss will LOVE it (possibly).

Photo: Annie Shillito (Elsie)

Dogs don't appreciate cultural breaks. They want beaches, woods and fields. Here's our pick of places that welcome dogs with open paws.

ENGLAND

St Ives, Cornwall
Stride the coastal path to Zennor (six miles), on to The Gurnard's Head pub (three miles) for lunch, then bus it back to St Ives.

Bodmin Moor, Cornwall
Trek up to the two highest points in Cornwall (OS Exp 109) and look to both coasts on a clear day. The remains of an iron age hill fort rewards you at the summit.

Daymer Bay, Cornwall
Lovely large sandy bay, one of the few open to dogs all year round, with proper waves.

Branscombe, Devon
Unspoilt pebble beach in pretty Branscombe where dogs can romp lead-free 50m in either direction of the car park and café. From here, a coastal walk.

Durdle Door, Dorset
Dogs on leads permitted all year round; also at Lulworth Cove and Worbarrow Bay. Dogs off-lead (except May-Sept) at Studland Shell Bay, a short drive east.

Camber Sands, East Sussex
When the tide is out dogs get a brilliant run on the sand. Well-managed beaches with Minnis Bay the favourite – but no dogs May-Sept.

Saxon Shore Way, Kent
On the long-distance footpath to the white cliffs of Dover you cross four wonderful

Photo: Angharad Barnes (Inca)

nature reserves: Conver Creek, Harty Ferry, the village of Oare and Faversham. Dogs on leads please.

Botany Bay, Broadstairs, Kent

Big old-fashioned sandy beach with rock pools and famous chalk stacks, off limits to dogs in summer (May-Sept 10am-6pm). Dogs welcome all year on Dumpton Gap beach. And gallops on the top for drying wet dogs off.

Groton Wood, Suffolk

Ancient woodland, enchanting walks: bluebells, nightingales, toads, newts and brimstone butterflies.

Wells-next-the-Sea, Norfolk

One area is dog-friendly all year round but at nesting time dogs are on leads. Big dogs go mad for the wide open spaces of nearby Holkham; at low tide the sands reach to the horizon.

Worcester Woods Country Park, Worcestershire

Acres of oak woodland, wildflower meadows and two gentle, circular walks perfect for elderly pooches.

Danes Dyke, Yorkshire

A small, away-from-it-all, award-winning beach – sand, pebbles, rock pools, clean water – reached from the car park down a steep road one mile west of Flamborough Head.

Rievaulx to Byland, Yorkshire

Not one but two ruined and magnificent abbeys in the North York Moors with a beautiful and varied six-mile walk between them.

St Bees, Cumbria

A great family beach three miles from Whitehaven – be sure to scoop every poop. For serious walkers, link up with the

Photo: Alec Studerus (Jago)

Coast to Coast Walk that runs from St Bees on the west to Robin Hoods Bay on the east – glorious.

Bamburgh, Northumberland
A vast, big skies, dog-happy beach with dunes, overlooked by magnificent Bamburgh Castle.

SCOTLAND

Culzean Castle & Country Park, Ayeshire
A 'castle in the air' perched high above the crashing waves of the Firth of Clyde, with miles of woodland walks. Leads on please for the deer park and swan pond.

Craigower, near Pitlochry, Perthshire
High-up open heathland with stunning long views, rare butterflies and scattered Scots pines. Dogs on the lead when crossing the golf course.

Hermitage, near Dunkeld, Perthshire
A woodland walk though huge Douglas firs to a folly overlooking the crashing Black Linn waterfall – best keep dogs and toddlers on leads.

Barry Mill, Carnoustie, Angus
It is a lovely walk with the dog up to Barry Mill, for the splash of the waterwheel and the smell of grinding corn: milling demos on Sundays.

Calgary Bay, Isle of Mull
Silver sands and crystal waters, exquisite on a fine day, atmospheric on a misty one. Unrestricted romps for dogs – but please think of humans too. (And the gulls and waders.)

Photo: Chris Banks (Undie)

WALES

Conwy Mountains
There's walking here as adventurous as anywhere in Snowdonia – but on a smaller scale.

Elan Valley
From Rhayader to Devil's Bridge, and some of the remotest hiking south of the Cairngorms. Miles of peaty plateaus, a few sheep, wheeling red kites and five larch-lapped Victorian reservoirs with associated viaducts and dams.

Rhossili Bay, Swansea
Miles of pristine sand at the tip of the Gower Peninsula, reached via many steps. There's enough space for dogs to run free all year – and a colourful selection of kites to bark at.

St David's Head Walk
Circular three-hour walk from Whitesands Bay, the first bit inland, the second along the wind-buffeted coastal path. Thrill to the Hats and Barrels – the rocks and reefs that still pose a threat to boats passing through these tidal races.

Usk Valley Walk
One gorgeous stretch of this 48-mile route from Brecon to Caerleon and the sea, is along the fish-rich river bank between Usk and Abergavenny. Every bit as pretty as the Wye.

Glanusk Estate, Crickhowell
Luscious acres roll as far as the eye can see – plus ancient Celtic standing stones, a bridge over the river Usk, a private chapel, farm buildings and stables, 120 different species of oak, opera (though not for the dog), and country shows galore.

Broad Haven, Bosherston, Pembs
Beautiful sheltered sand and dune bay reached via boardwalks across the famous lily ponds. Bow-wow heaven.

Photo: Jo Boissevain (Dora)

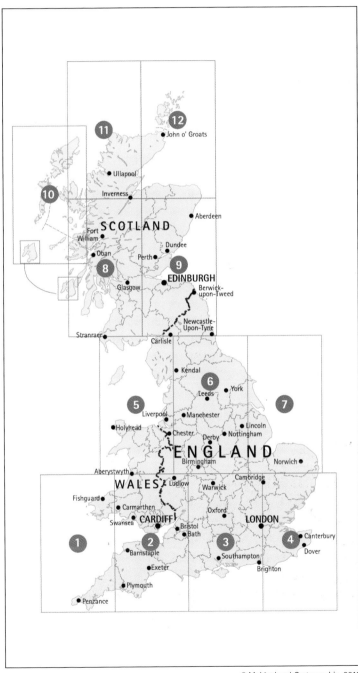

© Maidenhead Cartographic, 2011

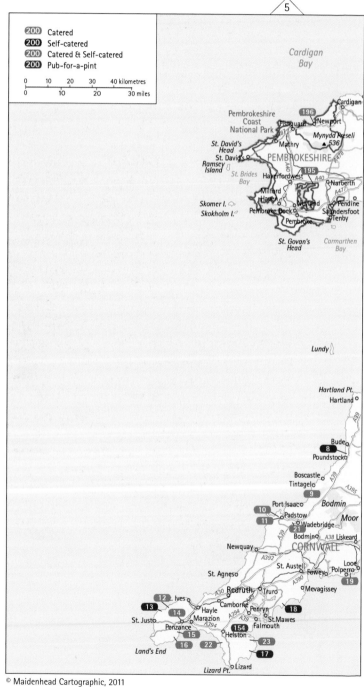

© Maidenhead Cartographic, 2011

Map 2

31

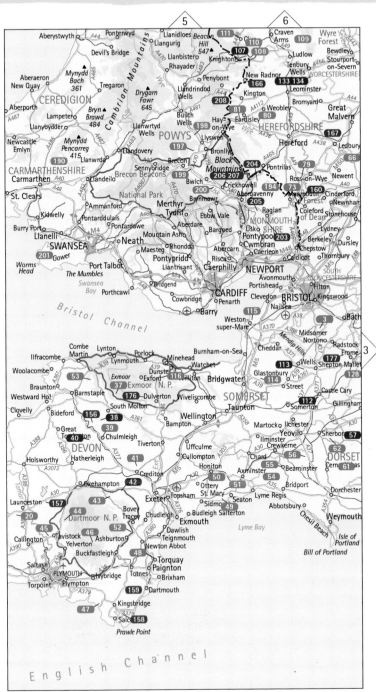

© Maidenhead Cartographic, 2011

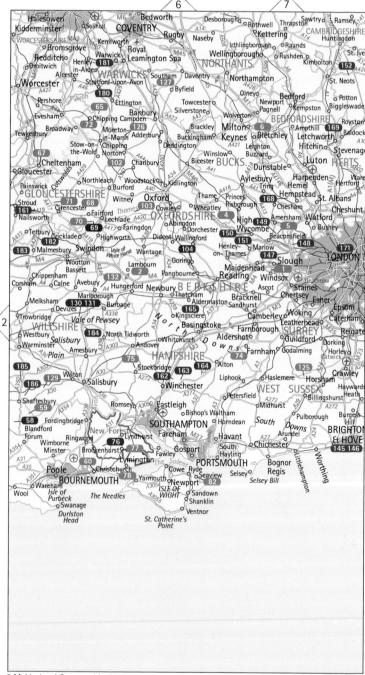

Map 4   33

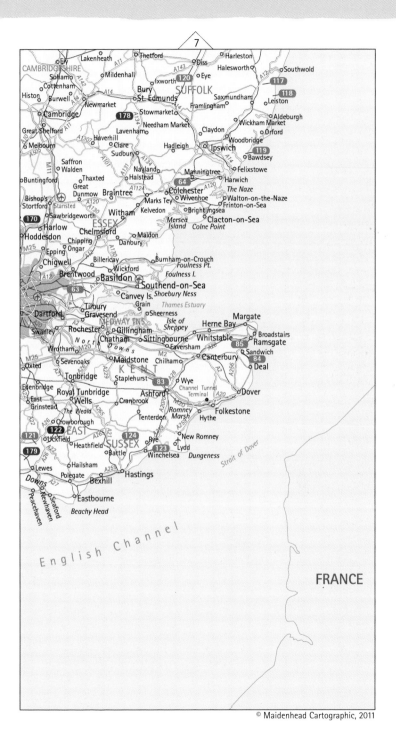

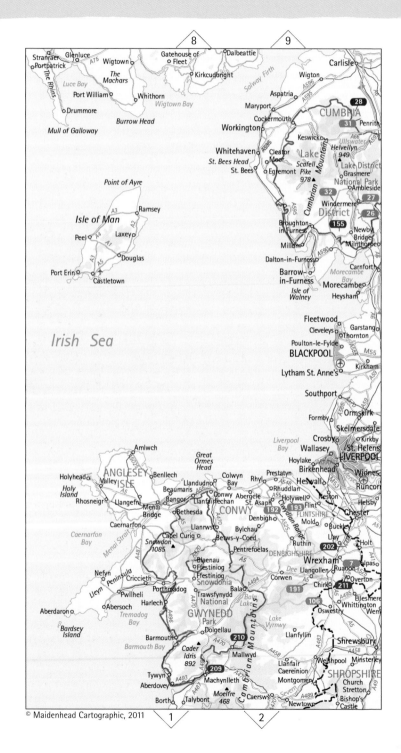

Map 6   35

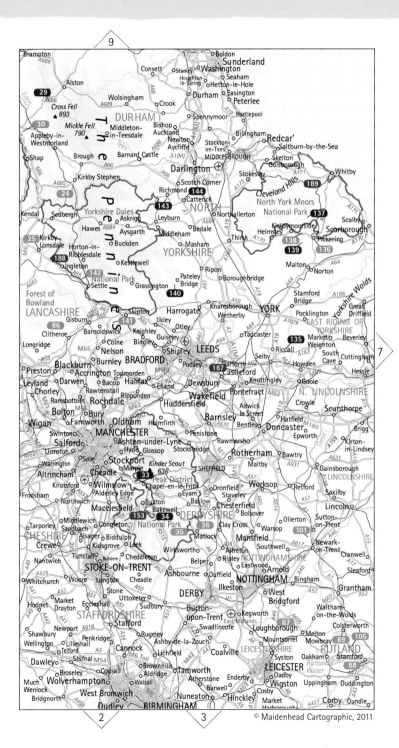

© Maidenhead Cartographic, 2011

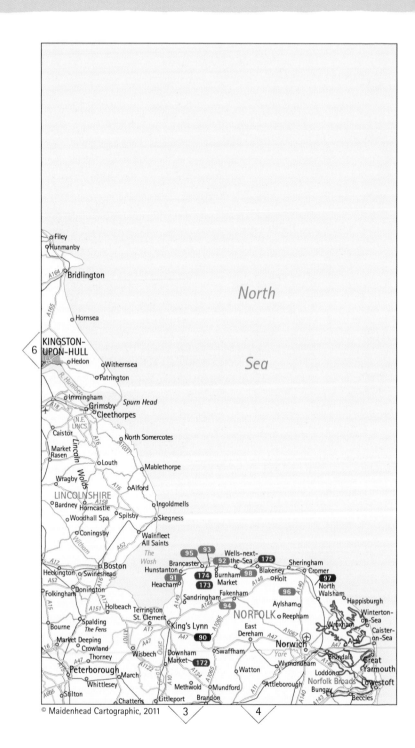

North

Sea

○ Filey
○ Hunmanby
A164 ○ Bridlington
A165
○ Hornsea
KINGSTON-
UPON-HULL
6 ○ Hedon
R. Humber ○ Withernsea
○ Patrington
○ Immingham Spurn Head
A18 Grimsby
○ Cleethorpes
N.E.
LINCS
○ Caistor
○ North Somercotes
Market
Rasen
A16 ○ Louth Mablethorpe
Lincoln
○ Wragby Wolds
LINCOLNSHIRE
○ Bardney Horncastle
A158 ○ Alford
○ Woodhall Spa Spilsby ○ Ingoldmells
Witham ○ Skegness
○ Coningsby Wainfleet
A52 All Saints
The
A17 Wash 95 93 Wells-next- 175
Heckington ○ Swineshead Boston Brancaster 92 the-Sea Sheringham
A52 Hunstanton 174 Burnham 98 Blakeney ○ Cromer
○ Donington Heacham 91 Market A148 ○ Holt 97
○ Folkingham 173 North
A15 Holbeach Sandringham Fakenham 96 Walsham
A151 Terrington A149 ○ Aylsham Happisburgh
○ Bourne ○ Spalding St. Clement 94 Winterton-
The Fens King's Lynn NORFOLK Wroxham on-Sea
Market Deeping A17 East ○ Reepham Caister-
○ Crowland A47 90 Dereham A1067 Acle on-Sea
○ Thorney Wisbech Downham A47 ○ Swaffham Norwich
Peterborough A47 Market 172 Yare Brundall
○ March A1122 ○ Watton Wymondham Loddon Great
○ Whittlesey A10 A134 A1065 Norfolk Broads Yarmouth
○ Stilton Methwold ○ Mundford Attleborough Bungay Lowestoft
○ Chatteris Littleport Brandon A11 A143 ○ Beccles

3   4

Map 8

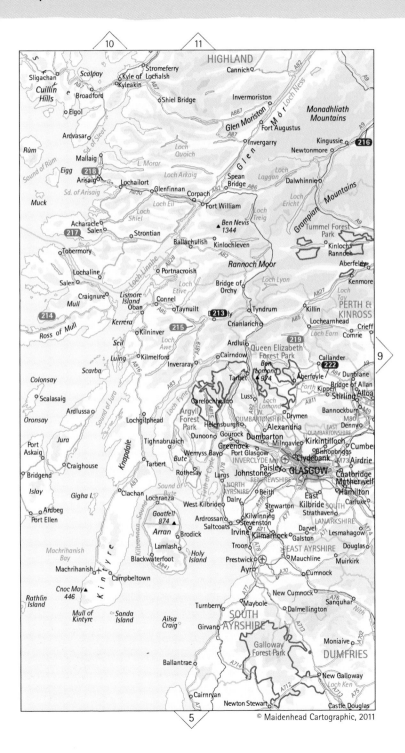

© Maidenhead Cartographic, 2011

ABERDEENSHIRE

Grantown-on-Spey
Carrbridge
Aviemore
Glenmore Forest Park
Cairngorm Mountains
Tomintoul
Rhynie
Correen Hills
Alford
Oldmeldrum
Ellon
Inverurie
Kintore
Dyce
Aberdeen

212
Aboyne
Braemar
Ballater
Grampian Mountains
Dee
Banchory
Peterculter

Stonehaven

Blair Atholl
Pitlochry
Ballinluig
Blairgowrie
Dunkeld
Coupar Angus
Rattray
Meigle
Bridge of Cally
Alyth
Kirriemuir
Glamis
Forfar
Sidlaw Hills
Dundee
Monifieth
Buddon Ness
ANGUS
Strathmore
Brechin
Montrose
Arbroath
Carnoustie
Laurencekirk
Inverbervie

PERTH & KINROSS
Perth
Bridge of Earn
Auchterarder
Ochil Hills
Newburgh
Newport-on-Tay
St. Andrews
Firth of Tay
North Sea

Kinross
Dollar
Lochgelly
Glenrothes
Dunfermline
Cowdenbeath
Markinch
Ladybank
Cupar
Leven
Buckhaven
Elie
Anstruther
Crail
Isle of May
CLACKMANNAN

Grangemouth
Bo'ness
Falkirk
Linlithgow
Inverkeithing
Burntisland
Firth of Forth
North Berwick
East Linton
Dunbar
EDINBURGH
Musselburgh
Haddington
Bathgate
Livingston
WEST LOTHIAN
Whitburn
Dalkeith
EAST LOTHIAN
Tranent
Bonnyrigg
MIDLOTHIAN
Penicuik
Pentland Hills
Lammermuir Hills
Meikle Says Law 520
Duns
St. Abb's Head
Grantshouse
Eyemouth
Ayton
220
Berwick-upon-Tweed

SOUTH LANARKSHIRE
Lanark
Biggar
Broughton
Peebles
Moorfoot Hills
Lauder
Stow
SCOTTISH
Greenlaw
Gordon
Coldstream
Holy Island

Culter Fell 748
Abington
Elvanfoot
Broad Law 830
Innerleithen
Yarrow
Selkirk
BORDERS
Galashiels
Melrose
Newton
St. Boswells
Kelso
Belford
Bamburgh
Wooler
221
Jedburgh
The Cheviot Hills
The Cheviot 815
Alnwick

Leadhills
Lowther Hills
Moffat
Beattock
Thornhill
Teviotdale
Hawick
Bonchester Bridge
Northumberland National Park
AND GALLOWAY
Langholm
Lockerbie
Dumfries
Border Forest Park
99
100
NORTHUMBERLAND
Morpeth
Bedlington
Cramlington
Ashington
Blyth
Whitley Bay
Newbiggin-by-the-Sea
Amble

Gretna
Longtown
Corbridge
Prudhoe
Hexham
Tyne
NEWCASTLE-UPON-TYNE

Map 10   39

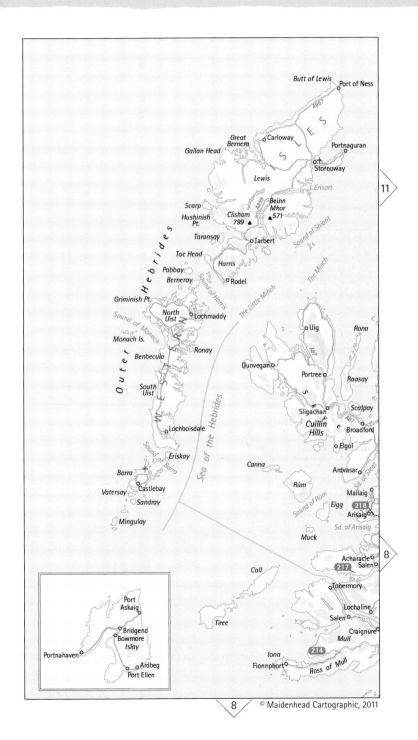

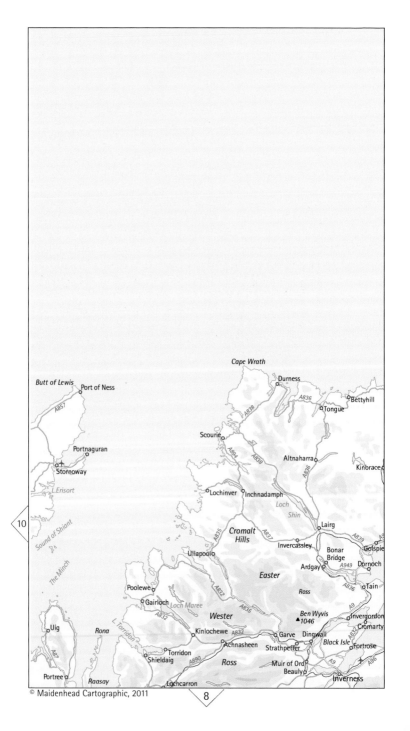

Map 12   41

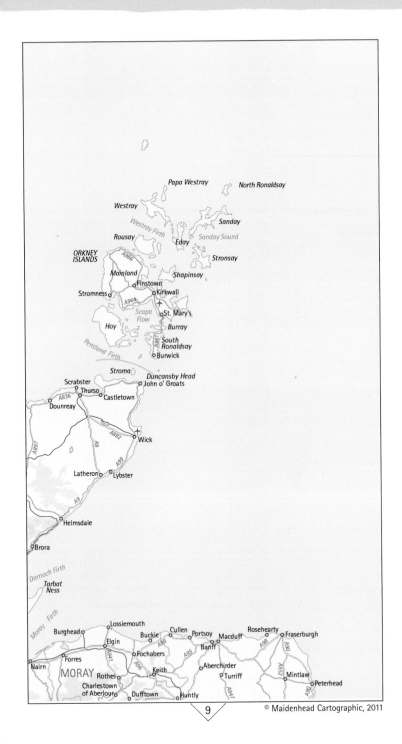

© Maidenhead Cartographic, 2011

England

The Christopher Hotel

The Christopher, an old coaching inn, sits quietly on Eton High Street, with the school running away to the north and Windsor Castle a short walk across the river. Many years ago the hotel stood opposite the school, but was politely asked to move as too many boys were popping in for refreshments; remarkably, it obliged. Recently a new broom has swept through, bringing with it colour and comfort in equal measure. A brasserie-style restaurant and a half-panelled bar stand either side of the coach arch and both come in similar vein with warm colours, stripped floors and big windows that look onto the street. In the restaurant you can stop for a bite, perhaps whitebait, wild boar sausages, lemon meringue pie; in the bar you'll find sofas, armchairs and champagne by the glass. Bedrooms – some in the main house, others stretching out at the back in motel-style – have comfy beds, padded heads, crisp white linen, a sofa if there's room. Those in the main house have the character, three are in the old magistrate's court, all have internet access and adequate bathrooms.

Price	£145-£186. Singles from £105.
Rooms	34: 25 twins/doubles, 9 singles.
Meals	Breakfast £10-£12.50.
	Lunch & dinner from £8.
Closed	Never.

Dogs in need of some exercise can romp around the big field behind

Janet Tregurtha
110 High Street, Eton,
Windsor SL4 6AN
Tel   +44 (0)1753 852359
Email   reservations@thechristopher.co.uk
Web   www.thechristopher.co.uk

Entry 1   Map 3

The Queen's Arms Hotel

This inn is utterly gorgeous, with tons of character, fabulous food, super bedrooms and staff that care. The location, too, couldn't be better: you're bang in the middle of the Lambourne Valley – prime English horse racing country – with a couple of paddocks abutting the inn and a lively crowd gathering in the bar. Inside are panelled walls, bold colours, gilt mirrors, art by the truckload and a fire that burns all day. There's a mannequin in the restaurant, seemingly dressed for a regimental dinner, and you can expect delicious food from head chef Kevin Chandler and his team: duck-eggs benedict, rare-breed sausages, baked Alaska with raspberry sauce. Bedrooms are perfectly formed: expect smart colours, wooden beds, Vi-Spring mattresses and bathrobes in excellent shower rooms. One room has its own poker table, all are named after grand old companies – Cordings of Piccadilly, Farlows of Pall Mall – and their artwork adorns the walls. You can fish the Kennet or ride out locally; this is rural England at its finest. Fantastic.

Price	£80–£139.
Rooms	8 doubles.
Meals	Lunch from £7.
	Dinner, 3 courses, about £25.
Closed	Rarely.

 A brimming biscuit jar for visiting canines & walking maps with routes straight from the door

Adam Liddiard
Newbury Road, East Garston,
Newbury RG17 7ET
Tel   +44 (0)1488 648757
Email   info@queensarmshotel.co.uk
Web   www.queensarmshotel.co.uk

Entry 2   Map 3

The Hunters Rest Inn

Astride Clutton Hill with fine views over the Cam valley the inn began life in the 1750s – as a hunting lodge. Eighty years later it became a smallholding and tavern. It's a big place, rambling around a large central bar, part wood, part stone, its bar topped with copper. There's plenty of jostling space so get ready to order from the Butcombe, Otter and guest ales and the Original Broad Oak and Pheasant Plucker ciders. Get cosy amongst the old oak and pine settles, the odd sofa and the tables to fit all sizes, the quirky wine-label wallpaper, the horse and country paraphernalia, the fires crackling away. Food is hale and hearty: shepherd's pie, pickled beetroot, crusty bread, wild mushroom risotto. Children are well looked after and there's a miniature railway in the garden. The fun continues upstairs with rooms that range from traditional four-poster with antiques to contemporary chic. All are distinctive, all have views, several look south to the Mendips; others have private terraces. Stylish bathrooms have bold tiles, roll top baths and thick towels. A most enjoyable 'sprack and spry' Somerset hideaway.

Price	£90-£125. Singles £65-£75.
Rooms	5: 4 doubles, 1 twin.
Meals	Lunch & dinner £8.25-£17.95.
Closed	Rarely.

 Private fields on the doorstep & tennis balls for fun

Paul Thomas
King Lane, Clutton Hill,
Clutton, Bristol BS39 5QL

Tel	+44 (0)1761 452303
Email	paul@huntersrest.co.uk
Web	www.huntersrest.co.uk

Entry 3   Map 2

Three Horseshoes Inn

London may be only an hour's drive, but you'll think you've washed up in the 1960s. Red kites circle a bowl of deep countryside, smoke curls from cottages that hug the hill. As for the Three Horseshoes, you find flagstones and an open fire in the tiny locals' bar, exposed timbers and country views in the airy restaurant. Simon, chef/patron, has cooked in The Connaught, Chez Nico, Le Gavroche – all the best places – and dinner is a treat, the homemade piccalilli worth the trip alone. Come for lunch and dig into baked camembert with garlic and rosemary, stay for dinner and try tiger prawns, boeuf bourguignon, then poached pear with chocolate mousse. Guests have a private entrance, stairs lead up to super-smart rooms with silky quilts, goose down pillows, funky furniture, Farrow & Ball paints. Also: views of the Chilterns and two garden rooms (nice and quiet). Breakfast indulgently, hike in the hills, walk by the Thames, hop over to Windsor. In summer you can eat on the terrace while ducks circle a sunken phone box in the pond. Only in England.

Price	£90–£150.
Rooms	6: 2 doubles, 2 garden rooms, 2 suites.
Meals	Lunch from £6.50. Bar meals from £7.50. Dinner from £15. Sun lunch £27.50. Not Sun night or Mon lunch.
Closed	Rarely.

 Dog biscuits in the bedrooms & at the bar

Simon Crawshaw
Horseshoe Road, Radnage,
High Wycombe HP14 4EB

Tel	+44 (0)1494 483273
Email	threehorseshoe@btconnect.com
Web	www.thethreehorseshoes.net

Entry 4   Map 3

Buckinghamshire B&B

Spindrift

A long, architect-designed 1933 house in a charming, sleepy village, home of the Quaker Movement; timbers from the *Mayflower* came to rest in an old barn nearby. Much of the house is open to guests and Norma is an accomplished cook; fruits, herbs and vegetables appear on the table, flowers are beautifully arranged. Traditional bedrooms are super comfortable with excellent beds, powerful new showers, and pretty floral curtains. Swim in the heated pool, walk the stunning countryside, or just slump in the sitting room with its French windows open to the scented garden.

Price	£130. Singles £75.
Rooms	2: 1 double, 1 twin.
Meals	Lunch £25.
	Dinner, 4 courses with wine, £30.
	Packed lunch £12.50. Pub 2 miles.
Closed	Never.

 Big village green to play on & treats galore – & a village wood teeming with smells & sounds

	Norma Desmond-Mawby
	Jordans HP9 2TE
Tel	+44 (0)1494 873172
Mobile	+44 (0)7963 661788
Email	john@spindrift.biz
Web	www.spindrift.biz

Entry 5   Map 3

Buckinghamshire B&B

South Lodge

Handy for the M1, this interestingly developed single-storey building appears pleasant enough. But clever Julia has introduced modern English art, dramatic lighting and contemporary furniture. A dark slate corridor lit by fluorescent multicoloured ceiling sticks leads to big airy bedrooms (one is as large as a suite) with memory mattresses and hi-spec bathrooms; all generous, all different. Velux blinds are solar-powered, heating is underfoot, rainwater is harvested for loos. You have your own patio overlooking a colourful garden, you can walk to the Stables Theatre, and Woburn Abbey is nearby. Great for house parties.

Price	£126–£148. Singles from £63.
Rooms	3: 2 doubles, 1 suite/family room.
Meals	Supper, 2 courses, £18.
	Pubs/restaurants within 0.5 miles.
Closed	Occasionally.

 Both dog-friendly rooms have access to the garden

	Julia Cox
	33 Cross End, Wavendon,
	Milton Keynes MK17 8AQ
Tel	+44 (0)1908 582946
Mobile	+44 (0)7989 541182
Email	info@culturevultures.co.uk
Web	www.culturevultures.co.uk

Entry 6   Map 3

Mulsford Cottage

Delicious! Not just the food (Kate's a pro chef) but the sweet whitewashed cottage with its sunny conservatory and vintage interiors, and the green Cheshire countryside that bubble-wraps the place in rural peace. Chat – and laugh – the evening away over Kate's superb dinners, lounge by the sitting room fire, then sleep deeply in comfy bedrooms: cane beds, a bright red chair, a vintage desk. The double has a roll top bath, the twin a tiny shower-with-a-view. Step out to birdsong and the 34-mile Sandstone Trail to Shropshire. Wales starts just past the hammock, at the bottom of the large and lovely garden.

Price	£80. Singles £45.
Rooms	2: 1 twin; 1 double with separate bath.
Meals	Dinner from £18. Pub 1.5 miles.
Closed	Rarely.

Mulsford mutt souvenir: a hymn sheet of 'How much is that Doggie in the Window' in Latin & Baskerville font

Kate Dewhurst
Mulsford, Sarn,
Malpas SY14 7LP

Tel	+44 (0)1948 770414
Email	katedewhurst@hotmail.com
Web	www.mulsfordcottage.co.uk

Entry 7   Map 5

The Look Out

A stone skim's away from one of Cornwall's loveliest bays – what a treat. Expect a warm greeting from bright and cheerful owners who welcome you with a Cornish cream tea – and there are pet donkeys, highland cattle and pigs to feed, groom and hug. This is the perfect coastal hideout. After a day's surfing or shell collecting on the privately owned beach, dine out on your decking, with a barbecue and bright blue picnic table. Inside couldn't be cosier, thanks to a well-stocked wood-burner surrounded by sofas and an all-in-one living and dining space. The lovely pine kitchen fits neatly along one wall, and there are quirky nautical touches to catch the eye. The seaside feel continues upstairs into super fresh bedrooms with spacious bathrooms, and the master room that's a delight: a telescope for stargazers and remote lighting and sound. Tuck into your locally sourced breakfast hamper before you and your dog head off to see what's on the horizon. There are 20 acres of private land around you, Bude and Padstow are close and walks start with that beach. You'll be as happy as a clam.

Price	£750–£1,250 per week.
Rooms	House for 4.
Meals	Self-catering.
Closed	Never.

 The South West Coastal Path is on the spot

Jane Montague
Wanson Mouth,
Bude EX23 0DF

Mobile	+44 (0)7880 798111
Email	info@thelookoutincornwall.co.uk
Web	www.thelookoutincornwall.co.uk

Entry 8   Map 1

The Mill House Inn

You coast down a steep winding lane to the 1760s mill house in its woodland setting, with Trebarwith's spectacular beach – all surf and sand a ten-minute walk away. It's quite a setting. Back at the inn, the bar combines the best of Cornish old and Cornish new: big flagged floor, wooden tables, chapel chairs, two leather sofas by a wood-burning stove. The swanky dining room overlooking the burbling mill stream is light, elegant and very modern. Settle down to fish chowder; rib-eye steak with wild mushroom and pink peppercorn fricassée; rose, jasmine and orchid panna cotta. Bar meals are more traditional, they do lovely barbecues in summer and, be warned, a band often plays at the weekend. In keeping with the peaceful seaside setting, simple bedrooms are uncluttered with a fresh feel, and the smaller standard rooms have good shower rooms. Room character and comfort have been raised following some essential upgrading. Coastal trails lead to Tintagel, official home of the Arthurian legends. Walking, biking, surfing, crabbing... you couldn't possibly be bored.

Price	£75–£130.
Rooms	8: 7 doubles, 1 family room.
Meals	Lunch from £7.50. Dinner from £12. Sunday lunch, 3 courses, £17.85.

 A perfect place for mutts to stay, often frequented by 'Dodger', star of the TV programme *Doc Martin*

Mark & Kep Forbes
Trebarwith,
Tintagel PL34 0HD

Tel	+44 (0)1840 770200
Email	management@themillhouseinn.co.uk
Web	www.themillhouseinn.co.uk

Woodlands Country House

A big house in the country, half a mile west of Padstow, with long views across the fields down to the sea. Pippa and Hugo came west to renovate and have done a fine job. You get an honesty bar in the sitting room, a croquet lawn by the fountain and stripped floors in the airy breakfast room, where a legendary feast is served each morning. Spotless bedrooms are smart and homely, some big, some smaller, all with a price to match, but it's worth splashing out on the bigger ones, which are away from the road and have watery views. Expect lots of colour, pretty beds, floral curtains, Frette linen. One room has a four-poster, another comes with a claw-foot bath, there are robes in adequate bathrooms. All have flat-screen TVs and DVD players, with a library of films downstairs. WiFi runs throughout, there's a computer guests can use, taxis can be ordered – but make sure you book restaurants in advance, especially Rick Stein's or Jamie Oliver's Fifteen. Hire bikes in town and follow the Camel trail, take the ferry over to Rock, head down to the beach, walk on the cliffs – bow-wow heaven.

Price	£98-£138. Singles from £74.
Rooms	8: 4 doubles, 3 twins/doubles, 1 four-poster.
Meals	Picnic £18. Restaurants in Padstow, 0.5 miles.
Closed	20 December-1 February.

For dog walking there's the refreshing pooch-tastic coastal path, plus local pub & restaurant maps

Hugo & Pippa Woolley
Treator,
Padstow PL28 8RU
Tel +44 (0)1841 532426
Email info@woodlands-padstow.co.uk
Web www.woodlands-padstow.co.uk

Entry 10 Map 1

The Seafood Restaurant

In 1975 a young chef called Rick Stein opened a restaurant in Padstow; the rest is history. Now he has three more, a deli and a pâtisserie, a seafood cookery school and 40 cossetting bedrooms. Despite this success his homespun philosophy has never wavered: buy the freshest seafood on the quay from the fisherman, cook it simply and eat it with friends. It is a viewpoint half the country seems to share. Come out of season when you can make the most of the coast, and the beaches (most of them!) are open to dogs. Walk up to the lighthouse on Trevose Head, paddle in the estuary, then drop into the lively restaurant for a fabulous meal, perhaps razor clams with garlic and parsley, chargrilled Dover sole with sea salt and lime, apple and quince tartlet with vanilla ice cream. Book in for the night and a table in the restaurant is yours – though beautiful bedrooms are so seductive you'll find them almost impossible to leave. They are scattered about town, some above the restaurant, others over at the bistro or just around the corner. Expect the best fabrics, gorgeous bathrooms, and the odd terrace with estuary views.

Price	£97–£280. £20 per dog per night.
Rooms	40: 6 doubles, 8 twins/doubles, 16 four-posters, 10 doubles.
Meals	Lunch £29.95. Dinner £55. Tasting menu £67.
Closed	Christmas.

A fleecy blanket to snuggle in – perfect after a run to the lighthouse

Rick & Jill Stein
Riverside, Padstow PL28 8BY

Tel	+44 (0)1841 532700
Email	reservations@rickstein.com
Web	www.rickstein.com

The Gurnard's Head

The coastline here is utterly magical and the walk up to St Ives is hard to beat. Secret beaches appear at low tide, cliffs tumble down to the water and wild flowers streak the land pink in summer. As for the hotel, you couldn't hope for a better base. It's earthy, warm, stylish and friendly, with airy interiors, colour-washed walls, stripped wooden floors and fires at both ends of the bar. Logs are piled up in an alcove, maps and art hang on the walls, books fill every shelf; if you pick one up and don't finish it, take it home and post it back. Rooms are warm and cosy, simple and spotless, with Vi-Spring mattresses, crisp white linen, throws over armchairs, Roberts radios. Downstairs, super food, all homemade, can be eaten wherever you want: in the bar, in the restaurant or out in the garden in good weather. Snack on rustic delights – pork pies, crab claws, half a pint of Atlantic prawns – or tuck into more substantial treats, maybe mussels with white wine, pork loin with grain mustard, then lemon posset and rhubarb. Picnics are easily arranged and there's bluegrass folk music in the bar most weeks.

Price	£95–£165. Singles from £75. Half-board from £70 p.p.
Rooms	7: 4 doubles, 3 twins/doubles.
Meals	Lunch from £4.50. Dinner, 3 courses, about £27.50.
Closed	24 & 25 December & 4 days in mid-January.

Welcome biscuits, dog towels & bowls, & reams of notes on good walks

Charles & Edmund Inkin
Zennor, St Ives TR26 3DE
Tel   +44 (0)1736 796928
Email   enquiries@gurnardshead.co.uk
Web   www.gurnardshead.co.uk

Entry 12   Map 1

Wheal Rose

Just above the sandy cove of Portheras, on Britain's most scenic coast, a tiny lane leads down to a detached farmhouse with stunning views. The old part of the cottage has all the charm you would expect and has been beautifully redone: spacious yet cosy sitting room with painted beams in pale colours, a log-burner for nights in, cool Cornish art in alcoves and window sills, and a dog basket and dog bowls for your best friend. This is a great cottage for family get-togethers as there is plenty for everyone to do: take the 15-minute walk down to the cove for a bracing dip, or idle away an afternoon watching the seals. If you fancy spoiling yourself with a Cornish cream tea, it's a gentle stroll across the fields to The Old School House and Gallery at Morvah. Or stride out along wild stretches of coastal path through historic mining landscapes dotted with ancient field systems, towards Zennor and St Ives. As dusk falls, light the barbecue, pour a glass of your favourite tipple, and watch the sun descend into the ocean. Note too the comforting presence of the Lighthouse at Pendeen Watch.

Price	£630–£1,490 per week.
Rooms	Cottage for 7.
Meals	Self-catering.
Closed	Rarely.

 A ten-minute walk to the Cornish coastal path & our local sandy cove, where dogs may frolic all year round

Nicky Gregorowski
Higher Chypraze, Morvah,
Pendeen, Penzance TR19 7TU
Tel   +44 (0)1386 881454
Email   gregorowski@hotmail.com
Web   www.whealrose.co.uk

The Abbey Hotel

The Abbey is a rare gem, a hotel that refuses to enter the modern world, choosing instead to linger in its serenely elegant past. The feel is of a smart country house, and the drawing room – roaring fire, huge gilt mirror, walls of books, rugs on stripped floors – is hard to beat. Drinks are brought to you, there's a bust of Lafayette, exquisite art and huge arched windows that rise to the ceiling and open onto the loveliest walled garden; step out in summer for afternoon tea or a breakfast to remember. The house dates from 1660 and has views to the front of Penzance harbour and St Michael's Mount. Country-house bedrooms are grandly quirky; in one you pull open a cupboard to find an en suite shower. Sink into big comfy beds wrapped up in crisp linen. There are chandeliers, quilted bedspreads, French armoires, plump-cushioned armchairs. You breakfast indulgently in a panelled dining room with a fire crackling and assorted busts and statues for company. Kind staff go the extra mile and point you in the right direction; St Ives, Zennor, Mousehole and the Minack all wait.

Price	£105–£200. Suite £150–£210. Singles from £75. Flat £115–£170.
Rooms	7 + 1: 4 doubles, 1 twin, 1 family room, 1 suite. Self-catering flat for 4.
Meals	Restaurants nearby.
Closed	Rarely.

 A tasty sausage at breakfast

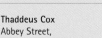

Thaddeus Cox
Abbey Street,
Penzance TR18 4AR
Tel   +44 (0)1736 366906
Email   hotel@theabbeyonline.co.uk
Web   www.theabbeyonline.co.uk

Entry 14   Map 1

Old Coastguard Hotel

Not much happens in Mousehole. The Spanish sacked the place in 1595 and since then it's been pretty quiet. As for the Old Coastguard, it sits bang on the water with lush lawns running down to the sea. There are decks on two levels to make the most of it all, while eight bedrooms have balconies with views across jostling boats to an ancient harbour. Follow the coastal path down and you'll find fishermen mending their nets before heading out to catch lobster, scallops and crab, much of which will land on your plate. Expect to eat well, perhaps deep fried crispy squid, crab linguine with chilli and garlic, treacle tart with vanilla ice cream. Airy interiors mix seaside colours to great effect. You'll find stripped boards, tongue-and-groove panelling, walls of glass to frame the view. Bedrooms come in uncluttered style: most look out to sea, you get white walls to soak up the light, flat-screen TVs, DVD players, robes in sparkling bathrooms. There's a small reading room and free internet access, then 20 palm trees in the garden. Head west for the Minack, then north to Zennor and St Ives. Wonderful.

Price	£120–£180. Suite £190–£210.
Rooms	14: 11 doubles, 2 twins/doubles, 1 suite.
Meals	Lunch from £4.95. Dinner about £25.
Closed	9 January–10 February.

The coastal path is at the bottom of garden... & blankets, bowls & towels are provided for afterwards

Tamsyn Bond
The Parade, Mousehole,
Penzance TR19 6PR

Tel	+44 (0)1736 731222
Email	bookings@oldcoastguardhotel.co.uk
Web	www.oldcoastguardhotel.co.uk

Entry 15   Map 1

The Cove

You're lost in the lanes west of Penzance with a pirate's cove at the end of the garden. The position here is fabulous, with beautiful local walks and views from the terrace that shoot out to sea. As for the Cove, well, it's not your average hotel. The trick here is that every apartment comes with a cool little kitchen, so you can look after yourself if you want. Not that you have to – the hotel has a fabulous restaurant and will cater to your every need, from Easter to November. Most people tend to do a bit of both and it works particularly well for young families, so much so there's a kids' club in summer. An airy seaside elegance runs throughout (white walls, coastal art, lots of glass to bring in the light), but the hub of the hotel is the terrace, where loungers circle the pool. Rooms – some huge, others smaller – all have a similar style: sisal matting, aqua blue fabrics, comfy beds, super little bathrooms. As for the restaurant, you can nip down for breakfast, lunch or a rather good dinner, perhaps Serrano ham with black figs, poached lobster with a rocket salad, a plate of West Country cheeses.

Price	Studios: £115–£195.
	Apartments: £115–£375.
	Min. 7 nights mid-July to Aug.
Rooms	15: 2 studios, 13 apartments.
Meals	Full English brought to you, £9.95.
	Lunch from £5. Dinner £22–£40.
Closed	Nov–pre-Easter.
	Self-catering open all year.

Beautiful coastal walks from the door

	Lee Magner
	Lamorna,
	Penzance TR19 6XH
Tel	+44 (0)1736 731411
Email	contact@thecovecornwall.com
Web	www.thecovecornwall.com

Entry 16   Map 1

Kilter House

A charming and stylish house a mile from the sea. Come for peace, privacy and comfort in spades. The house is large, with its fabulous country kitchen the hub. A long farmhouse table, sofas and a fireplace at one end, all the gadgetry at the other – ideal for a lazy family breakfast or an evening with friends. In the sitting room, deep sofas front a log-filled fireplace; after a hike, snuggle up with the dogs and toast your toes. Upstairs are bedrooms with large beds and crisp linen; bathrooms are immaculate, one with a corner bath, and if you are two families together, you get a staircase each. For children there are bunk beds, table football, gates on the stairs. Outside is an enormous garden with a lawn where animals and children can play to their hearts' content, and a lovely courtyard with sunloungers at the front: fire up the barbecue. Down the road is pretty Coverack, a seaside village with rockpools and sand at low tide and a pub to retreat to when it's high. The coastal path runs through the village and beyond is the Helford river, one of Cornwall's most special secrets.

Price	£650–£2,050 per week.
Rooms	House for 9.
Meals	Self-catering.
Closed	Never.

 Doggie guide to local walks & dog-friendly beaches. Tennis balls supplied for garden games

Harriet Gordon-Brown
Coverack,
Helston TR12 6TN
Tel   +44 (0)1254 826179
Email   info@kilterhouse.com
Web   www.kilterhouse.com

Entry 17   Map 1

Round House East

Like sentries guarding the village pub and green below are four 1820s roundhouses with pretty thatched roofs – and crosses to keep the devil away. Ingenious how everything fits so neatly within the curving walls of yours (from solid wood floors to fitted wardrobes), a warm quirky bolthole for two. Local art and retro touches – a tide clock, a 50s sideboard, bold upholstery – rub shoulders with vast TVs (in sitting room and cosy upstairs bedroom). In the kitchen extension, past the lime green fridge, is a glass dining table overlooking the pretty cottage garden. Take a morning espresso out to your lounger and watch wood pigeons peck and seagulls swoop. When night falls, soak in the roll top bath… then retire to a gothic super-sized bed under a vaulted ceiling, where an Art Deco mirror and a pink-and-purple rug continue the fun retro theme. Bring bicycles, dogs, flip flops for the beach and walking boots for the South West Coastal Path; the Roseland Peninsula is awash with coves and seaside restaurants. Or take the King Harry Ferry to Truro – one of the world's most scenic ferry routes.

Price	£379-£955 per week.
Rooms	House for 2.
Meals	Self-catering.
Closed	Never.

 Toy cupboard filled with squeakies, balls & tug toys to take to the beach

Ian Rose
Pendower Road, Veryan,
Truro TR2 5QL

Tel	+44 (0)20 7483 4630
Email	enquiries@roundhousecornwall.co.uk
Web	www.roundhousecornwall.co.uk

Entry 18   Map 1

Talland Bay Hotel

The position here is magical. First you plunge down rollercoaster lanes, then you arrive at this delicious hotel. Directly in front, the sea sparkles through pine trees, an old church crowns the hill and two acres of lawns end in a ha-ha, where the land drops down to the bay. Vanessa came to renovate and has done so magnificently, breathing new life into this venerable old hotel. There's a sitting room bar in blue and white, a roaring fire in the half-panelled dining room, refurbished bedrooms that take your breath away. Masses of art hangs on the walls, there are vast sofas, polished flagstones, a gravelled terrace for afternoon tea. Follow the coastal path over the hill, then return for an excellent dinner, perhaps chicken liver pâté with pistachio brioche, fillet of sea bream with olives and lemon, hot chocolate fondant with white chocolate sorbet. And so to bed. All rooms have been refurbished and are ready to pamper you rotten. Expect rich colours, vast beds, beautiful linen, the odd panelled wall. One has a balcony, a couple open onto terraces, all have seriously swanky bathrooms.

Price	£100-£200. Suites £155-£225. Half-board from £80 p.p.
Rooms	22: 17 twins/doubles, 3 suites, 2 singles.
Meals	Lunch from £4.95. Dinner £32-£38.
Closed	Never.

Special mini dog cupcakes on arrival & food mats to guzzle them from

Vanessa Rees
Porthallow, Looe PL13 2JB
Tel   +44 (0)1503 272667
Email   info@tallandbayhotel.co.uk
Web   www.tallandbayhotel.co.uk

Entry 19   Map 1

Hornacott

Little dog Teddy considers the garden a very good spot for rabbit watching, and so it is, in its lovely valley setting, with seats in corners for humans poised to catch the evening sun. The peaceful house is named after the hill and you have a private entrance to your airy suite: a room with a large bed plus a lofty sitting room with a balcony and windows that look down onto the valley. With CD player, music, chocolates and magazines you are truly self-contained. Jos, a kitchen designer, and Mary-Anne love having guests and living the slow life – busily! Expect top-notch local produce and free-range eggs for breakfast.

Roskear

Drive down the fields to this 17th-century working farmhouse, a blissfully peaceful escape. A large sitting room with log fire, a warm and smiling hostess, happy dogs, comfortable bedrooms, a cheerful Aga, fabulous estuary views – country life at its most charming. Delicious breakfasts are served on blue china, doors open to the garden on sunny days and there are acres of woodland and grassland to explore. Good restaurants include Rick Stein's, the ferry takes you to Rock, surfing is a short drive and the Camel cycle trail is nearby (hire bikes locally). Uncomplicated, good value B&B.

Price	From £95. Singles £50.	Price	From £70. Singles £35.
Rooms	2: 1 suite; 1 twin with separate shower.	Rooms	2: 1 double with separate bath; 1 twin/double sharing bath (let to same party only).
Meals	Dinner, 3 courses, £20. BYO. Pubs/restaurants 4.5 miles.	Meals	Pubs/restaurants 0.5-6 miles.
Closed	Christmas.	Closed	Rarely.

 Teddy says, "If we have dogs to stay I will share my biscuits & sometimes an extra sausage too"

Friendly resident dogs to play with, & a free range field to run in

Jos & Mary-Anne Otway-Ruthven
South Petherwin,
Launceston PL15 7LH
Tel   +44 (0)1566 782461
Email   otwayruthven@btinternet.com
Web   www.hornacott.co.uk

Rosina Messer-Bennetts
St Breock, Wadebridge PL27 7HU
Tel   +44 (0)1208 812805
Mobile   +44 (0)7748 432013
Email   rosina@roskear.com
Web   www.roskear.com

Entry 20   Map 2

Entry 21   Map 1

Cornwall

Halzephron House

The coastal path runs through the grounds and the view is to die for – you can see St Michael's Mount on a clear day. Be greeted by homemade biscotti and organic coffee roasted in Cornwall: lovely Lucy and Roger – foodies, designers – have a café and shop in the cottage next door. Bedrooms are contemporary, quirky and full of charm. Across the walled garden are the Cabin and the Observatory, each an enchanting nest for two, plus well-behaved dog – drift off under goosedown to the lapping waves below. You can walk to three amazing beaches, a 13th-century church, a golf course and a gastropub. Heaven.

Cornwall

The Hen House

Greenies will be delighted: Sandy and Gary, truly welcoming, are passionately committed to sustainability and happy to advise on the best places to eat, visit and walk; there are OS maps on loan too. Enlightened souls will adore the spacious colourful rooms, the bright fabrics, the wildflower meadow with inviting sun loungers, the pond, the tai chi, the fairy-lit courtyard at night, the scrumptious locally sourced breakfasts, the birdsong. There's even a sanctuary room for reiki and reflexology set deep into the earth in this generous, peaceful, dog-inviting retreat.

Price	£80–£130.
Rooms	3: 1 suite. Cabin: 1 suite. Observatory: 1 double.
Meals	Pub 0.25 miles.
Closed	Rarely.

Garden access to the coastal path – & magnificent beaches in both directions

Lucy & Roger Thorp
Gunwalloe,
Helston TR12 7QD
Tel   +44 (0)1326 241719
Email   lucy@halzephronhouse.co.uk
Web   www.halzephronhouse.co.uk

Entry 22   Map 1

Price	From £80. Singles £70.
Rooms	3: 2 doubles. Barn: 1 double.
Meals	Pub/restaurant 1 mile.
Closed	Rarely.

Runs around the exquisite wildflower meadow, safely fenced, specially for dogs

Sandy & Gary Pulfrey
Tregarne, Manaccan,
Helston TR12 6EW
Tel   +44 (0)1326 280236
Mobile   +44 (0)7809 229958
Email   henhouseuk@aol.com
Web   www.thehenhouse-cornwall.co.uk

Entry 23   Map 1

The Black Swan

This fabulous small hotel is hard to fault. Bang in the middle of a pretty village surrounded by blistering country it's all things to all men: a smart restaurant, a lively bar, a village shop; and they hold a music festival here in September. A stream runs through an enormous garden, where you can eat in good weather as dogs play; the hens live in one corner. Inside, warm country interiors fit the mood perfectly. You get fresh flowers, tartan carpets, games on the piano, books galore. There's a locals' bar for local ales and a sitting-room bar with an open fire, but the hub of the hotel is the main bar. You can eat wherever you want, including the airy restaurant at the front where you dig into delicious country food (the meat is from the fields around you), perhaps smoked trout terrine, steak and venison casserole, lemon and ginger syllabub. (They even sell food and biscuits for dogs.) Excellent bedrooms are fantastic for the money: pretty colours, beautiful linen, smart furniture, super bathrooms. The Lakes and Dales are close, and children are made as welcome as dogs. A very happy place. *Two dog-friendly rooms available.*

Price	£75–£100. Suites £115–£125. Singles £50.
Rooms	14: 11 twins/doubles, 2 suites, 1 single.
Meals	Lunch from £3.95. Dinner, 3 courses, £20–£30.
Closed	Christmas Day.

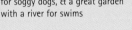 Drying facilities & free dog towels for soggy dogs, & a great garden with a river for swims

Alan & Louise Dinnes
Ravenstonedale,
Kirkby Stephen CA17 4NG
Tel   +44 (0)15396 23204
Email   enquiries@blackswanhotel.com
Web   www.blackswanhotel.com

Entry 24   Map 6

The Sun Inn

Extreme pleasure awaits those who book into The Sun. Not only is this ancient inn a delight to behold – thick stone walls, wood-burners, windows onto a cobbled passageway, beer pumps ready for action – but the town itself is dreamy, another jewel of the north. The inn backs onto St Mary's churchyard, where wild flowers prosper and bumble bees ply their trade. Potter across and find 'one of the loveliest views in England, and therefore the world' to quote Ruskin. Herons fish the river, lambs graze the fields, hills soar into a vast sky. Turner painted it in 1825. Back at The Sun, all manner of good things. Warm interiors, recently refurbished, come in elegant country style, keeping the feel of the past while dressing it up in smart clothes. You'll find old stone walls, boarded floors, cosy window seats, newspapers in a rack. Airy, uncluttered bedrooms upstairs are just as good; expect trim carpets, comfy beds, crisp white linen, super bathrooms. Finally, the food – homemade soups, mussels in white wine, loin of local lamb, apple and chocolate pudding. Don't miss it.

Price	£100-£150. Singles from £70.
Rooms	11: 8 doubles, 1 twin/double, 2 family rooms.
Meals	Lunch from £8.95. Dinner from £14.95. Not Monday lunch.
Closed	Never.

Iced water in the bar for visiting dogs & bowls & towels in the bedrooms

Mark & Lucy Fuller
6 Market Street, Kirkby Lonsdale,
Carnforth LA6 2AU

Tel	+44 (0)15242 71965
Email	email@sun-inn.info
Web	www.sun-inn.info

Entry 25   Map 6

Masons Arms

A perfect Lakeland inn tucked away two miles inland from Windermere. You're on the side of a hill with huge views across lush fields to Scout Scar in the distance. In summer, all pub life decants onto a spectacular terrace – a sitting room in the sun – where window boxes and flowerbeds tumble with colour. The inn dates from the 16th century and is impossibly pretty. The bar is wonderfully traditional with roaring fires, flagged floors, wavy beams, a cosy snug... and a menu of 40 bottled beers to quench your thirst. Rustic elegance upstairs comes courtesy of stripped floors, country rugs and red walls in the first-floor dining room – so grab a window seat for fabulous views and order delicious food, anything from a sandwich to Cumbrian duck. Apartments (in the pub) and cottages (with bunk beds and sofabeds for children) are a steal; all come with fancy kitchens and breakfast hampers can be arranged. You get cool colours, comfy beds and Bang & Olufsen TVs. Best of all, most have a private terrace; order a meal in the restaurant and they'll bring it to you here. Brilliant.

Price	£75–£140. Cottages £110–£165.
Rooms	5 + 2: 5 apartments. 2 self-catering cottages: 1 for 2-4, 1 for 2-6.
Meals	Breakfast hampers £15–£25. Lunch & dinner £5–£30.
Closed	Never.

 Lots of lovely local walks

John & Diane Taylor
Cartmel Fell,
Grange over Sands LA11 6NW
Tel   +44 (0)15395 68486
Email   info@masonsarmsstrawberrybank.co.uk
Web   www.strawberrybank.com

Entry 26   Map 5

Linthwaite House Hotel & Restaurant

Windermere sparkles half a mile below, a chain of peaks rises beyond – no great surprise to discover that the terrace acts as a sitting room in summer. In fourteen acres of hillside gardens, Linthwaite is a haven for your dogs. This is a grand Edwardian country house run in informal style where everything is a treat: wonderful bedrooms, gorgeous interiors, glorious food, attentive staff. The house dates from 1900 and is soundproofed by 15 acres of trim lawns, formal gardens and wild rhododendrons. Totter up through a bluebell wood to find a small lake surrounded by fields where you can fish, swim or retreat to a summerhouse and fall asleep in the sun. The house is no less alluring with logs piled high by the front door, fires smouldering, sofas waiting and a clipped colonial elegance in the conservatory sitting room. Sublime food is served in mirrored surroundings while gorgeous bedrooms come in a contemporary country-house style. Those at the front have lake views, you can stargaze from the suites. Best of all, the Linthwaite can suggest dog walks that vary in distance, stamina and terrain – and a guide should you want one!

Price	Half-board £126-£204 p.p. Suites £197-£308 p.p. Singles from £155.
Rooms	30: 22 doubles, 5 twins/doubles, 3 suites.
Meals	Lunch from £6.95. Dinner for non-residents £52.
Closed	Rarely.

 Lake District for excited hounds & a tarn nearby to splash in

Mike Bevans
Crook Road, Bowness-on-Windermere,
Windermere LA23 3JA

Tel	+44 (0)15394 88600
Email	stay@linthwaite.com
Web	www.linthwaite.com

Entry 27   Map 5

Scales Plantation

High in the wilds of the North Lakes, in the woods around Scales Farm, Tabatha and Rob Wilson have created a cluster of unusual camping retreats. Three shepherd's hut camps each with a timber kitchen a step away sit in semi-circular clearings on the edge of the forest, with views towards Bowscale Fell and Mount Skiddaw. Feather down duvets and sheepskin rugs soften one double bed and two bunks, there are full kitchen facilities and a fire pit for campfire cooking; the kids will be in heaven. With beautiful walks across the fells on your doorstep, the camps could almost be an extension of the Lake District. And the woodland canopy has been thinned to allow wildlife such as the resident red squirrels to flourish. You can get trail advice or hire bikes just down the road and head into the hills, then come back to the rustic comfort of the hut for a toasting by the wood-burner. You'll receive a list of local, seasonal produce that you can order before your stay, free-range eggs are on the house and the pub is just over two miles. Note, this is a working farm so keep a close eye on your dog!

Price	From £65 per night.
Rooms	3 shepherd's huts for 4.
Meals	Self-catering.
Closed	Never.

 At the foot of the North Lakes Fells & next to Greystoke Forest: endless scope for owners to be dragged around by their dogs

Canopy & Stars
Berrier,
Penrith CA11 0XE
Tel   +44 (0)1275 395447
Email   enquiries@canopyandstars.co.uk
Web   www.canopyandstars.co.uk

Entry 28   Map 5

The Lodge

The grandly named Lodge sits alone in a clearing by a wide sweep of woodland on the banks of the Eamont. While it blends perfectly into the remote landscape and the exterior is woody, simple and homely, the interior comes as a surprise, with its lovely serene colours and several stylish touches. From the upstairs 'master' bedroom – with views that make the most of the spot – a wrought-iron spiral staircase drops down into the centre of the well-equipped kitchen/sitting room. Find comfy armchairs facing a wood-burner, a double sofabed for extras, and sliding doors that open to a veranda and summer breezes; occasionally deer come to the river bank for a drink. Eden Hall estate offers plenty of scope for hiking and cycling as well as private stretches of river so you can catch your supper – then cook up a storm on the four-hob gas oven. There's plenty more: you can arrange for a chef to come out and cook, book a full hamper before you arrive, or arrange for a masseuse to come and ease away hiker's pains. And then there's the Lake District, a short drive away, great yomping territory for you and your dog.

Price	From £175 per night.
Rooms	Cabin for 4.
Meals	Self-catering.
Closed	Never.

 Suggestions for dog-friendly walks. Water, food bowl & dog bed all provided

Canopy & Stars
Eden Hall, Penrith CA11 8ST

Tel	+44 (0)1275 395447
Email	enquiries@canopyandstars.co.uk
Web	www.canopyandstars.co.uk

George & Dragon

Charles Lowther has found a chef who does perfect justice to the slow-grow breeds of beef, pork and lamb produced on the Lowther Estate — and you'll find lovely wines to match, 16 by the glass. Ales and cheeses are local, berries and mushrooms are foraged, vegetables are home-grown… and his signature starter, twice-baked cheese soufflé with a hint of spinach — is divine. As for the long low coaching inn, it's been beautifully restored by craftsmen using wood, slate and stone, and painted in colours in tune with the period. Bare wooden tables, comfy sofas, intimate alcoves and crackling fires make this a delightful place to dine and unwind; old prints and archive images tell stories of the 800-year-old estate's history. Outside is plenty of seating and a lawned play area beneath fruit trees. Upstairs are ten bedrooms of varying sizes (some small, some large and some above the bar), perfectly decorated in classic country style. Carpeting is Cumbrian wool, beds are new, ornaments come with Lowther history, showers are walk-in, baths (there are two) are roll top, and breakfast is fresh and delicious.

Price	£90–£140. Singles from £70.
Rooms	10 twins/doubles.
Meals	Lunch & dinner from £9.95.
Closed	Boxing Day.

 A welcome doggie treat for all hounds

Juno Leigh
Clifton, Penrith CA10 2ER
Tel   +44 (0)1768 865381
Email   enquiries@georgeanddragonclifton.co.uk
Web   www.georgeanddragonclifton.co.uk

Cumbria

Johnby Hall

You are ensconced in the quieter part of the Lakes and have independence in this Elizabethan manor house – once a fortified Pele tower, now a family home. Two suites (one in the converted granary) are fresh and light: each has its own sitting room with lots of books and pictures, squashy sofas, pretty fabrics and whitewashed walls. Beds have patchwork quilts, windows have stone mullions and there is absolute quiet. Henry gives you sturdy breakfasts, and good home-grown suppers by a roaring fire in the great hall; he and Anna can join you or leave you in peace. Walks from the door are sublime. *Dogs welcome in one room (the Studio).*

Price	£100–£110. Singles £75–£80.
Rooms	2: 1 suite for 2.
	Granary: 1 family suite.
Meals	Supper, 2 courses, £20. Pub 1 mile.
Closed	Rarely.

 A vast garden for dogs to explore full of exciting whiffs, & ten acres of private woodland

Henry & Anna Howard
Johnby,
Penrith CA11 0UU
Tel   +44 (0)17684 83257
Email   bookings@johnbyhall.co.uk
Web   www.johnbyhall.co.uk

Entry 31   Map 5

Cumbria

Yew Tree Farm

Everything here is special: 600 acres of sheep and cattle, a farmhouse once owned by Beatrix Potter, a spinning gallery on the side of the barn, one of the best known buildings in the Lakes. Jon farms the rising hills, Caroline (a member of the Mountain Rescue team) looks after guests with great warmth. Inside, ancient panelling, vast flagstones and William Morris wallpaper shine. There's a fire at breakfast (home-cured bacon, home-laid duck eggs), Ms Potter's furniture, letters from Wordsworth and Ruskin in a cabinet. Bedrooms are traditional with original wood, smart fabrics and views of the valley. Unmissable.

Price	£104–£124. Singles £70.
Rooms	3: 1 twin/double, 1 four-poster;
	1 four-poster with separate bath.
Meals	Dinner, 3 courses, £30. Supper
	£15 (min. 6).
Closed	Rarely.

 Juicy marrowbone from the on-farm butchery & reams of fantastic walks & tarns for swimming nearby

Jon & Caroline Watson
Coniston LA21 8DP
Tel   +44 (0)1539 441433
Mobile +44 (0)7732 757043
Email   info@yewtree-farm.co.uk
Web   www.yewtree-farm.com

Entry 32   Map 5

The Old House, Cote Bank Farm

You'll love this cluster of old stone buildings where history and peace intertwine – and the natural spring that feeds the farm makes the most wonderful tea. This cottage for two, the 'end' of a Tudor farmhouse, was built around 1560 and is an upside-down house, with kitchen, bedroom and bathroom upstairs, and sitting room down. Dark by day, cosy by night, it has a mix of old and new furniture and an inglenook the length of one wall – logs are provided. The kitchen is a good size, the bedroom is light, well-proportioned and roomy; creamy fabric soars from carved bedhead to wooden beam and a swag of dried flowers hangs on rose-tinted walls. Beautiful mullioned windows contain the original glass; scratched onto one pane in perfect copybook script: "George Kyrke came to the Coate Bank 1692." Perch on an oak window seat and gaze onto sheep-clad hills... The owners, friendly, energetic and well-travelled, live in the hamlet and offer you dog bowls and brushes and all you need to know about walking Kinder Scout, the highest point in the Peaks. You wake to birdsong and the setting is sublime. *Also Cherry Tree Cottage for 4-6.*

Price	£250–£415 per week.
Rooms	Cottage for 2.
Meals	Self-catering.
Closed	Never.

 Doggie treat walks with countryside smells: rabbits, badgers, foxes. Fresh spring water for thirsty pups on their return

Pamela & Nick Broadhurst
Buxworth,
High Peak SK23 7NP
Tel   +44 (0)1663 750566
Email   cotebank@btinternet.com
Web   www.cotebank.co.uk

Entry 33   Map 6

Wheeldon Trees Farm Cottages

Deborah and Martin fell in love with this lush corner of England by chance and set about renovating their cluster of farmyard cottages with gusto. The result: nine modern homes clothed in warm limestone, put together with a feel for comfort and a passion for green living. Find sleek leather sofas and original oak beams, Denby china in open-plan kitchens, and lovely views from fresh modern bedrooms. All the houses bar one are two-storey and gaze over the valleys, and each has its own patio – and personality, thanks to local art, antiques and curios from the owners' travels. Groups are taken care of too, with a communal Long Room for cooking, dining and games. Animals graze on the farm's 12 acres and each hen has a name – you can order a tasty breakfast box that includes the farm's eggs. A web of walking and cycling trails stretches through the Peak District while lively market towns are an easy bus ride away. As for pooches, they're spoilt rotten, with a catalogue of treats including spare leads and pet food forks, stair gates and dog tags, in case Dodger gets lost. They've thought of everything!

Price	£325-£695 per week.
Rooms	8 cottages (sleeps 28 in total).
Meals	Self-catering.
Closed	Rarely.

 Toys & treats, bags & scoops, plus a special doggie exercise area with a tap & towels for muddy paws

Deborah & Martin Hofman
Earl Sterndale,
Buxton SK17 0AA
Tel   +44 (0)1298 83219
Email   stay@wheeldontreesfarm.co.uk
Web   www.wheeldontreesfarm.co.uk

Entry 34   Map 6

The Peacock at Rowsley

The Peacock dates to 1652. It was once the dower house to Haddon Hall and stands by the bridge in the middle of the village. It opened as a coaching inn 200 years ago and its lawns run down to the river Derwent. Fishermen come to try their hand, but those who want to walk can follow the river up to Chatsworth. Later, sweep back over gentle hills and return for a night at this rather swish hotel. Old and new mix harmoniously inside. Imagine mullioned windows, hessian rugs, aristocratic art, then striking colours that give a contemporary feel. French windows in the restaurant open onto a pot-festooned terrace in summer, while the fire in the bar smoulders all year. Rooms come in different shapes and sizes, all with a surfeit of style: crisp linen, good beds, Farrow & Ball colours, the odd antique. Serious food waits in the restaurant, perhaps squab pigeon with chocolate jelly, Derbyshire rib-eye with Madeira sauce, ginger crème brûlée with pear sorbet. Three circular walks start from the front door, so you can walk off any excess in the hills that surround you.

Price	£155–£257.50. Singles from £85. Half-board from £107.50 p.p.
Rooms	16: 6 doubles, 7 twins, 1 four-poster, 2 singles.
Meals	Lunch from £4.25. Dinner £52.50. Sunday lunch £20.50–£27.50.
Closed	Rarely.

Towels on offer for muddy paws & tasty leftovers

Jenni MacKenzie
Bakewell Road, Rowsley,
Matlock DE4 2EB

Tel	+44 (0)1629 733518
Email	reception@thepeacockatrowsley.com
Web	www.thepeacockatrowsley.com

Entry 35   Map 6

The Devonshire Arms at Beeley

An old stone pub on the Chatsworth estate that carries the family name. The Duke and Duchess of Devonshire have renovated in fine style. Character comes courtesy of stone walls, roaring fires, flagged floors and timber frames, but the feel is fresh and elegant, with Designer's Guild fabrics and Farrow & Ball paints. A sympathetic extension houses the restaurant, where contemporary art adds much colour and a wall of glass looks onto the village. Scoff your bacon and eggs here, pop in for lunch, walk all day, then return for a good supper, perhaps Brixham scallops, Beeley lamb, Mrs Hill's lemon tart. In summer, sit out on the terrace with a pint of Chatsworth Gold and watch walkers pour off the hill. Bedrooms are split between the inn and next-door Brookside House. Expect extravagant headboards, period colours, beautifully dressed beds and super bathrooms (one has a claw-foot tub in the room). Also, all the expected gadgets: Bose sound systems, flat-screen TVs, DVD players, iPod docks. The Derbyshire Dales are all around and you can walk over the hill to Chatsworth.

Price	£137–£207.
Rooms	8: 4 doubles, 3 twins/doubles, 1 suite.
Meals	Lunch from £9.95. Dinner, 3 courses, about £25.
Closed	Never.

A pooch-friendly walk across beautiful countryside on the Chatsworth Estate, straight from the inn

Alan Hill
Beeley, Matlock DE4 2NR

Tel	+44 (0)1629 733259
Email	res@devonshirehotels.co.uk
Web	www.devonshirebeeley.co.uk

Entry 36   Map 6

Heasley House

The sort of place you chance upon, only to return again and again. Everything here is lovely. It's a beautiful house in a sleepy village lost in a wild Exmoor valley, with stylish interiors, delicious food and very attractive prices. Inside, Paul and Jan have overseen a total refurbishment, recovering the grandness of a Georgian mine captain's house, then dressing it up in contemporary clothes. You find stripped boards, stone walls, timber frames, a frieze on the fireplace. Harmonious colours run throughout, fires burn in the sitting rooms, there is original art, a fancy bar and fresh flowers everywhere. Airy bedrooms are more than comfy with big beds, good linen and lovely bathrooms. Those at the front have country views, those in the eaves have beams. All have flat-screen TVs, DVD players, bathrobes and armchairs. Spin down to the restaurant for a feast of local Devon produce, perhaps fennel soup with smoked salmon, Exmoor lamb with puy lentils, rhubarb and orange crumble with clotted cream. Paths lead out, so follow the river into the woods or head north for cliffs at the coast. Brilliant – and so hospitable.

Price	£150. Suite £170. Singles from £115.
Rooms	7: 6 twins/doubles, 1 suite.
Meals	Dinner £26–£32.
Closed	Christmas Day, Boxing Day & February.

 Dogs are allowed almost everywhere, pigs' ears are always available & there's fantastic walking from the door

Paul & Jan Gambrill
Heasley Mill, South Molton EX36 3LE
Tel   +44 (0)1598 740213
Email   enquiries@heasley-house.co.uk
Web   www.heasley-house.co.uk

Little Comfort Farm Cottages

Folded deep into Devon hills is a slice of green heaven. Five sturdy stone cottages have eased themselves into the landscape, and been gently tweaked and updated over the years – welcome to Jackie and Roger's working organic farm. Their passion makes this place. Slip off walking boots at your door and escape into a homely haven – an easy mix of lived-in sofas and and log-burner, and DVDs for lazy nights in. Bathrooms are simple, bedrooms cosy with pine, flowery curtains and country views. The local shop will stock your fridge and freezer, you can buy sausages, bacon, lamb, beef, eggs and apple juice on the farm; Jackie even does delicious meals. This is a gift for young families – morning trailer rides, lamb feeding, a barn filled with toys. And dog heaven, with private access to a river valley walk and maps for dogs off and on lead. It would also make a blissful retreat for couples outside of the busiest times. Walk miles, fish in the lake, switch off, head for the endless sands of Saunton, Putsborough and Woolacombe. And if you fancy a day's shopping in Barnstable, there's a good friendly kennels nearby.

Price	£327–£1,787 per week.
Rooms	5 cottages for 4-10.
Meals	Home-cooked meals available.
Closed	Never.

Fabulous farm walks, rivers to splash in & a list of the best dog-friendly pubs, gardens & beaches

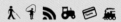

Roger & Jackie Milsom
Braunton EX17 4SU
Tel   +44 (0)1271 812414
Email   info@littlecomfortfarm.co.uk
Web   www.littlecomfortfarm.co.uk

Entry 38   Map 2

The Globe Inn

A super little inn that mixes old and new to great effect. Once the village reading room, it stands in a tiny square in the shade of the church; bell ringers practice on Thursday nights. Inside, funky interiors hide behind smart 17th-century walls. Huge lampshades hang low above the bar, there are flickering candles, shiny flagstones and a sofa in front of a roaring fire — settle in with a pint of Speckled Hen. The restaurant is altogether different. Once the village library, its original panelling is listed and you eat amid a riot of wood, with gothic-style mirrors leaning against the wall and red silk curtains draped around Georgian windows. It's a perfect spot for a little indulgence, so feast on bouillabaisse, tiger prawns, fillet of pork, roast pheasant with red onions, peppers and Madeira... and apple crumble and vanilla ice cream. Recently refurbished bedrooms have lots of style: a wall of colour, big mirrors, super beds, fancy showers. As for this patch of England, it is both glorious and ignored — a must-visit! Chulmleigh Fair, first held under royal charter in 1206, takes place at the end of July.

Price	£60–£120.
Rooms	5: 2 doubles, 1 twin, 2 four-posters.
Meals	Lunch & bar meals from £4.95. Dinner from £8.50. Sunday lunch £25.
Closed	Never.

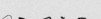 Beautiful hiking country for you & your dog

	Church Street, Chulmleigh EX18 7BU
Tel	+44 (0)1769 580252
Email	info@theglobeinnchulmleigh.co.uk
Web	www.theglobeinnchulmleigh.co.uk

Horry Mill

Pied fly-catchers, a babbling brook, 20 acres of natural woodland, wild flowers, ducks, chickens, cattle lowing – rural bliss. Mobile phones don't work, the only tune you will hear is birdsong: a place for a bucolic escape. This was once a miller's cottage, destroyed by fire in the 18th-century and rebuilt using the old beams and timbers. Sonia has accentuated the original features (the big fireplace in the beamed sitting room stacked with logs, the wide oak stairs, the gleaming floor boards in the bedrooms) and added good solid cottage furniture, a flat-screen TV, games and books, an old iron bedstead with crisp white linen, nice china and a window seat overlooking the cottage garden. Milk and newspapers can be delivered at weekends and the welcoming owners who live in the Millhouse a little way away are on hand should you need them. There are walks in all directions, for dogs and owners zippy or slothful, birdsong all day, and Simon's pièce de résistance: a beautiful, wooden thatched summerhouse a step from your door. Peaceful, untouched and a perfect place for stargazing.

Price	£330–£600 per week.
Rooms	Cottage for 4.
Meals	Self-catering.
Closed	Rarely.

 20 acres of woodland for wonderful walks

Simon & Sonia Hodgson
Hollocombe,
Chulmleigh EX18 7QH
Tel   +44 (0)1769 520266
Email   horrymill@aol.com
Web   www.horrymill.com

Entry 40   Map 2

The Lamb Inn

This 16th-century inn is nothing short of perfect, a proper local in the old tradition with gorgeous rooms and the odd touch of scruffiness to add authenticity to earthy bones. It stands on a cobbled walkway in a village lost down Devon's tiny lanes, and those lucky enough to chance upon it will leave reluctantly. Outside, all manner of greenery covers its stone walls; inside there are beams, but they are not sandblasted, red carpets with a little swirl, sofas in front of an open fire and rough-hewn oak panels painted black. Boarded menus trumpet wonderfully priced food – carrot and orange soup, whole baked trout with almond butter, an irresistible tarte tatin. There's a cobbled terrace, a walled garden, an occasional cinema, an open mic night… and a back bar, where four ales are hand-pumped. Upstairs, six marvellous bedrooms elate. One is large with a bath and a wood-burner in the room, but all are lovely with super-smart power showers, sash windows that give village views, hi-fis, flat-screen TVs, good linen and comfy beds. Dartmoor waits but you may well linger. There's Tiny, the guard dog, too.

Price	£65–£105.
Rooms	6: 5 doubles, 1 twin/double.
Meals	Lunch from £8.
	Dinner, 3 courses, £15–£25.
Closed	Rarely.

A map for good dog walks & a Bonio biscuit to keep tails wagging

Mark Hildyard & Katharine Lightfoot
Sandford,
Crediton EX17 4LW

Tel	+44 (0)1363 773676
Email	thelambinn@gmail.com
Web	www.lambinnsandford.co.uk

Entry 41   Map 2

Higher Eggbeer Farm

Buried in the pages of the Domesday Book is a record of Higher Eggbeer Farm: a 900-year-old thatched longhouse on the edge of Dartmoor. There are medieval farm buildings and 14 acres of pasture, and guests and their dogs are free to roam – and meet the pigs, cows, chickens, ducks, kittens, and tiny Pete the pony. William and Sally Anne's rustic home will charm you straight away; you get one whole wing. Find a huge inglenook fireplace in the drawing room, rose pink walls, a piano, bright art and heaps of books. In the country kitchen, a dresser and sunny walls. Up the creaky staircase, two adjoining bedrooms with sloping floors and spectacular valley views. And across the tiny lobby, a museum piece of a bathroom, big, beamy and carpeted. William and Sally Anne, who keep a room for B&B, leave you to unravel the delights of this deeply rural place. Ramble Dartmoor from the front door, visit Castle Drogo, spend a day in the cathedral city of Exeter. Or head for the north or south Devon coasts: you're halfway between the two. Two pubs are walking distance – Sally Anne will lend you a torch.

Price	£250–£675 per week.
Rooms	Wing for 5.
Meals	Self-catering.
Closed	Rarely.

 Huge garden for romping in & all manner of play things for your pooch

Sally Anne Selwyn & Alistair Scott Lawson
Cheriton Bishop, Exeter EX6 6JQ
Tel   +44 (0)1647 24427
Mobile   +44 (0)7850 136131
Email   ascottlawson@gmail.com

Entry 42   Map 2

Mill End

Another Dartmoor gem. Mill End is flanked by the Two Moors Way, one of the loveliest walks in England. It leads along the river Teign, then up to Castle Drogo – not a bad way to follow your bacon and eggs. As for the hotel, inside is an elegant country retreat. There are timber frames, nooks and crannies, bowls of fruit, pretty art. Warm, uncluttered interiors are just the ticket, with vases of flowers on plinths in the sofa'd sitting room and smartly upholstered dining chairs in the airy restaurant. Bedrooms come in country-house style: white linen, big beds, moor views, the odd antique. You might find a chandelier, a large balcony or padded window seats. All come with flat-screen TVs, some have big baths stocked with lotions. Back down in the restaurant, where the mill wheel turns in the window, you find delicious food, perhaps mushroom and tarragon soup, Dartmoor lamb with fondant potato and rosemary jus, chocolate tart. Little ones have their own high tea at 6pm; dogs are made to feel part of the family. In the morning there's porridge with cream and brown sugar, as well as the usual extravagance.

Price	£135-£155. Suites £170-£230. Singles from £67.50. Half-board from £100 p.p.
Rooms	15: 9 doubles, 2 twins, 1 family, 3 suites.
Meals	Lunch by arrangement. Sunday lunch from £15.95. Dinner £36-£39.50.
Closed	2 weeks in Jan.

Doggie heaven! Great walks on the moors & a boot room for after

Peter & Sue Davies
Chagford,
Newton Abbot TQ13 8JN
Tel   +44 (0)1647 432282
Email   info@millendhotel.com
Web   www.millendhotel.com

Entry 43   Map 2

The Elephant's Nest Inn

Overseas visitors will give a rapturous smile as they enter the main bar, all polished oak beams, flagstone floors and crackling fires… you almost imagine a distant Baskerville hound baying. This is an atmospheric inn that serves properly home-cooked food – very local, very seasonal and British with a twist: perhaps antipasto of pastrami, rosette saucisson and Black Forest ham, or South Devon sirloin with mushrooms, vine tomatoes and French fries; sweet tooths will surely drool over Mrs Cook's fabulous lemon posset with blueberry compote. When suitably sated, slip off to the annexe and a nest of your own in one of three rather fun, wonderfully quiet and extremely comfortable rooms. Wake to a pretty garden with views to Brentor church and Dartmoor, even, perhaps, a cricket match to watch: the pub has its own ground and club. Settle back to the thwack of willow on leather with a pint of Palmer's IPA – or Doom Bar, Jail Ale from Princetown, and guest ales from O'Hanlon's, Otter, Cotleigh, Teignworthy and Butcombe. What's more, the pub is as dog-friendly as they come.

Price	£80–£90.
Rooms	3 twins/doubles.
Meals	Lunch & dinner £8.95–£19.95.
Closed	Rarely.

   Pigs' ears & assorted treats provided, & well-behaved dogs on leads are welcome throughout the pub

Hugh & Denise Cook
Horndon, Mary Tavy,
Tavistock PL19 9NQ
Tel   +44 (0)1822 810273
Email   info@elephantsnest.co.uk
Web   www.elephantsnest.co.uk

Entry 44   Map 2

The Horn of Plenty

This country-house hotel has been thrilling guests for 40 years and it doesn't take long to work out why; the view, the food, the staff and the rooms: all deliver in spades. The house goes back to 1860 and was built for the captain of the mines, who could peer down the valley and check his men were at work; these days it's the Tamar snaking through the hills below that catches the eye. Inside you find the essence of graceful simplicity: stripped floors, gilt mirrors, exquisite art and flowers everywhere. Bedrooms are just as good. Some have terraces that look down to the river, others come in country-house style with vast beds, old armoires, shimmering throws and rugs on stripped floors; bathrooms are predictably divine. As for the food, well, it's the big draw, so expect to eat well, perhaps Falmouth Bay scallops with a carrot purée, Devonshire lamb with a Madeira sauce, then nougat parfait with caramelised pineapple and a coconut sorbet. Best of all are the staff, who couldn't be more helpful. Tavistock, Dartmoor and The Eden Project are all within striking distance.

Price	£95–£295. Singles from £85. Half-board from £82.50 p.p.
Rooms	10 twins/doubles.
Meals	Lunch £19-50–£24.50. Dinner £49.50.
Closed	Never.

 Tasty treats, five acres of garden, plus beautiful walks in the Tamar Valley & on Dartmoor

Julie Leivers & Damien Pease
Gulworthy,
Tavistock PL19 8JD
Tel   +44 (0)1822 832528
Email   enquiries@thehornofplenty.co.uk
Web   www.thehornofplenty.co.uk

Entry 45   Map 2

Prince Hall Hotel

An avenue of beech trees sweeps you down to this peaceful hotel in six acres of woodland and lawns with views to the back across majestic Dartmoor. Inside, a warm country house comes with colour and comfort in equal measure. Follow your dog's nose to find beautiful sofas in front of the fire, an airy bar where doors open onto a smart terrace, and wooden floors in a refurbished restaurant where you (but not your dog) dine on super food from the finest local suppliers – perhaps honey glazed pork belly with pear purée, and white chocolate cheesecake with spearmint jelly. Bedrooms come in different shapes and sizes. Expect wallpaper, white linen, dressing mirrors and warm florals. The more expensive rooms have the view; a couple have fancy bathrooms too. Outside, lawns run down to paddocks, the river passes beyond, then nothing but moor and sky. Foxgloves and primroses bring colour in spring. Dogs are greeted like old friends, maps for walks are provided, as are doggy poop bags and a bin. You can even choose to eat with your dog in tow: take breakfast and dinner in the bar, or by the fire in the lounge.

Price	£100–£180. Singles from £80.
Rooms	8: 4 doubles, 4 twins/doubles.
Meals	Lunch from £5.95.
	Dinner £33.95–£39.95.
Closed	Never.

 A Bonio in your room, dog biscuits at reception... & towels, hose, spare leads, emergency dog food & water bowls just in case

Fi & Chris Daly
Two Bridges, Princetown,
Yelverton PL20 6SA
Tel   +44 (0)1822 890403
Email   info@princehall.co.uk
Web   www.princehall.co.uk

Entry 46   Map 2

The Henley Hotel

A small house above the sea with fabulous views, super bedrooms and some of the loveliest food in Devon. Despite such credentials it's Martyn and Petra who shine most brightly, and their kind, generous approach makes this a memorable place to stay. Warm Edwardian interiors come with stripped wood floors, seagrass matting, Lloyd Loom wicker chairs, the odd potted palm. Below, the Avon estuary slips gracefully out to sea: at high tide surfers ride the waves; at low tide you can walk on the sands. There's a pretty garden with a path tumbling down to the beach, binoculars in each room, a wood-burner in the snug and good books everywhere. Bedrooms are a steal (one is huge). Expect warm yellows, crisp linen, tongue-and-groove panelling and robes in super little bathrooms. As for Martyn's table d'hôte dinners, expect something special. Fish comes daily from Kingsbridge market, you might have warm crab and parmesan tart, roast monkfish with a lobster sauce, then hot chocolate soufflé with fresh raspberries. Gorgeous Devon is all around. Don't miss it.

Price	£120–£144. Singles from £80. Half-board option.
Rooms	5: 3 doubles, 2 twins/doubles.
Meals	Dinner £36.
Closed	November–March.

 Your hosts love dogs, beaches are right outside & lovely countryside is all around

Martyn Scarterfield & Petra Lampe
Folly Hill, Bigbury-on-Sea,
Kingsbridge TQ7 4AR
Tel   +44 (0)1548 810240
Email   thehenleyhotel@btconnect.com
Web   www.thehenleyhotel.co.uk

Entry 47   Map 2

The Cary Arms at Babbacombe Bay

The Cary Arms hovers above Babbacombe Bay with huge views of water and sky that shoot off to Dorset's Jurassic coast. It's a cool little place – half seaside pub, half dreamy hotel – and it makes the most of its spectacular position: five beautiful terraces drop downhill towards a small jetty, where locals fish. The hotel has six moorings in the bay, you can charter a boat and explore the coast. Back on dry land the bar comes with stone walls, wooden floors and a fire that burns every day. In good weather you eat on the terraces, perhaps a pint of prawns, Dover sole, wet chocolate cake; groups of friends can enjoy their own barbecues. Dazzling bedrooms come in New England style; two are dog-friendly, as are the cottages, and come with private terraces – just the job for sea-soaked fur coats. You get decanters of sloe gin, flat-screen TVs, fabulous beds, super bathrooms. Back outside, you can snorkel on mackerel reefs or hug the coastline in a kayak. If that sounds too energetic, head to the treatment room (bookable in advance) and let someone else take the dogs for a walk. All is possible here.

Price	£155–£260. Suite £310–£360. Singles from £105. Cottages £770–£2,565 p.w.
Rooms	8 + 3: 6 doubles, 1 twin/double, 1 family suite. 4 s/c cottages for 2-8.
Meals	Lunch from £7.95. Dinner £25–£35.
Closed	Never.

 Treats, bags & towels – & their own dinner dish on the menu

Jen Podmore
Beach Road,
Torquay TQ1 3LX
Tel   +44 (0)1803 327110
Email   enquiries@caryarms.co.uk
Web   www.caryarms.co.uk

Entry 48   Map 2

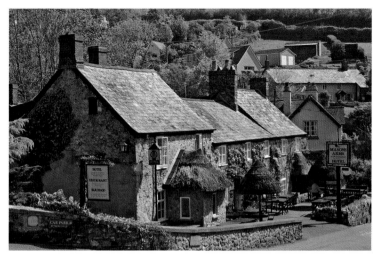

Masons Arms

Lose yourself in tiny lanes, follow them down towards the sea, pass the Norman church, roll up at the Masons Arms. It stands in a village half a mile back from the pebble beach surrounded by glorious country, with a stone terrace at the front from which to gaze upon lush hills. It dates back to 1350 – a cider house turned country pub – and the men who cut the stone for Exeter Cathedral drank here, hence the name. Inside, simple, authentic interiors are just the thing: timber frames, low beamed ceilings, pine cladding, whitewashed walls and a roaring fire over which the spit roast is cooked on Sundays. Some bedrooms are above the inn, others are behind on the hill. Those in the pub are small but cosy (warm yellows, check fabrics, leather bedheads, super bathrooms); those behind are bigger, quieter and more traditional; they overlook a garden and share a private terrace with valley views that tumble down to the sea. Footpaths lead out – over hills, along the coast – so follow your nose, then return for super food: seared scallops, lamb cutlets, saffron and honey crème brûlée.

Price	£70–£140. Suites £150–£175.
Rooms	21: 8 doubles, 6 twins/doubles, 6 four-posters, 1 family room.
Meals	Lunch from £7.50. Bar meals from £9.95. Dinner, 3 courses, £20–£25. Sunday lunch from £9.95.
Closed	Never.

 Wonderful windy walks along the Jurassic Coast

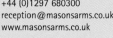

Paul Couldwell
Branscombe,
Seaton EX12 3DJ
Tel   +44 (0)1297 680300
Email   reception@masonsarms.co.uk
Web   www.masonsarms.co.uk

Combe House Devon

Combe is immaculate, an ancient house on a huge estate, the full aristocratic works. You spin up a long drive, pass Arabian horses running wild in the distance, then skip through the front door and enter a place of architectural splendour. A fire roars in the warm panelled hall, the muralled dining room serves ambrosial food, the sitting room/bar in racing green opens onto the croquet lawn. Best of all is the way things are done: the feel is more home than hotel and you may mistake yourself for lord of the manor – a battalion of household staff to attend to your every whim. Wander around and see 600-year old flagstones, original William Morris wallpaper, Victorian kitchen gardens that provide much for the table, beehives for breakfast honey. Rooms are fabulous: stately fabrics, wonderful beds, gorgeous bathrooms, outstanding views. The vast suite, once the laundry press, is now the stuff of fashion shoots and comes with a vast copper bath. There are 3,500 acres for dogs to explore and fabulous food to keep you going, but it's Ruth and Ken who win the prize; they just know how to do it.

Price	£199-£364. Suites £399-£419. Half-board from £148.50 p.p. Cottage £399-£419 (B&B per night).
Rooms	15 + 1: 10 twins/doubles, 1 four-poster, 4 suites. Self-catering cottage for 2.
Meals	Lunch £27-£32. Dinner £49.
Closed	Rarely.

3,000 acres: ample to please the most demanding hound

Ruth & Ken Hunt
Gittisham,
Honiton EX14 3AD
Tel   +44 (0)1404 540400
Email   stay@combehousedevon.com
Web   www.combehousedevon.com

Entry 50   Map 2

Devon   B&B

Glebe House

Set on a hillside with fabulous views over
the Coly valley, this late-Georgian vicarage
is now a heart-warming B&B. The views
will entice you, the hosts will delight you
and the house is filled with interesting
things. Chuck and Emma spent many years
at sea – he a Master Mariner, she a chef –
and have filled these big light rooms with
cushions, kilims and treasured family
pieces. There's a sitting room for guests, a
lovely conservatory with a vintage vine,
peaceful bedrooms with blissful views and
bathrooms that sparkle. All this, two sweet
pygmy goats, wildlife beyond the ha-ha and
the fabulous coast a hike away.

Devon   B&B

Hooks Cottage

At the end of a long bumpy track, the
hideaway mine captain's house may have
few original features but the woodland
setting is gorgeous. Mary and Dick have a
finely judged sense of humour; labradors
Archie and Cobble will charm you. It is
simple, rural, close to the Moors, with
woodland birds and a gentle river to
unwind stressed souls. Carpeted bedrooms
have a faded floral charm and pretty stream
views; bathrooms are plain. Enjoy local
sausages and Mary's marmalade for
breakfast, a lovely garden and amazing
bluebells in spring; walks from the house
are sublime. Your horse is welcome too.

Price	From £70. Singles £45.
Rooms	3: 1 double, 1 twin/double, 1 family.
Meals	Dinner, 3 courses £25. Pubs/restaurants 2.5 miles.
Closed	Christmas & New Year.

 Afternoon tea for guests comes with a Bonio for the dogs... 15 acres of countryside, too

Emma & Chuck Guest
Southleigh, Colyton EX24 6SD
Tel   +44 (0)1404 871276
Mobile   +44 (0)7867 568569
Email   emma_guest@talktalk.net
Web   www.guestsatglebe.com

Entry 51   Map 2

Price	From £65. Singles from £40.
Rooms	2: 1 double en suite (wc across landing); 1 twin with separate bath.
Meals	Pub/restaurant 2 miles.
Closed	Rarely.

 12 acres of land to roam & a swim in the river – let Archie & Cobble be your guides!

Mary & Dick Lloyd-Williams
Bickington,
Ashburton TQ12 6JS
Tel   +44 (0)1626 821312
Email   hookscottage@yahoo.com
Web   www.hookscottage.co.uk

Entry 52   Map 2

Bratton Mill

Absolute privacy down the long lane to a thickly wooded and beautifully secluded valley: watch for dragonflies, red deer, buzzards and the flash of the kingfisher. Breakfast may be served in summer by the Exmoor trout stream. To the backdrop of the rushing water is the house, filled with treasure – including Marilyn, who spoils you with elegant china, flowers, embroidered linen and a decanter of port. Or choose independence in a prettily furnished folly in the garden, opening onto a terrace and a hop from the water. Strolls and hikes from the door, and invaluable advice on good value, dog-friendly places to eat.

Price	£95–£125. Singles £60.
Rooms	2: 1 twin/double. Extra single available. Folly: 1 double & kitchen.
Meals	Pub within walking distance.
Closed	Rarely.

  Lots of local, dog-friendly knowledge: wonderful walks from the front door along coastal paths & beaches

Marilyn Jacobs Holloway
Bratton Fleming,
Barnstaple EX31 4RU
Tel   +44 (0)1598 710026
Email   contact@brattonmill.co.uk
Web   www.brattonmill.co.uk

Entry 53   Map 2

The Shave Cross Inn

Fancy a pint of Branoc and a spicy salad of jerk chicken? Once a busy stop-off point for pilgrims and monastic visitors (whose crowns were shorn whilst staying), the cob-and-flint pub now sits dreamily off the beaten track at the end of several very narrow lanes. It was rescued from closure by the Warburtons, back from the Caribbean. Life has stepped up a gear and the old tavern thrives – thanks largely to the exotic and delicious cuisine, and the swish bedrooms in a new stone building next door. Where else in deep Dorset can you tuck into Louisiana blackened chicken with cream and pepper sauce? There's simple pub grub for less adventurous palates, while surroundings remain strictly traditional: flagged floors, low beams, country furniture and vast inglenook. Named after the surrounding hills, those seven smart bedrooms flourish big sleigh beds and grand four-posters, stone floors and oak beams and a host of pleasing extras – fresh coffee, plasma screens, bathrobes, posh smellies. The meandering garden, with goldfish pool, wishing well and play area, is gorgeous. The Jurassic coast awaits.

Price	£160–£190. Singles £95. £15 for two dogs per stay.
Rooms	7 doubles.
Meals	Lunch & dinner £9.95–£16.50.
Closed	Never.

 Two daft Harlequin Great Danes to welcome you, & miles of footpaths through beautiful countryside

Roy & Mel Warburton
Shave Cross,
Bridport DT6 6HW
Tel   +44 (0)1308 868358
Email   roy.warburton@virgin.net
Web   www.theshavecrossinn.co.uk

Entry 54   Map 2

BridgeHouse Hotel

Beaminster – Emminster in Thomas Hardy's *Tess* – sits in a lush Dorset valley. From the hills above, rural England goes on show: quilted fields lead to a country town, the church tower soars towards heaven. At BridgeHouse stone flags, mullioned windows, old beams and huge inglenooks sweep you back to a graceful past. This is a comfortable hotel in a country town – intimate, friendly, quietly smart. There are rugs on parquet floors, a beamed bar in a turreted alcove, a sparkling dining room with Georgian panelling. Breakfast is served in the brasserie, where huge windows look onto the lawns, so watch the gardener potter about as you scoff your bacon and eggs. Delicious food – local and organic – is a big draw, perhaps seared scallops, Gressingham duck, champagne sorbet. And so to bed. Rooms in the main house are bigger and smarter, those in the coach house are simpler, less expensive and welcome dogs; all are pretty with chic fabrics, crisp linen, flat-screen TVs and stylish bathrooms. There are river walks, antique shops and Dorset's Jurassic coast.

Price	£116–£200. Singles from £76. Half-board (min. 2 nights) from £83 p.p.
Rooms	13: 6 twins/doubles, 2 four-posters, 1 single. Coach House: 3 doubles, 1 family room.
Meals	Brasserie lunch/dinner from £12. Dinner, £27.50–£40.
Closed	Never.

Lots of lovely walks & dogs are welcome in the bar

Mark & Jo Donovan
3 Prout Bridge,
Beaminster DT8 3AY

Tel	+44 (0)1308 862200
Email	enquiries@bridge-house.co.uk
Web	www.bridge-house.co.uk

The Acorn Inn

Perfect Evershot and rolling countryside lie at the door of this 400-year-old inn deep in Thomas Hardy country. Hardy called the inn the Sow and Acorn and let Tess rest a night here; had he visited today he might have let her stay longer. Red Carnation Hotels, under the guidance of chef Jack Mackenzie and Alex Armstrong-Wilson, are reviving its fortunes. This is very much a traditional inn: as much a place for locals to sup pints of Otter Ale and swap stories by the fire in the flagstoned bar, as for foodies to sample some good food sourced within 25 miles. Walk through to the dining room and the atmosphere changes to rural country house with smartly laid tables, terracotta tiles, soft lighting and elegant fireplaces; food is taken seriously, take scallops with pumpkin and vanilla purée and chorizo dressing and roast pork belly with sherry vinegar jus, or a rare roast beef and horseradish sandwich in the bar. Bedrooms creak with age and style; uneven floors, antiques, bright fabric wall-coverings, beautiful draperies to soften grand four-posters, and smart new bathrooms. Hardy would approve.

Price	£99–£119. Four-posters £119–£139. Suite £149–£189. Singles £79–£139. £10 per dog per night.
Rooms	10: 3 doubles, 3 twins, 3 four-posters, 1 suite.
Meals	Lunch & dinner £4–£18.95.
Closed	Rarely.

 All doggie arrivals are given a treat & a guide to local paths & dog-friendly excursions

Jack Mackenzie &
Alex Armstrong-Wilson
Evershot, Dorchester DT2 0JW

Tel	+44 (0)1935 83228
Email	stay@acorn-inn.co.uk
Web	www.acorn-inn.co.uk

Prides Cottage

Tucked between two ancient hill forts is the pretty hamlet of Child Okeford. Snug in its middle, opposite the post office, is a listed 17th-century thatch cottage with old beams, wonky windows, ancient bread oven and secret staircase – yet it is refreshingly light and airy. Find white walls, contemporary lighting and sandy wooden floors covered by sumptuous Middle Eastern rugs – and a list of the best dog-friendly pubs in Dorset. Upstairs, the bedrooms are similarly bright with fresh white sheets and tasteful throws, the delightful master room with a high brass-knobbed bed and its own cast-iron fireplace. The second room is more compact but tuck yourself into the window seat and catch the views – they stretch for up Hambledon Hill to the woods. If you're feeling energetic you can set off on the 184-metre hike to the top direct from your front door – or choose from one of ten walks from the village along the Stour: bliss for mutts who love a swim. On lazy days, relax in the enchanting, safely fenced cottage garden: its rockery, climbing rose and small terrace make it a pretty spot for summer dining.

Price	£385-£770 per week.
Rooms	Cottage for 4.
Meals	Self-catering.
Closed	Rarely.

 72 footpaths in & around the village, close to the old railway line for flat mud-free rambles

Kate Partridge & Richard Choat
High Street, Child Okeford,
nr Blandford Forum DT11 8EH
Tel   020 763 98698 / 0772 5245066
Email   info@pridescottage.co.uk
Web   www.pridescottage.co.uk

Entry 57   Map 2

Coach Cottage

Off the village street, up the walkers' track, past a few cottages and there's yours, sweetly 18th-century and fronted by a garden of roses – just enough space to sit out in summer. Enter a sitting/dining room bursting with character and painted white, with an open-plan feel and a staircase at one end. Floors have been laid with light oak, fresh walls have been Farrow & Ball'd, deep-red cushions and curtains create warmth, a Victorian fireplace holds a trusty wood-burner – a characterful marriage of old and new. A few steps down is the little kitchen, its pine units painted a lovely blue, its racks glowing with pots and pans. The bathroom too is downstairs, too – no space up! – stocked with luxurious towels. After exploring Studland, Brownsea Island and the thrilling, fossil-lined coast, wend your way up the narrow stairs to cosy bedrooms behind old latch doors and charming brass beds with bright woollen throws. If the cottage is a treat then so is the village, in glorious countryside under Hambledon Hill – not too big, not too small, with a cinema in the village hall, several pubs and some great little shops.

Price	£300-£550 per week.
Rooms	Cottage for 3.
Meals	Self-catering.
Closed	Rarely.

Right on the footpath to Hambledon Hill – fabulous for dogs. The river Stour is nearby for a splash, too

Kate Partridge & Richard Choat
Coach Lane, Child Okeford DT11 8EJ
Tel   020 763 98698 / 0772 5245066
Email   info@coachcottage.co.uk
Web   www.coachcottage.co.uk

Entry 58   Map 3

The King John Inn

You're on the Dorset/Wiltshire border, lost in blissful country, with paths that lead into glorious hills. Tumble back down to this super inn. Alex and Gretchen have refurbished every square inch and the place shines. Expect airy interiors, a smart country feel, a sun-trapping terrace and a fire that crackles in winter. Originally a foundry, it opened as a brewery in 1859, and, when beer proved more popular than horseshoes, the inn was born. You'll find three local ales on tap but great wines, too – Alex loves the stuff and has opened his own shop across the courtyard; take home a bottle if you like what you drink. As for the food, it's as local as can be with game straight off the Rushmore estate and meat from over the hill; the sausages are a thing of rare beauty. Country-house bedrooms are the final treat. Some are bigger than others, three are in the Coach House, all come with wonderful fabrics, padded headboards, crisp white linen and super bathrooms (one has a slipper bath). In summer, a terraced lawn gives views over a couple of rooftops onto the woods. A perfect spot.

Price	£115-£165.
Rooms	8: 6 doubles, 2 twins/doubles.
Meals	Lunch from £6.95. Bar meals from £8.95. Dinner, 3 courses, £25-£30. Sunday lunch £30.
Closed	Rarely.

 Dog treats behind the bar & VIP dog beds

Alex & Gretchen Boon
Tollard Royal,
Salisbury SP5 5PS
Tel   +44 (0)1725 516207
Email   info@kingjohninn.co.uk
Web   www.kingjohninn.co.uk

Entry 59   Map 3

Captain's Club Hotel

A sparkling hotel on the banks on the Stour, where a tiny ferry potters along the river dodging swans and ducks. The hotel has its own launch and those who want to skim across to the Isle of White can do so in style. Back on dry land, locals flock in day and night and the big bar hums with merry chatter as they sink into sofas, sip cocktails or dig into a crab sandwich. There's live music every night, newspapers at reception and doors that open onto a pretty terrace, perfect in good weather. Bedrooms all have river views and come in an uncluttered contemporary style, with low-slung beds, crisp white linen, neutral colours and excellent bathrooms. None are small, some are huge with separate sitting rooms, apartments have more than one bedroom, thus perfect for families and friends. Residents have free access to the spa (hydrotherapy pool, sauna, four treatment rooms). Dinner comes in an ultra-airy restaurant, where you dig into tasty brasserie-style food, perhaps goats cheese soufflé, Gressingham duck, pear mousse with Kir royale sorbet. Pretty Christchurch is a short walk upstream.

Price	£199–£259. Apartments £289–£649.
Rooms	29: 17 doubles, 12 apartments for 2-6.
Meals	Bar meals all day from £6. Restaurant lunch from £14.50; dinner £30-£35.
Closed	Never.

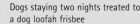 Dogs staying two nights treated to a dog loofah frisbee

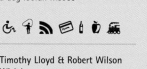

Timothy Lloyd & Robert Wilson
Wick Lane,
Christchurch BH23 1HU
Tel   +44 (0)1202 475111
Email   reservations@captainsclubhotel.com
Web   www.captainsclubhotel.com

Entry 60   Map 3

Old Causeway Bakery

In an unpretentious village, a quirky gem. Abundant flower arrangements and bold colours glow alongside oils; prints and antiques are dotted around; bookcases bow with the weight of walking guides; and Henry and Bertie – the resident hounds – will tell you all about the best beaches and off-the-track walks. In the self-contained bakery wing is a theatrical boudoir: gold drapes, a chaise longue. The main house bedrooms are more serene but still eclectic, with antiques and tapestry-upholstered headboards, and bathrooms are super throughout. Full English breakfasts are all locally sourced, and served whenever you like.

Munden House

When the sun shines, you'll think you're in Provence. Gardens and terraces abound at this small, intimate hotel, with assorted outbuildings that have been beautifully stitched together. Expect golden stone, a thatched roof and long views over open country. Stone walls soar to a beamed ceiling in the sitting room, a grand piano sits in the dining room. Pretty bedrooms in the main house have lots of colour, crisp white linen and good little bathrooms. The garden suites where dogs are welcome are bigger. One has a galleried bedroom; another has doors onto the side terrace, one has a shaded deck. Delicious dinners wait, too.

Price	£85–£95. Wing £100–£120. Singles £75–£85.
Rooms	3: 2 doubles. Bakery Wing: 1 double.
Meals	Pub 30 yds.
Closed	Rarely.

 Walks straight from the garden gate into fields: maps & books of circular & waterside walks to borrow

Price	£80–£120. Singles from £70.
Rooms	7: 2 doubles, 1 twin/double, 1 four-poster, 3 garden studios.
Meals	Dinner, 3 courses, £25.
Closed	Christmas.

 Complimentary dog treats offered

Sandra Williams & Simon Boggon
Hazelbury Bryan,
Sturminster Newton DT10 2BH
Tel   +44 (0)1258 817228
Mobile   +44 (0)7825 815796
Email   sandrasimonbw@btinternet.com
Web   www.oldcausewaybakery.co.uk

Entry 61   Map 2

Annie Fabbri & Colin Fletcher
Mundens Lane,
Alweston,
Sherborne DT9 5HU
Tel   +44 (0)1963 23150
Email   stay@mundenhouse.co.uk
Web   www.mundenhouse.co.uk

Entry 62   Map 2

The Bell Inn & Hill House

A 600-year-old timber-framed coaching inn, as busy today with happy locals as it was when pilgrims stopped on their way to Canterbury. Everything here is a treat: hanging lanterns in the courtyard, stripped boards in the bar, smartly dressed staff in the restaurant, copious window boxes bursting with colour. This is a proper inn, warmly welcoming, with thick beams, country rugs, panelled walls and open fires. Stop for a pint of cask ale in the lively bar, then potter into the restaurant for sensational food, perhaps stilton ravioli, grilled Dover sole, orange and passion fruit tart. Christine grew up here, John joined her 35 years ago; both are much respected in the trade, as is Joanne, their loyal manager of many years and Master Sommelier. An infectious warmth runs throughout this ever-popular inn. As for the bedrooms, go for the suites above the shop: cosy, individual, very traditional. In the morning stroll up the tiny high street to breakfast with the papers at elegant Hill House, then head north into Constable country or east to the pier at Southend. London is close.

Price	£50–£60. Suites £85.
Rooms	15: 7 doubles, 3 twins, 5 suites.
Meals	Lunch & dinner from £11.95.
	Bar meals from £8.95.
	Not bank holidays.
Closed	Christmas Day & Boxing Day.

Wonderful walking on the doorstep with field & woodland smells

Christine & John Vereker
High Road,
Horndon on the Hill,
Stanford le Hope SS17 8LD

Tel	+44 (0)1375 642463
Email	info@bell-inn.co.uk
Web	www.bell-inn.co.uk

Entry 63   Map 4

The Mistley Thorn

This Georgian pub stands on the high street and dates back to 1746, but inside you find a fresh contemporary feel that will tickle your pleasure receptors. The mood is laid-back with a great little bar, an excellent restaurant and bedrooms that pack an understated punch. Downstairs, an open-plan feel sweeps you through high-ceilinged rooms that flood with light. Expect tongue-and-groove panelling, Farrow & Ball colours, blond wood furniture and smart wicker chairs. Climb up to excellent rooms for smartly dressed beds, flat-screen TVs, DVD players and iPod docks. You get power showers above double-ended baths, those at the front have fine views of the Stour estuary, all are exceptional value for money. Back down in the restaurant dig into delicious food; Sherri runs a cookery school next door and has a pizzeria in town. Try smoked haddock chowder, Debden duck with clementine sauce, chocolate mocha tart (if you stay on a Sunday or Monday, dinner is free). Best of all: special dog meals on request. Constable country is all around and history, too; the Witch-Finder General once lived on this spot.

Price	£80–£105. Singles from £65.
Rooms	7: 4 doubles, 3 twins/doubles.
Meals	Lunch from £7.95.
	Dinner, 3 courses, about £25.
Closed	Rarely.

 A doggie bag filled with homemade biscuits, towels for muddy paws & a scrumptious sausage for breakfast

David McKay & Sherri Singleton
High Street,
Mistley CO11 1HE
Tel   +44 (0)1206 392821
Email   info@mistleythorn.co.uk
Web   www.mistleythorn.co.uk

Charingworth Manor

This grand old Cotswold manor house stands in blissful country with huge views from its lovely garden shooting south for three miles. Outside, creepers roam on 14th-century walls, while inside you find ancient beams and a roaring fire, painted panelling in the sitting room, mullioned windows in the drawing room, and flickering candles by the score in the low-ceilinged restaurant. Bedrooms – all recently refurbished – come in the same soothing contemporary style: neutral colours, padded headboards, excellent linen, flat-screen TVs. Some open onto private terraces, others have the odd beam, all have white robes in excellent bathrooms. Those in the main house tend to be elegantly traditional – old armoires, window seats, fine views. Elsewhere, there's lots to do: tennis, croquet on the lawn, a small gym, an indoor pool, a steam room and sauna, sun loungers too. Parasols shade pretty tables and chairs on the terrace, perfect for cream teas. As for dinner, try asparagus soup, chump of lamb, lemon mousse with a black pepper sorbet. Sunday night prices are a steal, and Stratford is close.

Price	£145-£205. Suites £245-£350. Singles from £110. Half-board from £105 p.p.
Rooms	26: 20 twins/doubles, 6 suites.
Meals	Lunch from £14.95. Sunday lunch £14.95-£19.95. Dinner about £35.
Closed	Never.

 Four rooms open straight onto the garden – 55 acres. Spot-on for dogs to stretch their legs

	Michael Eastick
	Charingworth,
	Chipping Campden GL55 6NS
Tel	+44 (0)1386 593555
Email	info.charingworthmanor@classiclodges.co.uk
Web	www.classiclodges.co.uk

Entry 65   Map 3

Corse Lawn House Hotel

Baba is old-school, so is Corse Lawn. The service is excellent, the food is delicious and generous prices make it a must for those in search of an alternative to contemporary minimalism. This fine Queen Anne manor house was built on the ruins of a Tudor inn where Cromwell is thought to have slept before the battle of Worcester (1651). It is now the hub of a small community. The Rotary Club dine once a week, shooting parties gather in winter, locals come to celebrate. At the front, a willow dips its branches into the country's last surviving coach-wash; in summer you can sit out under parasols and dig into a cream tea while ducks glide by. Inside, slightly eccentric furnishings prevail. There are palms in the swimming pool, a sofa'd bistro for light meals, an open fire in the sitting room, a paddock at the back for visiting horses. Big bedrooms are eminently comfortable and come in warm colours with crisp linen, bowls of fruit, fresh milk and leaf tea; the four-poster looks onto the pond. As for the food, it's utterly delicious: game terrine, grilled lobster, sticky toffee pudding.

Price	£150–£170. Suites £185. Singles £95. Half-board from £80 p.p.
Rooms	18: 13 twins/doubles, 2 four-posters, 3 suites.
Meals	Lunch & dinner £10–£35.
Closed	Christmas Day & Boxing Day.

 Pups can motor about mown paths through fields & loll in grounds especially for dogs

Baba Hine
Corse Lawn,
Gloucester GL19 4LZ
Tel   +44 (0)1452 780771
Email   enquiries@corselawn.com
Web   www.corselawn.com

The Montpellier Chapter

The Montpellier Chapter stands at the vanguard of a new movement in cool hotels: loads of style, attractive prices, excellent service from staff who care. It mixes old-fashioned hospitality (you are met in reception and shown to your room) with new technology (you browse the wine list on an iPad). More than anything else, it's a great place to be as it fills with happy locals who bring an infectious buzz. Follow your nose and find a library bar, a Victorian conservatory and a funky interior courtyard for breakfast in good weather. The style is contemporary, the building is a grand Victorian townhouse that's been meticulously restored. Bedrooms – some big, others smaller – spoil you all the way with super-comfy beds, an excess of technology and bathrooms that take your breath away. You get iPods full of local info, Nespresso coffee machines, even a complimentary mini-bar. Excellent comfort food waits in the restaurant, perhaps scallops cooked with garlic and herbs, Shepherd's pie with swede mash, tarte tatin with crème chantilly. And there's an electric car to whisk you around town.

Price	£140-£245. Suite £400.
Rooms	61: 55 doubles, 5 twins/doubles, 1 suite.
Meals	Bar lunch from £7. Restaurant lunch & dinner £12.50-£15. A la carte from £25.
Closed	Never.

Snug dog beds, water & food bowls in the room, & recommended walks

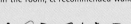

James Partridge
Bayshill Road, Montpellier,
Cheltenham GL50 3AS

Tel	+44 (0)1242 527788
Email	info@chapterhotels.com
Web	www.chapterhotels.com

Entry 67   Map 3

The New Inn at Coln

The New Inn is old – 1632 to be exact – but well-named nonetheless; a top-to-toe renovation has recently swept away past indiscretions. These days, it's all rather smart. The pub stands in a handsome Cotswold village with ivy roaming on original stone walls and a sun-trapping terrace where roses bloom in summer. Inside, airy interiors come with low ceilings, painted beams, flagged floors and fires that roar. There are padded window seats, eastern busts, gilt mirrors and armchairs in the bar. Bedrooms are a treat, all warmly elegant with perfect white linen, flat-screen TVs and good little bathrooms (a couple have claw-foot baths). There are wonky floors and the odd beam in the main house, while those in the old dovecote come in bold colours and have views across water meadows to the river; walks start from the front door. Bibury, Burford and Stow are all close, so spread your wings, then return for a wonderful meal, perhaps grilled goat's cheese with poached pear, roasted lemon sole with pink grapefruit, vanilla panna cotta with plum crumble.

Price	£115–£160. Singles from £105. Half-board from £82.50 p.p. £20 per dog per night.
Rooms	14 doubles.
Meals	Lunch from £5.95. Dinner, 3 courses, about £30. Sunday lunch from £12.50.
Closed	Never.

  B&B for dogs too: scrumptious sausages to start the day

Stuart Hodges
Main Street, Coln St Aldwyns,
Cirencester GL7 5AN
Tel   +44 (0)1285 750651
Email   info@new-inn.co.uk
Web   www.new-inn.co.uk

Entry 68   Map 3

Otter Camp

Great Farm is a family-run farm in Whelford, a perfect place from which to explore the gentle English villages of the Cotswolds. Otter Camp consists of two shepherd's huts and a fisherman's hut, set in a clearing. The river bank forms a boundary to the front, there's woodland at the rear, and sheep and cattle nearby – keep the dogs on leads. Wend your way along the leafy path through the trees and cross the narrow footbridge over the river – children will find it idyllic. The first shepherd's hut is your bedroom, with a full-size double bed and a traditional wood-burning stove. The second, alongside, has a modern shower, a basin and a loo. The fisherman's hut – again, all yours – with comfy chairs and wind-up radio, is a great little place to curl up with a book and shelter from the midday sun. There's a firepit, a gas stove, you're stocked with the staples, and Leonie can provide a hamper of local ingredients for breakfasts and picnics; dinners too can be delivered. A ladder on the bank gives access to the river for paddling, swimming and fishing… if you're lucky, you'll spot an otter.

Price	From £95 per night.
Rooms	Shepherd's hut for 2.
Meals	Self-catering.
Closed	Never.

 Dog bowls & a mystery treat provided

Canopy & Stars
Thatched Cottage, Whelford,
Fairford GL7 4EA
Tel +44 (0)1275 395447
Email enquiries@canopyandstars.co.uk
Web www.canopyandstars.co.uk

Kempsford Manor

On the edge of the Cotswolds, a huge 17th-century village manor surrounded by mature trees, and beautifully tended gardens (the snowdrops are wonderful) leading to an orchard and canal walk. Crunch up the gravelled drive to find floor-to-ceiling windows, dark floors with patterned rugs, wood panelling, a piano and a library. Spacious bedrooms have super garden views; one comes with a Chinese theme, rugs, blankets and a pretty quilt; bathrooms are functional and old-fashioned. Stoke up on Zehra's homemade muesli and bread and ask her advice on the finest dog walks. Return for dinner; vegetables are deliciously home-grown.

The Guest House

You get your own new timber-framed house with masses of light and space, a terrace, and spectacular valley views. The living room has wooden floors, lovely old oak furniture and French windows onto a safe two-acre garden where dogs may roam free. Sue brims with enthusiasm, gives you a list of dog-friendly pubs and is a flexible host: breakfast can be over in her kitchen or continental in yours. Look forward to the papers, eggs from the hens, delicious dinners with produce from the veg patch. The bedroom is a charming up-in-the-eaves room with colourful linen and a big comfy bed; a fresh, simple wet room is downstairs.

Price	£65–£70. Singles from £40.
Rooms	3: 2 doubles, 1 single sharing 2 bathrooms.
Meals	Dinner by arrangement. Pub 200 yds.
Closed	Rarely.

 Delicious dog breakfasts of scrambled eggs, cosy dozes by a log fire – & dog-sitting!

Zehra I Williamson
High Street, Kempsford,
Fairford GL7 4EQ
Tel   +44 (0)1285 810131
Mobile   +44 (0)7980 543882
Email   info@kempsfordmanor.com
Web   www.kempsfordmanor.com

Entry 70   Map 3

Price	From £120.
Rooms	Cottage: 1 double, sitting room, sofabed & kitchenette.
Meals	Dinner, 2 courses, from £12; 3 courses, from £20. Pub 1 mile.
Closed	Rarely.

Walks with our dogs in the day & friendly dog-sitting at night

Sue Bathurst
Manor Cottage,
Bagendon,
Cirencester GL7 7DU
Tel   +44 (0)1285 831417
Email   heritage.venues@virgin.net
Web   www.cotswoldguesthouse.co.uk

Entry 71   Map 3

The Court

Just off Chipping Campden high street this huge honey-hued Jacobean house has been in the family since it was built in 1624 by Sir Baptist Hicks. Dogs sound the alarm when you knock... step inside to find a relaxed faded splendour. Delicate ornaments sit on exquisite antiques, family portraits and spectacular oils line the walls; up winding stairs, bedrooms (some with TVs) have comfy beds, books, a mix of beautiful and functional furniture and breathtaking views of rooftops or gardens. Jane's friendly housekeeper cooks your Aga breakfast – eggs and jams are from the garden. The walking is superb, Hidcote and Kiftsgate are close.

Steep Meadow

An understated exterior belies the charm of Helen and John's modern home. Built into the hillside, bedrooms give a hare's-eye view of woods and wildlife; the guest sitting room above, with a wall of sliding glass, is a comfortable eyrie peering over the Forest of Dean. Recycled wood and bricks warm light and generous bedrooms, gleaming bathrooms have homemade soaps and dogs get their own shower. Meals from the Aga are superb; eggs, bacon, sausages, pork and honey from the Meadow's lively menagerie set you up for walks from the door, and Jake the rescue dog will hand yours the wonderful Ruff Guide to the Forest of Dean.

Price	£40-£70.	Price	£78-£88. Singles £38.
Rooms	4: 2 family suites; 1 double, 1 family suite, each with separate bath.	Rooms	3: 2 doubles, 1 single.
Meals	Pub/restaurant 30 yds.	Meals	Dinner, 2 courses, £14; 3 courses, £17. Pub/restaurant 400 yds.
Closed	Christmas, Easter, Whitsun bank holiday & half term.	Closed	Rarely.

 Dog biscuits & treats at breakfast, good walks locally – just keep an eye out for sheep!

 A scrumptious dog's breakfast: poached egg on wholemeal dog biscuits garnished with crispy bacon rind

Jane Glennie
Calf Lane,
Chipping Campden GL55 6JQ
Tel   +44 (0)1386 840201
Email   j14glennie@aol.com
Web   www.thecourtchippingcampden.co.uk

Helen Theophilus
Staunton,
Coleford GL16 8PD
Tel   +44 (0)1594 832316
Email   helen@steepmeadow.co.uk
Web   www.steepmeadow.co.uk

Entry 72   Map 3

Entry 73   Map 2

The Anchor Inn

A super-smart country dining pub, renovated recently in imperious style. The house is Edwardian with 14th-century roots, and its treasure-trove interiors are full of beautiful things: timber frames, wavy beams, oils by the score, trumpets and pith helmets, a piano in the bar. Old photographs of Charterhouse School cover the walls, there are sofas by the fire in the panelled bar and busts on plinths in the airy restaurant, where you dine on proper English food: devilled kidneys, lemon sole, treacle tart with clotted cream. Doors open onto a lawned garden with country views, so come in summer for lunch in the sun. Bedrooms upstairs are seriously indulging. Expect beautifully upholstered armchairs, seagrass matting, fine linen on comfy beds, flat-screen TVs. There are power showers, huge towels and bathrobes, too. One suite is open to the rafters and comes with Nelson and friends framed on the wall; another has an enormous window that opens onto a private balcony. Don't come looking for a gastropub; do come looking for good ales, sublime food and old-world interiors. A treat!

Price	£110-£140.
Rooms	5: 4 doubles, 1 suite.
Meals	Lunch & dinner £6.50-£19.
Closed	Christmas Day.

 A brimming biscuit jar for visiting canines & walking maps with routes straight from the door

Amy Greener
Lower Froyle,
Alton GU34 4NA
Tel   +44 (0)1420 23261
Email   info@anchorinnatlowerfroyle.co.uk
Web   www.anchorinnatlowerfroyle.co.uk

Entry 74   Map 3

The Peat Spade

Hampshire is as lovely as any county in England, deeply rural with lanes that snake through glorious countryside. As if to prove the point, the Peat Spade serves up a menu of boundless simplicity and elegance. First there's this dreamy thatched village in the Test valley, then there's the inn itself, packed to the gunnels with lip-licking locals for Sunday lunch in early February (and there's a 4pm sitting to satisfy demand). A Roberts radio on the bar brings news of English cricket, gilt mirrors sparkle above smouldering fires, fishing rods hang from the ceiling (fish the Test while you're here) and a pith helmet sits in an alcove. There's a horseshoe bar, flowers everywhere, varnished wood floors and claret walls. Upstairs, a snug residents' sitting room, a roof terrace for summer breakfasts and a couple of bedrooms above the bar. Others are in next-door Peat House, all are as lovely as you'd expect. Fired Earth colours, sisal matting, big wooden beds, crisp white linen – the works. There's no space left to describe how utterly wonderful the food is, but be assured it is.

Price	From £130.
Rooms	6: 2 doubles, 1 twin.
	Peat House: 3 doubles.
Meals	Lunch & dinner £5-£25.
Closed	Christmas.

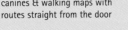 A brimming biscuit jar for visiting canines & walking maps with routes straight from the door

Paul Whitburn
Longstock,
Stockbridge SO20 6DR

Tel	+44 (0)1264 810612
Email	info@peatspadeinn.co.uk
Web	www.peatspadeinn.co.uk

Waterfall Cottage

The 1840 cottage is set in gardens planted by a Chelsea gold-medallist. Embraced by stream, waterfall and trees, its lawns lead directly to New Forest heathland and forest dotted with ponies and deer... quintessentially English, a magical place. John used to paddle in the stream as a boy – his aunt (the gardener) used to live here – now there's a lovely new summerhouse too, perfect for curling up in with a good book. Inside, the cottage is light and sunny and full of family antiques and some of Naomi's paintings and John's photographs. Restored parquet floors, velvet drapes, fresh flowers, Aga and working coal and log fire create cottage cosiness. Off a big landing are three eiderdowned bedrooms: the master with its own dressing room and tiny, wisteria-clad balcony, the second double with hugely wide floorboards and goatskin rugs, the little single with sloped ceiling and Victorian bed. Pubs, shops, bike-hire and horse-drawn carriages are a mile off; walks are on the spot. And everywhere, the song of birds and stream: it's like stumbling upon a hidden corner of England.

Price	£440-£1,050 per week.
Rooms	Cottage for 5.
Meals	Self-catering.
Closed	Never.

 Bow-wow heaven: out of the back gate & straight into open forest

Naomi King
Burley,
New Forest BH24 4HR

Tel	+44 (0)1722 334337
Email	naomi4law@btinternet.com
Web	www.newforestcottage.biz

Entry 76   Map 3

The Master Builder's House Hotel

The position here is faultless: lawns roll down to the Beaulieu river, curlews race across the water, a vast sky hangs overhead. The house, built in 1729, was home to shipwrights who served the British fleet and Nelson's favourite vessel, *Agamemnon*, was built here. Inside, newly refurbished interiors mix contemporary flair with classical design. Expect earthy colours and a roaring fire in the yachtsman's bar, then huge sofas and watery views in the sitting room. Bedrooms in the main house are nothing short of gorgeous: huge beds, pots of colour, fabulous views, super bathrooms. Those in the annexe are simpler, but cosy – good value for money. Back downstairs, the dining room swings to an informal beat. You get wooden booths, smart rugs and doors that open onto a terrace which looks the right way. You can eat here in summer or barbecue on the lawn, perhaps grilled lobster, a rib-eye steak, then custard tart with nutmeg ice cream. Stride out on the footpaths that sweep along the river, dive into the forest to cycle and ride or lose yourself in acres of silence.

Price	£105–£180. Singles from £95. Half-board from £82.50 p.p. £20 per dog per night.
Rooms	24: 5 doubles, 3 suites. Annexe: 11 doubles, 5 twins/doubles.
Meals	Lunch from £7.50. Dinner, 3 courses, £25–£30.
Closed	Never.

B&B for dogs too: scrumptious sausages to start the day

Colin Curran
Bucklers Hard, Beaulieu,
Brockenhurst SO42 7XB

Tel +44 (0)1590 616253
Email enquiries@themasterbuilders.co.uk
Web www.themasterbuilders.co.uk

Bay Trees

Step in from the village street and you find yourself in a striking hall where the guest book perches on the music stand! Comfortable bedrooms are spotless and warm, with a hint of luxury; the double has French windows opening to a lush suntrap of a garden, a wonderful surprise, full of arbours and weeping willow and a brook at the end with a seat for two. Breakfasts are in gourmet style, served in the conservatory overlooking the magnolia. The shingle beach with views to the Isle of Wight is a sprint away.

Price	£80–£130. Singles from £50.
Rooms	4: 1 double, 1 four-poster; 1 triple, 1 single sharing bath (2nd room let to same party only).
Meals	Restaurants/pubs 100 yds.
Closed	Rarely.

  Large garden to explore – plus exciting forest walks & leisurely strolls in the pleasure garden

Mark & Sarah Clayson
8 High Street, Milford-on-Sea,
Lymington SO41 0QD
Tel   +44 (0)1590 642186
Email   sarah.clayson@btinternet.com
Web   www.baytreebedandbreakfast.co.uk

Entry 78   Map 3

Glewstone Court Country House Hotel & Restaurant

Those in search of the small and friendly will love it here. Bill and Christine run Glewstone with great style, instinctively disregarding the bland new world in favour of a more colourful landscape. Their realm is this attractive country house, once owned by Guy's Hospital. Inside, an eclectic collection of art and antiques fills the rooms. Eastern rugs cover stripped wood floors, resident dog Ben snoozes in front of the fire – may yours be equally content – and guests gather in the drawing-room bar to eat, drink and make merry. Outside, there's croquet on the lawn in the shade of an ancient cedar of Lebanon, while back inside a fine Regency staircase spirals up to a galleried landing. Warmly comfortable bedrooms wait. A couple are huge, those at the front have long views across to the Forest of Dean, those at the back overlook cherry orchards; one room on the ground floor opens onto the garden. Fabulous food, much local, is reason enough to come, with Herefordshire beef served pink with a claret gravy at lunch on Sunday. The Forest of Dean and the Wye valley are close.

Price	£125-£145. Singles £60-£85.
Rooms	9: 6 doubles, 1 four-poster, 1 single, 1 suite.
Meals	Lunch from £12.50. Dinner, 3 courses, about £30. Sunday lunch £20.
Closed	25-27 December.

 A copy of 'Ben's Favourite Walks' is for keeps: the best strolls around Ross-on-Wye

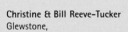

Christine & Bill Reeve-Tucker
Glewstone,
Ross-on-Wye HR9 6AW
Tel   +44 (0)1989 770367
Email   glewstone@aol.com
Web   www.glewstonecourt.com

Entry 79   Map 2

Garnstone House

Come for peace and quiet in the Welsh Marches, good food and lovely, humorous, down-to-earth hosts. The atmosphere is easy, and the furniture a lifetime's accumulation of eclectic pieces and pictures and prints of horses, hounds and country scenes. After dinner and good conversation, climb the picture-lined stairs to a comfortingly carpeted bedroom – either a twin or a double – and a bathroom that is properly old-fashioned. Delicious breakfasts, good dinners and a stunning garden to explore – the variety and colour of the springtime flowers are astonishing and the clematis is a glory.

Winforton Court

Dating from 1500, the Court is dignified in its old age: undulating floors, great oak beams, thick walls, a long gallery for family parties. It is a dramatic, colourful home with exceptional timber-framed bedrooms; one room has an Indian-style bathroom and roll top bath, the sumptuous suite has a sitting area with sofas. Choose a book from the small library and relax by a warming log fire in the elegant guest sitting room; all is immaculate. Your hosts are delightful and generous: decanters of sherry, bedside chocolates, delicious breakfasts. Visit Hay, walk down to the Wye, relax in the splendid garden.

Price	From £80. Singles from £45.	Price	£90-£115. Singles from £75.
Rooms	2: 1 double, 1 twin, each with separate bath.	Rooms	3: 1 double, 1 four-poster, 1 four-poster suite.
Meals	Dinner from £25. Pub/restaurant 1 mile.	Meals	Pub/restaurant 2-minute walk.
Closed	Rarely.	Closed	20-30 December.

   Walks from the door & a great big garden to play in

   Dog treats in the room, towels for muddy paws & a sausage or two for breakfast

Dawn & Michael MacLeod
Weobley HR4 8QP
Tel   +44 (0)1544 318943
Email   macleod@garnstonehouse.co.uk
Web   www.garnstonehouse.co.uk

Jackie Kingdon
Winforton HR3 6EA
Tel   +44 (0)1544 328498
Email   jackie@winfortoncourt.co.uk
Web   www.winfortoncourt.co.uk

Seaview Hotel

Everything here is a dream. You're 50 yards from the water in a small seaside village that sweeps you back to a nostalgic past. Locals pop in for a pint, famished yachtsmen float in for a meal, those in the know drop by for a luxurious night in indulging rooms. The bar has nautical curios nailed to its walls, the terrace buzzes with island life in summer, the restaurants hum with the contented sighs of happy diners. The whole show is orchestrated by Andrew and a battalion of kind staff, who book taxis, carry bags, send you off in the right direction. Interior designer Graham Green oversaw the fabulous refurbishment; some rooms come in smart country-house style (upholstered four-posters, padded headboards), others are contemporary (cool colours, fancy bathrooms). Three new apartments have blossomed from a converted bank next door, another is on the way. Don't miss the food. The hotel has its own farm – home-reared meat, home-grown vegetables, home-laid eggs, while the crab ramekin is an island institution. There's a treatment room, too, for expert pampering.

Price	£125-£220. Suites from £210.
Rooms	29: 14 twins/doubles, 3 four-posters. New wing: 4 doubles, 3 twins/doubles, 5 family suites.
Meals	Lunch & dinner £5-£35.
Closed	One week at Christmas.

Hand-written note to welcome your dog & a treat on the bed

Andrew Morgan
High Street, Seaview PO34 5EX
Tel   +44 (0)1983 612711
Email   reception@seaviewhotel.co.uk
Web   www.seaviewhotel.co.uk

Elvey Farm

This ancient Kentish farmhouse stands in six acres of blissful peace half a mile up a private drive. It's a deeply rural position, a nostalgic sweep back to old England. White roses run riot on red walls, a cooling vine shades the veranda, trim lawns are flanked by colourful borders. Inside you find timber frames at every turn, but the feel is airy and contemporary with smart furniture sitting amid stripped boards and old beams. Bedrooms come in similar vein. The two in the main house are big and very family-friendly, while those in the stable block are seriously indulging with sweeping wooden floors, chunky beds wrapped in crisp cotton, small sitting areas with flat-screen TV/DVDs, and fabulous wet rooms (two have slipper baths). The four-poster suite comes with a hot tub in a secret garden, but all open onto the veranda, beyond which tables and chairs are scattered across the lawn. As for the restaurant, seasonal menus of Kentish fare offer long-lost treats: potted ham, hop-pickers pie… and gypsy tart. Leeds Castle is close; the *Darling Buds of May* was filmed in the village.

Price	£105–£225.
Rooms	11: 2 suites for 4.
	Stables: 1 four-poster, 4 suites.
	Oast: 2 doubles. Granary: 2 suites.
Meals	Dinner £23–£28. Sunday lunch £12.95.
Closed	Never.

 Rabbit holes, footpaths & fields.
Rooms open to the garden

Jeff Moody & Simon Peek
Pluckley,
Ashford TN27 0SU
Tel   +44 (0)1233 840442
Email   bookings@elveyfarm.co.uk
Web   www.elveyfarm.co.uk

Entry 83   Map 4

The Bell Hotel

Sandwich, a Cinque port, is England's best-preserved medieval town. It's tiny, dates to the 12th century, and timber-framed houses are found all over town. The Bell stands opposite the old toll gate, where the river Stour glides past on its way to the sea. You can follow it down to Sandwich Bay past the famous Royal St George's golf course. Back at the hotel, oak revolving doors propel you into an elegant world of golden hues, smouldering logs and vintage luggage piled up in a corner. Open-plan interiors flow from restaurant to conservatory to bar. All are smart and airy, with blond wood and halogen lighting giving a contemporary feel. Doors open onto a terrace in summer, while locally sourced seasonal food hits the spot perfectly. Bedrooms come in different sizes and mix comfort and style in equal measure. The bigger ones with river views are fabulous, but all have warm colours, sparkling bathrooms, digital radios and WiFi access. Canterbury is a 20-minute drive, Broadstairs, a pretty seaside town, is worth a peek.

Price	£110-£165. Suites £190-£210. Singles from £95. Half-board from £80 p.p.
Rooms	37: 29 twins/doubles, 4 family rooms, 2 singles, 2 suites.
Meals	Lunch from £5. Dinner £15-£30. Sunday lunch £15.50.
Closed	Never.

Cosy bedding, treats & towels

Matt Collins
1 Upper Strand Street,
Sandwich CT13 9EF

Tel	+44 (0)1304 613388
Email	reservations@bellhotelsandwich.co.uk
Web	www.bellhotelsandwich.co.uk

Entry 84   Map 4

The Royal Harbour Hotel

A delightfully quirky townhouse hotel that stands on a Georgian crescent with magnificent views of harbour and sea. Simplicity, elegance and a quiet eccentricity go hand in hand. The sitting room is a dream with stripped floors, gorgeous armchairs, a crackling fire and an honesty bar. Beautiful things abound: a roll top desk, super art, potted palms, a miniature orange tree bearing fruit. There are binoculars with which to scan the high seas (Ramsgate was home to the Commander of the Channel Fleet), books by the hundred for a good read (Dickens's Bleak House is up the road in Broadstairs) and a library of DVDs for the telly in your room or the cinema in the basement (home to an inspiring film production company). Bedrooms at the front are tiny, but have the view, those at the back are bigger and quieter. The suite is enormous with a coal fire and French windows that open onto a balcony. All have good linen, excellent shower rooms and flat-screen TVs. Breakfast is a leisurely feast with cured hams from James's brother, a Rick Stein food hero.

Price	£99–£139. Singles from £79. Suite £198.
Rooms	19: 13 doubles, 2 family rooms, 3 singles, 1 suite.
Meals	Restaurants in town.
Closed	Rarely.

  Dog biscuits galore – & the low-down on the finest beaches in town

James Thomas
10-11 Nelson Crescent,
Ramsgate CT11 9JF

Tel	+44 (0)1843 591514
Email	info@royalharbourhotel.co.uk
Web	www.royalharbourhotel.co.uk

The Inn at Whitewell

It is almost impossible to imagine a day when a better inn will grace the English landscape. Everything here is perfect. The inn sits just above the river Hodder with five-mile views across blistering parkland to rising fells; doors in the bar lead onto a terrace where guests sit in a row and gaze upon it. Inside, fires roar, the papers wait, there are beams, sofas, maps and copies of *Wisden*. Bedrooms are exemplary and come with real luxury, perhaps a peat fire, a lavish four-poster, a fabulous Victorian power shower. All have beautiful fabrics, Egyptian linen and gadgets galore; many have the view — you can fall asleep at night to the sound of the river. There's a restaurant for splendid food (the Queen once popped in for lunch), so dig into seared scallops, Bowland lamb, a plate of cheese or something sweet; there are bar meals for those who want to watch their weight and the Whitewell fish pie is rightly famous. Elsewhere, a small vintners in reception, seven miles of private fishing and countryside as good as any in the land. Magnificent.

Price	£113–£162. Suite £191. Singles from £83.
Rooms	23: 9 twins/doubles, 13 four-posters, 1 suite.
Meals	Bar meals from £8. Dinner £25–£35.
Closed	Never.

 Lovely dog beds to borrow, water bowls in the bars, & river to swim in at the end of the garden

Charles Bowman
Dunsop Road, Whitewell,
Clitheroe BB7 3AT

Tel	+44 (0)1200 448222
Email	reception@innatwhitewell.com
Web	www.innatwhitewell.com

The Gorse House

Passing cars are less frequent than passing horses – this is a peaceful spot in a pretty village. The lasting impression of this 17th-century cottage is of lightness and space. There's a fine collection of paintings and furniture, and oak doors lead from dining room to guest sitting room. Country style bedrooms are simply done, the largest with three views; bathrooms are a little dated. The garden was designed by Bunny Guinness, the stables accommodate up to six horses and it's a stroll to a good pub dinner. The house is filled with laughter and the Cowdells are terrific hosts who absolutely love having guests to stay.

Price	From £60. Singles £35.
Rooms	3: 1 double, 1 family for 3.
	Stable: 1 triple & kitchenette.
Meals	Packed lunch £5. Pub 75 yds.
Closed	Rarely.

 Excellent guide to local walks & a free Bonio to keep tails wagging

Lyn & Richard Cowdell
33 Main Street, Grimston,
Melton Mowbray LE14 3BZ

Tel	+44 (0)1664 813537
Mobile	+44 (0)7780 600792
Email	cowdell@gorsehouse.co.uk
Web	www.gorsehouse.co.uk

Entry 87   Map 6

The Bull & Swan

A magical renovation, an ancient inn that stands a short walk from the middle of glorious Stamford. It's part of the Burghley estate – and the Order of Little Bedlam, a 17th-century aristocratic drinking club, would almost certainly have popped in for the odd snifter. Not that they had it this good. Step inside to find varnished wood floors, golden stone walls, fires smouldering all over the place and newspapers hanging on poles. At the bar venison Scotch eggs are impossible to resist, as are a raft of local ales and splendid wines. You eat wherever you want, here or in the dining room across the coach arch, where leather-backed settles take the strain and regal oils adorn the walls. As for beautiful bedrooms, they come in country-house style with huge beds, fabulous linen, warm colours and super-funky bathrooms. Most are big, all are delightful, mattresses are divine. Back downstairs, delicious food waits, perhaps stilton on toast, Burghley game pie, apple and blueberry crumble. And don't miss Burghley, a five-minute stroll, one of Britain's finest houses.

Price	£80–£110. Half-board from £70 p.p. £20 per dog per night.
Rooms	7: 5 doubles, 2 twins/family.
Meals	Lunch from £6. Dinner, 3 courses, £25–£30.
Closed	Never.

 B&B for dogs too: scrumptious sausages to start the day

	Ben Larter
	St Martins,
	Stamford PE9 2LJ
Tel	+44 (0)1780 766412
Email	enquiries@thebullandswan.co.uk
Web	www.thebullandswan.co.uk

Entry 88   Map 6

Brook House

A two-storey stable conversion in warm stone, in its own statue and bamboo-filled courtyard – all yours. Beyond is farmland as far as the eye can see. Downstairs: a fresh stylish feel to the sitting room with its Farrow & Ball 'matchstick' walls, cream sofa, tumbled limestone floors with underfloor heating and handy fridge. Up thick biscuit carpets to the spacious, semi-galleried bedroom with white cane furniture, sloped ceiling, pretty fabrics and (from the bath!) sunset views. Julian and Jenny have created a magical garden which is yours to explore – but stoke up with a hearty breakfast first. Wonderful walks abound.

Price	£92. Singles £70.
Rooms	Stables: 1 double & sitting/dining room.
Meals	Pubs/restaurants from 2 miles.
Closed	Christmas.

Biscuits for well-mannered mutts, & a kennel for those who prefer to spend the night outdoors

	Julian & Jenny McAlpine
	Gunby, Grantham NG33 5LF
Tel	+44 (0)1476 860010
Email	jennifermcalpine@aol.com
Web	www.honeyandmcalpine.co.uk

Entry 89 Map 6

Heron Cottage

A super spot for a family break – in the heart of lively Castle Acre village, next to the castle's ancient gateway, a skip from pubs, tea room and village green. The cottage itself is modern, fresh and smartly decorated, its inviting living room dotted with comfy sofas, a sisal rug on a wood floor, bookshelves laden with novels and magazines and a wood-burner that comes with a full basket of logs. The family kitchen is well-equipped and you eat together in a dining area bright with candlesticks, objets d'art and pots of scented lavender. Upstairs, fall back on large painted wooden beds scattered with cerise cushions, all top quality and spotlessly clean. Outside is a small courtyard garden, and the castle grounds behind are suitable for early morning pootles. For dog walkers, the Peddars Way rambles down the old Roman Road to the Norfolk Coast Path. For sightseers, it's a short drive to the 11th-century ruins of Cluniac Priory and historic Houghton Hall. For ornithologists, the bird-rich salt marshes lining the North Norfolk coast are an absolute must – but keep the dogs on leads!

Price	£250–£390 per week.
Rooms	Cottage for 4.
Meals	Self-catering.
Closed	Nov–March.

 An invaluable guide is provided to walks & dog-friendly beaches, pubs, cafés & restaurants

	Marian Sanders
	6 Bailey Gate,
	Castle Acre PE32 2AF
Tel	+33 (0)5 46 04 01 66
Email	marianatmoreau@hotmail.com

Entry 90   Map 7

Gin Trap Inn

An actor and a lawyer run this old English Inn. Steve and Cindy left London for the quiet life and haven't stopped since, adding a conservatory dining room at the back and giving the garden a haircut. The Gin Trap dates to 1667, while the horse chestnut tree that shades the front took root in the 19th century; a conker championship is in the offing. A smart whitewashed exterior gives way to a beamed locals' bar with a crackling fire and the original dining room in Farrow & Ball hues. Upstairs, you find three delightful bedrooms in smart country style. Two have big bathrooms with claw-foot baths and separate showers, all come with timber frames, cushioned window seats, Jane Churchill fabrics and the odd chandelier; walkers will find great comfort here. Come down for delicious food: Thornham oysters, shoulder of lamb, a plate of local cheeses. Ringstead – a pretty village lost in the country – is two miles inland from the coastal road, thus peaceful at night. You're on the Peddars Way, Sandringham is close and fabulous sandy beaches beckon.

Price	£78–£120. Singles from £39.
Rooms	3 doubles.
Meals	Lunch from £7. Dinner from £20.
Closed	Rarely.

Dog bowl & biscuit to come home to after a long walk

Steve Knowles & Cindy Cook
6 High Street, Ringstead,
Hunstanton PE36 5JU

Tel	+44 (0)1485 525264
Email	thegintrap@hotmail.co.uk
Web	www.gintrapinn.co.uk

Entry 91   Map 7

The Hoste Arms

Nelson was a local, but now it's farmers, fishermen and film stars who jostle at the bar and roast away on winter evenings in front of a roaring fire. In its 300-year history The Hoste has been a court house, a livestock market, a gallery and a brothel. These days it's more pleasure dome than inn and even on a grey February morning it was buzzing with life. The place has a genius of its own with warm bold colours, armchairs to sink into, panelled walls, a conservatory, its own art gallery. Fabulous food can be eaten anywhere and anytime, so dig into Brancaster mussels, Holkham venison, sticky toffee pudding. In summer life spills out onto tables at the front or you can dine on the terrace in the garden at the back. Rooms are all different: a tartan four-poster, an oak half-tester, leather sleigh beds in the Zulu wing, country-house elegance across the road in the Vine House; bathrooms are all predictably over the top (note the ladies' loo). Burnham Market is gorgeous, the north Norfolk coast is on your doorstep, there are vast sandy beaches for running off any excess – and don't miss afternoon tea!

Price	£122-£312. Half-board from £76.50 p.p.
	Dogs £10 per stay.
Rooms	49 + 3: 34 twins/doubles & suites.
	Vine House: 7 doubles.
	Railway Inn: 7 doubles, 1 carriage.
	3 railway cottages.
Meals	Lunch from £6. Dinner, £25-£30.
Closed	Never.

Christmas stockings & Easter Eggs...

Emma Tagg
Market Place, Burnham Market,
King's Lynn PE31 8HD
Tel   +44 (0)1328 738777
Email   reception@hostearms.co.uk
Web   www.hostearms.co.uk

Entry 92   Map 7

The White Horse

You strike gold at The White Horse. For a start, you get one of the best views on the North Norfolk coast – a long, cool sweep over tidal marshes to Scolt Head Island. But it's not just the proximity of the water that elates: the inn, its rooms and the delicious food all score top marks. Follow your nose and find a sunken garden at the front, a local's bar for billiards, a couple of sofas for a game of Scrabble, and a conservatory/dining room for the freshest fish. Best of all is the sun-trapping terrace; eat out here in summer. Walkers pass, sea birds swoop, sail boats glide off into the sunset. At high tide the water laps at the garden edge, at low tide fishermen harvest mussels and oysters from the bay. Inside, the feel is smart without being stuffy: stripped boards, open fires, seaside chic with sunny colours. Beautiful bedrooms in New England style come in duck-egg blue with spotless bathrooms. In the main house some have fabulous views, those in the garden open onto flower-filled terraces. The coastal path passes directly outside.

Price	£96–£190.
Rooms	15: 11 doubles, 4 twins.
Meals	Lunch & bar meals from £8.50.
	Dinner £13.50–£17.75.
	Sunday lunch £23.15.
Closed	Never.

 For the discerning dog, a stunning view & ramble along sandy beaches perfect for a paddle

Cliff Nye
Brancaster Staithe, King's Lynn
PE31 8BY
Tel   +44 (0)1485 210262
Email   reception@whitehorsebrancaster.co.uk
Web   www.whitehorsebrancaster.co.uk

Entry 93   Map 7

The Crown Inn

Kiwi TV chef Chris Coubrough bought his second Crown in 2008 (his first is at Wells-next-the-Sea). Right by the A148, overlooking the village green, it's a handy spot to rest and refuel while exploring the North Norfolk coast. For beyond the charming and spruced-up exterior lies a lovely big open-plan bar with low beams, rug-strewn tiles, fresh contemporary colours, shelves full of books and an assortment of well-scrubbed dining tables. Fishermen and farmers supply the produce for modern dishes listed on daily printed menus – and it's hard not to be tempted by Houghton Hall venison with braised red cabbage, sea bass with saffron and spring onion risotto, a slate of crayfish, prawns, cockles and brown shrimp (to share), and delicious warm apricot tart. It's all so relaxing and quietly pleasing why not book in for the night? Bedrooms are above, simple and stylish, with white brass beds and painted furniture, modern easy chairs and good quality fabrics, big lamps and lovely bathrooms with wooden floors. Double glazing guarantees a perfect night's sleep.

Price	£100–£125. Half board from £65 p.p.
Rooms	6: 5 doubles, 1 family room.
Meals	Lunch from £7.95.
	Dinner from £11.95.
	Sunday lunch, 3 courses, £21.95.
Closed	Rarely.

A dog bed, towel & biscuits on arrival

Chris Coubrough
The Green, East Rudham,
King's Lynn PE31 8RD
Tel   +44 (0)1485 528530
Email   reception@crowninnnorfolk.co.uk
Web   www.thecrowneastrudham.co.uk

Entry 94   Map 7

The Ship Inn Hotel

The swanky Ship is smack on the coast road and a ten-minute walk from Brancaster beach. Once a grim boozer, ignored by most, this cosy coastal bolthole is now the first port of call for post-beach drinks and tucker; kids and dogs are welcome. Grab a pint of Adnams and a crab sandwich, or linger over scallops with pea purée and pancetta… temptingly followed by pork belly with champ and cider jus, or chocolate brownie with vanilla ice cream. The bar is stylish, the food is locally sourced and the atmosphere in the dining areas is relaxed and informal. Be wowed by a quirky-chic décor: jute blinds, driftwood lights, slate-topped tables, striped fabrics, antique mirrors, objets d'art, and map-of-Norfolk wallpaper in the Map Room – it's a fun place to end a glorious day on the beach. Cosy, comfortable and imaginative rooms upstairs are a treat; most enjoyable are the bedsteads, each one different, each topped with a fat mattress and a fur or tartan throw; there are splashes of subtle colour, fresh coffee, fabulous bathrooms, some with roll-top baths and real coffee. A brilliant refuge for happy beach bums.

Price	£90–£175. Singles £70. Half board from £75 p.p.
Rooms	11: 7 doubles, 2 twins, 2 suites.
Meals	Lunch from £6.95. Dinner from £12.45. Sunday lunch, 3 courses, £21.95.
Closed	Rarely.

A dog bed, towel & biscuits on arrival

Chris Coubrough
Brancaster,
King's Lynn PE31 8AP
Tel   +44 (0)1485 210333
Email   reception@shiphotelnorfolk.co.uk
Web   www.shiphotelnorfolk.co.uk

Entry 95   Map 7

Saracens Head

Lost in the lanes of deepest Norfolk, an English inn that's hard to beat. Outside, Georgian red-brick walls ripple around, encircling a beautiful courtyard where you can sit for sundowners in summer before slipping into the restaurant for a good meal. Tim and Janie came back from the Alps, unable to resist the allure of this inn. A sympathetic refurbishment has brightened things up, but the spirit remains the same: this is a country-house pub with lovely staff who go the extra mile. Downstairs the bar hums with happy locals who come for Norfolk ales and good French wines, while the food in the restaurant is as good as it ever was, perhaps baked camembert, haunch of venison, treacle tart and caramel ice cream. Upstairs you'll find a sitting room on the landing, where windows frame country views, and six pretty bedrooms. All have been redecorated and have smart carpets, blond wood furniture, comfy beds and sparkling bathrooms. Breakfast sets you up for the day, so explore the coast at Cromer, play golf on the cliffs at Sheringham, or visit Blickling Hall, a Jacobean pile. Blissful stuff.

Price	From £95. Singles £65.
Rooms	6: 5 twins/doubles, 1 family room.
Meals	Lunch & dinner £6.50-£20.
	Not Mon & Tues lunch Sept-Jun.
Closed	Christmas.

Walks for dogs to take their owners on, towels for a rub down & wellies for guests who forgot theirs

Tim & Janie Elwes
Wolterton,
Norwich NR11 7LZ
Tel +44 (0)1263 768909
Email info@saracenshead-norfolk.co.uk
Web www.saracenshead-norfolk.co.uk

Entry 96 Map 7

The Willows Cottage

Two cottages – two staircases – woven into one, and a tiny sun room tucked onto the end. This is a sweet Norfolk brick and flint house, quintessentially English and idyllically positioned on a village road three miles from the coast. Over the garden gate is the Southrepps Common Nature Reserve, 12 hectares of reed beds and woodland bisected by boardwalks – a privileged spot. Step through the door and into the dining room to low ceilings, a wooden floor, a lovely homely feel. Then the kitchen: low-beamed, well-equipped, and a sparkling bathroom, white and light green. In the sitting room, modern artwork on the walls, books, sculptures, a berugged floor, squishy sofas and a wood-burner with logs on the house. Up those steep narrow stairs are inviting bedrooms with sloping ceilings, low windows and doors to duck; the twin is nautically themed, the double is a dream, with a carved mahogany bed and a glass chandelier. Feather toppers, scented candles, gorgeous linen… brilliant for families, walkers, romantic couples, and dogs, enticed with bowls, biscuit snacks, holiday tags and a list of all the best walkies.

Price	£395–£650 per week.
Rooms	Cottage for 4.
Meals	Self-catering.
Closed	Rarely.

 Snoopy the spaniel has whizzed up a welcome pack with lists of the best walks & beaches

Verity & David Sewell
Lower Street,
Southrepps NR11 8UL
Tel   +44 (0)1608 686351
Email   norfolkholidaycottage@gmail.com
Web   www.norfolk-cottage-holiday.co.uk

Entry 97   Map 7

The Crown Hotel

The interior of this handsome 16th-century coaching inn has been neatly rationalised yet is still atmospheric with its open fires, bare boards and easy chairs. And it's run by Chris Coubrough, an enterprising landlord who knows how to cook. Order pub food at the bar and eat it in the lounges or the lovely modern conservatory: a hearty serving of Brancaster mussels, paella with monkfish, crab claws, squid, clams and chorizo. Or, quite simply, the Crown beefburger with pepper relish and a pint of Adnams Bitter. Bold colours, modern art and attractively laid tables give life to the restaurant where local ingredients are translated into global ideas: steamed cod with ginger lemongrass and lime; Thai marinated duck breast with seared scallops and chilli jam. Bedrooms have had a classy makeover – all sport rich hues and fabrics, fat lamps, crisp linen and bright throws on big wooden beds; larger rooms have squashy sofas and DVD players. Beaches and bracing salt marsh walks are mere minutes away and the geese wheel above: this is birdwatching country!

Price	£90-£175. Singles from £70. Half-board from £75 p.p.
Rooms	12: 9 doubles, 1 twin, 2 family suites.
Meals	Lunch from £6.95. Dinner from £14.95. Sunday lunch, 3 courses, £21.95.
Closed	Rarely.

 A comfy bed, towel & biscuits on arrival for every pampered pooch

Chris Coubrough
The Buttlands,
Wells-next-the-Sea NR23 1EX
Tel   +44 (0)1328 710209
Email   reception@crownhotelnorfolk.co.uk
Web   www.thecrownhotelwells.co.uk

 Entry 98   Map 7

The Pheasant Inn

A really super little inn, the kind you hope to chance upon. The Kershaws run it with great passion and an instinctive understanding of its traditions. The stone walls hold 100-year-old photos of the local community; from colliery to smithy, a vital record of its past. The bars are wonderful: brass beer taps glow, anything wooden – ceiling, beams, tables – has been polished to perfection and the clock above the fire keeps perfect time. The attention to detail is a delight, the house ales expertly kept: Timothy Taylor's and Northern Kite. Robin cooks with relish, again nothing too fancy, but more than enough to keep a smile on your face – cider-baked gammon, grilled sea bass with herb butter, wicked puddings, Northumbrian cheeses; as for Sunday lunch, *The Observer* voted it the best in the North. Bedrooms in the old hay barn are as you'd expect: simple and cosy, good value for money. You are in the glorious Northumberland National Park – no traffic jams, no rush. Hire bikes and cycle round the lake, canoe or sail on it, or saddle up and take to the hills.

Price	£90–£100. Singles £50–£65. Half-board from £70 p.p.
Rooms	8: 4 doubles, 3 twins, 1 family room.
Meals	Bar meals from £8.95. Dinner, 3 courses, £18–£22.
Closed	25-27 December.

 Heavenly forest & lakeside walks

Walter, Irene & Robin Kershaw
Stannersburn, Hexham NE48 1DD
Tel   +44 (0)1434 240382
Email   stay@thepheasantinn.com
Web   www.thepheasantinn.com

Entry 99   Map 9

Battlesteads Hotel

In the land of castles, stone circles and fortified towers is Battlesteads, an old inn given a fresh lease of life by owners who aim to go as 'green' as possible. The boiler burns wood chips from local sustainable forestry, a poly-tunnel produces the salads, the waste composting involves the local school; no wonder the Slades have won a Green Tourism gold and Best Green Pub 2010. Enter a large, cosy, low-beamed and panelled bar with a wood-burning stove and local cask ales on hand pump. A step further and you find a spacious dining area: leather chairs at dark wood tables and a conservatory dining room that reaches into a sunny walled garden. The menus show a commitment to sourcing locally and the food is flavoursome. The Northumbrian fillet steak with Cumbrian blue cheese is meltingly tender, specials like halibut with leek fondue and spiced pea purée are scrummy. Exemplary is the housekeeping so bedrooms are spotless – and spacious, carpeted and comfortable. The newest are mini-suites, and there's wheelchair access on the ground floor. Hadrian's Wall is marvellously close.

Price	£105–£135. Singles £60–£85.
Rooms	17: 16 twins/doubles, 1 single.
Meals	Lunch & dinner from £7.95. Sunday lunch, 3 courses, £13.50.
Closed	Never.

 Doggie 'welcome pack' with a Bonio biscuit & towel for muddy paws. And dogs may dine with their owners if they wish

Richard & Dee Slade
Wark, Hexham NE48 3LS
Tel   +44 (0)1434 230209
Email   info@battlesteads.com
Web   www.battlesteads.com

Willoughby House

Past the village pub, through a gate, this three-storey brick farmhouse reflects its owners' skilful interior design. The house brims with tokens of its 18th century past, like meat hooks in the scullery-turned-sitting room, but feels ever so smart. Bedrooms are large and comfortable: climb up to Harry's room with its brass bed and toy soldiers over the fireplace; Edward's and George's share raftered loft space and a swish bathroom. Sarah rustles up delicious meals in a dining room embraced by poppy red walls and shutters. Get out on hikes or bikes; round the little village, or Southwell and Newark are close.

Price	£75-£95. Singles £55-£65.
Rooms	4: 1 twin/double; 1 double, 1 twin/double sharing bath (same party only); 1 double with separate bath/shower.
Meals	Dinner from £20. Packed lunch £7.50. Pub 3-min walk.
Closed	Christmas & occasionally.

Guide to nearby walks

Andrew & Sarah Nesbitt
Main Street, Norwell,
Newark NG23 6JN
Tel   +44 (0)1636 636266
Mobile   +44 (0)7789 965352
Email   willoughbybandb@aol.com
Web   www.willoughbyhousebandb.co.uk

Entry 101   Map 6

The Kingham Plough

You don't expect to find locals clamouring for a table in a country pub on a cold Tuesday in February, but different rules apply at the Kingham Plough. Emily, once junior sous chef at the famous Fat Duck in Bray, is now doing her own thing and it would seem the locals approve. You eat in the tithe barn, now a splendid dining room, with ceilings open to ancient rafters and excellent art on the walls. Attentive staff bring sublime food. Dig into game broth with pheasant dumplings, fabulous lamb hotpot with crispy kale, and hot chocolate fondant with blood orange sorbet. Interiors elsewhere are equally pretty, all the result of a delightful refurbishment. There's a piano by the fire in the locals' bar, a terrace outside for summer dining, fruit trees, herbs and lavender in the garden. Bedrooms, three of which are small, have honest prices and come with super-comfy beds, flat-screen TVs, smart carpets, white linen, the odd beam; one has a claw-foot bath. Arrive by train, straight from London, to be met by a bus that delivers you to the front door. The Daylesford Organic farm shop/café is close.

Price	£90–£130. Singles from £75.
Rooms	7 twins/doubles.
Meals	Lunch from £15. Bar meals from £5. Dinner, 3 courses, about £30. Sunday lunch from £17.
Closed	Christmas Day.

Scrumptious pigs' ears at the ready

Emily Watkins & Miles Lampson
The Green, Kingham,
Chipping Norton OX7 6YD
Tel   +44 (0)1608 658327
Email   book@thekinghamplough.co.uk
Web   www.thekinghamplough.co.uk

Entry 102   Map 3

The Trout at Tadpole Bridge

A 17th-century Cotswold inn on the banks of the Thames; pick up a pint, drift into the garden and watch life float by. Gareth and Helen bought The Trout after a two-year search and have cast their fairy dust into every corner: expect super bedrooms, oodles of style, delicious local food. The downstairs is open plan and timber-framed, with stone floors, gilt mirrors, wood-burners and logs piled high in alcoves. Bedrooms at the back are away from the crowd; three open onto a small courtyard where wild roses ramble on creamy stone – but you may prefer to stay put in your room and indulge in unabashed luxury. You get the best of everything: funky fabrics, trim carpets, monsoon showers (one room has a claw-foot bath), DVD players, flat-screen TVs, a library of films. Sleigh beds, brass beds, beautifully upholstered armchairs… one room even has a roof terrace. You can watch boats pass from the breakfast table, feast on local sausages, tuck into homemade marmalade courtesy of Helen's mum. Food is as local as possible, there are maps for walkers to keep you thin.

Price	£120. Suite £150. Singles from £80.
Rooms	6: 2 doubles, 3 twins/doubles, 1 suite.
Meals	Lunch & dinner £10.95–£19. Sunday lunch from £10.95.
Closed	Never.

 Local walking guides, tennis balls for the garden, & a chew for every visiting dog!

Gareth & Helen Pugh
Buckland Marsh,
Faringdon SN7 8RF

Tel	+44 (0)1367 870382
Mobile	+44 (0)7711 259406
Email	info@trout-inn.co.uk
Web	www.trout-inn.co.uk

Entry 103   Map 3

The Old School Room

Only an hour or so from London in the upmarket Thames valley with a leafy country lane feel. The small 1860s building is on a quiet road near the river leading to bigger neighbours, and the friendly owners live opposite in their own 17th-century cottage. Inside, find an insulated, high-ceilinged, functional living area with big armchairs and sofas clustered at one end, Victorian oak furniture and an open fire at the other – cosy on wintry nights – and a kitchen with all the gadgetry you need, but not a huge amount of work surface. No matter, there are heaps of good restaurants and pubs around. Off here is a small shower room with an enormous shower head and a bedroom with a big wrought-iron bed and a pretty patchwork quilt. Gorgeous leaded windows on both sides add a smattering of light. The Ridgeway footpath passes through the garden and the Chilterns are near, so stride off with the dog for a hearty hike. Oxford, Henley and the regatta are a car drive away, and Goring has a station if you prefer the train. Lovely to return to peacefulness, birdlife and the river Thames.

Price	£395-£575 per week.
Rooms	Cottage for 2.
Meals	Self-catering.
Closed	Xmas & New Year.

 Two walking routes for dogs, one including a swim in the river Thames

Jon Scourse
The Street,
North Stoke OX10 6BL
Tel +44 (0)1491 826479
Email jonscourse@btinternet.com
Web www.northstokecottages.co.uk

Entry 104   Map 3

The Olive Branch

A Michelin-starred pub in a sleepy Rutland village, where bridle paths lead out across peaceful fields. The inn dates to the 17th century and is built of Clipsham stone. Inside, a warm, informal rustic chic hits the spot perfectly; come for open fires, old beams, exposed stone walls and choir stalls in the bar. Chalk boards on tables in the restaurant reveal the names of the evening's diners, while the food – seared scallops with black pudding fritter, slow-roast pork belly with creamed leeks and apple sauce – elates. As do the hampers that you can whisk away for picnics in the country. Bedrooms in Beech House across the lane are impeccable. Three have terraces, one has a free-standing bath, all come with crisp linen, pretty beds, Roberts radios, real coffee. Super breakfasts – smoothies, boiled eggs and soldiers, the full cooked works – are served in a smartly renovated barn, with flames leaping in the wood-burner. The front garden fills in summer, the sloe gin comes from local berries, and Newark is close for the biggest antiques market in Europe. A total gem.

Price	£115-£195. Suite £175-£260. Singles from £97.50.
Rooms	6: 5 doubles, 1 family suite.
Meals	Bar meals £10.50. Dinner £14.50. Sunday lunch £24.95.
Closed	Rarely.

 Alfie the springer shares treats & walks. His top tip: sit by the youngest family member at meals (they may drop something!)

Ben Jones & Sean Hope
Main Street, Clipsham,
Oakham LE15 7SH
Tel   +44 (0)1780 410355
Email   info@theolivebranchpub.com
Web   www.theolivebranchpub.com

Pen-y-Dyffryn Country Hotel

In a blissful valley lost to the world, this small, traditional country house sparkles on the side of a peaceful hill. To the front, beyond the stone terraces that drip with aubretia, fields tumble down to a stream that marks the border with Wales. Outside, daffodils erupt in spring, the lawns are scattered with deckchairs in summer, paths lead onto the hill for excellent walks and there's a huge romping wood for the dogs right next door. Inside, colourful interiors are warmly attractive: Laura Ashley wallpaper and an open fire in the quirky bar; shuttered windows and super food in the yellow restaurant; the daily papers and a good collection of art in the sitting room. Bedrooms are stylish without being grand, most with great views. Four rooms in the adjoining coach house are dog-friendly and have their own private patios, you get silky curtains, padded bedheads, white linen. There's plenty of space for a gathering, and super food to help you celebrate; the smoked haddock at breakfast is divine. Printed dog walks lead you to all sorts of exciting places, including Offa's Dyke.

Price	£114-£166. Singles £86.
Rooms	12: 8 doubles, 4 twins.
Meals	Light lunch (for residents) by arrangement. Dinner £30-£37.
Closed	Rarely.

 A private patio for pooches, the perfect spot for their sundowner after a hard day's walk

Miles & Audrey Hunter
Rhydycroesau,
Oswestry SY10 7JD
Tel   +44 (0)1691 653700
Email   stay@peny.co.uk
Web   www.peny.co.uk

Entry 106   Map 5

Millstream Camp

The very pretty Millstream Camp is made up of two different spaces for a self-contained escape – and a dog's kennel replete with bed (though not bedding). The shepherd's hut, beautifully decorated with vintage items from the house, feather down pillows and a huge duvet filled with Welsh sheep's wool, serves as the dog-free sleeping space. The tipi, decked out with old Indian saris, campaign trunks and a lacquered table, is your sitting room. As well as a pair of day beds with vintage rugs to lounge around on, you also have a hammock and a seating area by the stream – dammed at the mill, on hot days, to create a magical bathing pool. Food and cooking are an essential part of a Millstream holiday. Carolyn runs cookery courses on site and 'food safaris': tours of local producers with ample opportunity for snacking. Back at the camp you can use the barbecue, the wood-burner or the campfire to hone your skills. There are pots of herbs, a vegetable garden and even a gas hob so you can cook up a storm. And an annotated map with resident dog Copper's favourite routes.

Price	From £90 a night.
Rooms	Hut for 2.
Meals	Self-catering.
	Pub/restaurant 4 miles.
Closed	October to March.

A tour of the grounds from resident lab Copper & a "proper bone" straight from the village butcher

Canopy & Stars
Lower Buckton Country House,
Buckton, Leintwardine SY7 0JU
Tel   +44 (0)1275 395447
Email   enquiries@canopyandstars.co.uk
Web   www.canopyandstars.co.uk

Entry 107   Map 2

Lower Buckton Country House

You are spoiled here in house-party style; Carolyn – passionate about Slow Food – and Henry, are born entertainers. Kick off with homemade cake in the drawing room with its oil paintings, antique furniture and old rugs; return for delicious nibbles when the lamps and wood-burner are flickering. Dine well at a huge oak table (home-reared pork, local cheeses, dreamy puddings), then nestle into the best linen and the softest pillows. A fabulous Dog Box is provided: bio bags, disposable gloves, food, towels. Paddle in the stream, admire the stunning views, find a quiet spot with a good book. And no cat chasers, please!

Price	£90. £10 per dog per night.
Rooms	3: 2 doubles; 1 twin/double with separate bath.
Meals	Dinner, 4 courses, £35. BYO wine. Pub/restaurant 4 miles.
Closed	Rarely.

 A tour of the grounds from resident lab Copper, & a "proper bone" straight from the village butcher

Henry & Carolyn Chesshire
Buckton, Leintwardine SY7 0JU
Tel   +44 (0)1547 540532
Mobile   +44 (0)7960 273865
Email   carolyn@lowerbuckton.co.uk
Web   www.lowerbuckton.co.uk

Entry 108   Map 2

Cleeton Court

Rare peace: a tiny lane leads to this part 14th-century farmhouse, immersed in the countryside with views over meadows and heathland. You have your own entrance, and the use of the pretty drawing room, elegantly comfortable with sofas and a log fire. Beamed bedrooms are delightfully furnished, one with a magnificent, chintzy four-poster and a vast bathroom; recline in the cast-iron bath with a glass of wine, gaze on views from the window as you soak. Bring your boots: the walking is superb, and charming Ros gives you a smashing, locally sourced breakfast to get you going. *Children over five welcome. Very well-behaved dogs only!*

Price	From £70. Singles £45-£50.
Rooms	2: 1 twin/double, 1 four-poster.
Meals	Packed lunch on request. Pubs/restaurants 1.5-4 miles.
Closed	Christmas & New Year.

 A Bonio at bedtime

Rosamond Woodward
Cleeton St Mary, Ludlow DY14 0QZ
Tel   +44 (0)1584 823379
Mobile   +44 (0)7778 903136
Email   roswoodward@talktalk.net
Web   www.cleetoncourt.co.uk

Entry 109   Map 2

Hopton House

Karen looks after her guests wonderfully – and that includes dog lovers, who are given a super stylish ground-floor room in the barn. Karen's house is a fresh and uplifting granary conversion with old beams, high ceilings and a sun-filled dining/sitting room overlooking the hills. The rooms in the barn, one up, one down (each with its own entrance) have beautifully dressed beds, silent fridges, good lighting, and deep baths (and showers). Karen's breakfasts of Ludlow sausages, home-laid eggs, fine jams and homemade marmalade set you up brilliantly for an eight-mile, dog-friendly, circular walk with no stiles. Superb.

Clun Farm House

These young relaxed owners make a great team. Susan gives you homemade marmalade at breakfast and seasonal produce at dinner; Anthony helps you discover the secrets of the village and the heavenly hills. Both are enthusiastic collectors of country artefacts and have filled their listed 15th-century farmhouse with eye-catching things; the cowboy's saddle by the old range echoes Susan's roots. Bedrooms have aged and oiled floorboards, fun florals and bold walls; bathrooms are small and simple. Walk Offa's Dyke and the Shropshire Way; return to a cosy wood-burner, a warm smile and a delicious dinner. Good value.

Price	From £105.
Rooms	3: 1 double. Barn: 2 doubles.
Meals	Restaurant 3 miles.
Closed	19-27 December.

A jar of biscuits for every dog & details of local dog-friendly pubs & places to visit

Karen Thorne
Hopton Heath,
Craven Arms SY7 0QD
Tel   +44 (0)1547 530885
Email   info@shropshirebreakfast.co.uk
Web   www.shropshirebreakfast.co.uk

Entry 110   Map 2

Price	From £75. Singles by arrangement.
Rooms	2: 1 double (with extra bunk bed room); 1 twin/double with separate shower.
Meals	Dinner from £25. Packed lunch £4. Pubs/restaurants nearby.
Closed	Occasionally.

Assorted dog chews, & towels on tap for muddy paws

Anthony & Susan Whitfield
High Street, Clun,
Craven Arms SY7 8JB
Tel   +44 (0)1588 640432
Mobile   +44 (0)7885 261391
Email   susanwhitfield@talk21.com
Web   www.clunfarmhouse.co.uk

Entry 111   Map 2

The Ancient Barn

Dive deep into the countryside to a cluster of farm buildings and this medieval cruck barn. Great wishbone-like beams open up above you, white lime-plastered walls and a heated flagstone floor set the tone, and art historian Anthea, full of warmth and friendliness, settles you in. Find a hotch-potch of sea-green sofas, wooden dining table, a pine dresser filled with good crockery, thick curtains and a smattering of art; the dated but decently equipped kitchen is to the side. Downstairs too is the double bedroom, cosy with king-sized brass bed and white Indian cover, beige linen curtains at new wooden windows, and thick towels in a new bathroom with walk-in shower. Upstairs is a simpler bedroom with a low cross beam between two beds (perfect for the agile!) and views to the farmhouse. Patio doors lead from the living room onto a little paved furnished area by the peaceful road, facing south-west so you can catch the afternoon sun. This is a child-friendly holiday home, with highchair, plastic cutlery, cot, heaps of books and games... and the thrill of tractors and cows on the spot.

Price	£325–£620 per week.
Rooms	Barn for 4.
Meals	Self-catering.
Closed	Never.

 Perfect walks for dogs, starting right outside the door

Anthea Peppin
Lower Cockhill Farm,
Castle Cary BA7 7NZ
Tel   +44 (0)1963 351288
Email   info@medievalbarn.co.uk
Web   www.medievalbarn.co.uk

Entry 112   Map 2

The Garden Studio, Hillview Cottage

A cosy cabin for two, clad inside and out in wood and smelling of pine. You're tucked in the Mendip hills, with chickens on the edge of the garden and relaxed owners living next door. There's a big soft bed with feather pillows and duvet, recycled Spanish rugs on new pine floors, comfy armchairs, books and magazines, and an electric fire that looks like a French stove. The sitting room and bedroom are one – somehow it feels better this way – all is light and relaxed, and you can store your stuff in the wardrobe of the shower room. French windows may be flung open on warm days, to a patio area with table, chairs and loungers and an above-ground pool (in summer) on your lawn. Make the most of the good pubs in the area, or bring some basics and whiz up a simple supper; the kitchen is small but has all you'll need: microwave, hob, dishwasher, and washing machine. For balmy evenings there's a grass tennis court and a croquet lawn, you can stroll to Wells in an hour and a half or take the car to Stourhead and Bath. A great little place for people and dogs – and walks start right outside the door. *2 B&B rooms in main house.*

Price	£280-£350 per week.
	B&B from £70.
Rooms	Studio for 2.
Meals	Breakfast available.
Closed	Never.

 Stride through the owners' fields to the dog-friendly village pub

Michael & Catherine Hay
Paradise Lane,
Croscombe, Wells BA5 3RN
Tel   +44 (0)1749 343526
Mobile   +44 (0)7801 666146
Email   cathyhay@yahoo.co.uk
Web   www.sawdays.co.uk/self-catering

Entry 113   Map 2

Edington House

Step back in time into this rambling, ancient English country house, where twists and turns link panelled rooms replete with silk curtains, portraits, fireplaces, chandeliers, objets d'art. Families will love exploring the countless sitting and dining rooms and large sweeping gardens: discover a pool, tennis court, Georgian summerhouse, kitchen garden, orchard and ponies. Your easy-going, well-travelled hosts (she Austrian, he English) want guests to enjoy it all. Bedrooms are just as grandiose, with draped floral fabrics, antiques and patterned wallpapers. Inge is a serious cook and suppers are a highlight.

Church House

Feel happy in this warm Georgian rectory with sweeping views over gardens, seaside homes and the Bristol channel. "We cannot imagine life without a dog," say Tony and Jane, generous people who love what they do. Bedrooms are large, pristine and indulgent with goose down duvets as soft as a cloud, swish modern bathrooms, huge towels and thoughtful extras (scrumptious biscuits, cosy hot water bottles). Breakfasts are a grand feast of eggs from their hens, organic sausages and homemade preserves, served on delightful china at a long mahogany table. Take the whole house and be cosseted – great for large gatherings. Superb.

Price	£110-£130. Singles £120.
Rooms	3: 1 four-poster, 1 double, 1 family suite for 3-4.
Meals	Dinner, 4 courses, £35. Supper, 2 courses, £20. Pub/restaurant 1 mile.
Closed	Christmas.

 Free meals, dogsitting, an orchard for romps with the resident dogs & lovely walks by the sea

Inge Sprawson
Edington TA7 9JS
Tel +44 (0)1278 722238
Email inge@edingtonhouse.co.uk
Web www.edingtonhouse.co.uk

Entry 114   Map 2

Price	From £80. Singles from £60.
Rooms	5: 4 doubles, 1 twin.
Meals	Pubs 400 yds.
Closed	Rarely.

 Treats, towels and – if your dog needs one – a crate so you don't need to bring yours

Jane & Tony Chapman
27 Kewstoke Road, Kewstoke,
Weston-super-Mare BS22 9YD
Tel +44 (0)1934 633185
Email churchhouse@kewstoke.net
Web www.churchhousekewstoke.co.uk

Entry 115   Map 2

North Wheddon Farm

Pootle through the vibrant green patchwork of Exmoor National Park and bowl down a pitted track to land in Blyton-esque bliss – a classic Somerset farmyard, crackling with geese and hens, round which is the gentleman farmer's house. Bedrooms are airy and comfortable with grand views, books, fresh flowers and small, but neat-as-a-pin bathrooms. Bring children and they will be in heaven, with eggs to collect and pigs to pat, or come just for yourself and a bit of indulgence. Food is 'River Cottage' style and much is home-reared, the walking is fabulous for miles and kind Rachael sends you off with a thermos of tea. *Self-catering also available.*

Price	£75–£80. Singles £38.50.
Rooms	3: 1 double, 1 twin/double; 1 single with separate bath.
Meals	Dinner from £24. Cold/hot packed lunch £7.50–£9.75. Pub 0.25 miles.
Closed	Rarely.

 Man's best friend is welcome on all West Somerset beaches all year round

 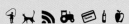

Rachael Abraham
Wheddon Cross TA24 7EX
Tel   +44 (0)1643 841791
Email   rachael@go-exmoor.co.uk
Web   www.northwheddonfarm.co.uk

 Entry 116   Map 2

The Westleton Crown

This is one of England's oldest coaching inns, with 800 years of continuous service under its belt. It stands in a village two miles inland from the sea at Dunwich, with Westleton Heath running east towards Minsmere Bird Sanctuary. Inside, you find the best of old and new. A recent refurbishment has introduced Farrow & Ball colours, leather sofas and a tongue-and-groove bar, and they mix harmoniously with panelled walls, stripped floors and ancient beams. Weave around and find nooks and crannies in which to hide, flames flickering in an open fire, a huge map on the wall for walkers. You can eat wherever you want, and a conservatory/breakfast room opens onto a terraced garden for summer barbecues. Fish comes straight off the boats at Lowestoft, local butchers provide local meat. Lovely bedrooms are scattered about and come in cool lime white with comfy beds, Egyptian cotton, flat-screen TVs. Super bathrooms are fitted out in Fired Earth, and some have claw-foot baths. Aldeburgh and Southwold are close by.

Price	£90–£215. Singles from £80.
Rooms	34: 26 doubles, 2 twins, 3 family rooms, 2 suites, 1 single.
Meals	Lunch & bar meals from £5.50. Dinner from £11.95. Sunday lunch £26.
Closed	Never.

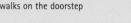

Biscuits, bowls, blankets & brilliant walks on the doorstep

Gareth Clarke
The Street, Westleton,
Saxmundham IP17 3AD
Tel   +44 (0)1728 648777
Email   info@westletoncrown.co.uk
Web   www.westletoncrown.co.uk

Entry 117   Map 4

The Ship

Once a great port, Dunwich is now a tiny (but famous) village, gradually sinking into the sea. Its well-loved smugglers' inn, almost on the beach, overlooks the salt marsh and sea and pulls in wind-blown walkers and birdwatchers from the Minsmere Reserve. In the old-fashioned bar – nautical bric-a-brac, flagged floors, simple furnishings and a stove that belts out the heat – you can tuck into legendary fish and chips washed down with a pint of Adnams. There's also a more modern dining room, but don't expect fancy food; what you get are traditional dishes in generous portions, bowls of soup with chunks of bread, and big platefuls of ham, egg and chips; in the evening, lamb, pea and mint casserole, or baked megrim in lemon butter. Up the fine Victorian staircase are spruced up bedrooms – simple, uncluttered, with period features, cord carpets, brass beds, old pine, little shower rooms. Rooms at the front have glorious salt marsh views, courtyard rooms are cosy with new pine, and the family room under the eaves is fabulous: single beds, a big futon-style bean bag, and a plasma screen for the kids.

Price	£85–£135.
Rooms	15: 11 doubles, 1 twin, 3 family rooms.
Meals	Lunch from £6.95.
	Bar meals from £9.75.
	Dinner from £9.95.
	Sunday lunch, 3 courses, £18.95.
Closed	Rarely.

Fabulous walks on beaches, heaths & forest

Matt Goodwin
St James's Street, Dunwich,
Saxmundham IP17 3DT

Tel	+44 (0)1728 648219
Email	info@shipatdunwich.co.uk
Web	www.shipatdunwich.co.uk

The Old Rectory

Through the front door to a generously proportioned and flagstoned hall and a smiling welcome from Christopher. Archways lead down the corridor to the library (cosy with maps, books and open fire) and a tall elegant staircase leads to spacious bedrooms, one with delightful bow windows and a view of the sea. There are sash windows and shutters, pelmets and antiques, heaps of good books. Outside: 20 acres of woodlands, meadows, paddocks, croquet lawn and vegetable garden (walled and wonderful). Walks galore on the Deben Peninsula, music at Snape Maltings; it's Suffolk at its best and peace reigns supreme.

Price	£75. Singles £50.
Rooms	3: 2 doubles, 1 twin. Extra bed available.
Meals	Dinner, 3 courses, £30. Supper, 2 courses, £20. Pub 5-minute walk.
Closed	Occasionally.

 Two Suffolk coastal footpath maps for all Sawday's guests with their dog

Christopher Langley
Alderton,
Woodbridge IP12 3DE
Tel   +44 (0)1394 410003
Email   clangley@keme.co.uk
Web   www.oldrectoryaldertonbandb.co.uk

Entry 119   Map 4

Oak House

A wonderful, higgledy-piggledy Suffolk pink farmhouse – and owners who love good food and adventure. Inside creaks with medieval character: lead windows, crooked stairs, low carved ceilings, inglenook fireplaces, a roll top bath, a bread oven (Tom plans pizzas). With Kathy's 60s Royal Doulton and dazzling colours you're in for some fun. Outside: fruit trees, trampoline, an unfenced pond (there's a hose and shampoo for very dirty dogs!) and a pheasant that breakfasts with Kathy's chickens. Over a candlelit dinner in the 15th-century kitchen, ask what treats hide in these quiet surroundings, from walks and castles to camels.

Price	£55-£90. Singles from £45. Child £10.
Rooms	2: 1 double; 1 double with separate bath.
Meals	Dinner from £18. BYO. Packed lunch £5.
Closed	Rarely.

Welcome pack with bed, bowls and biscuits. Dog-sitting & advice on local walks

Kathy Brooke
Mill Street,
Gislingham IP23 8JT
Tel   +44 (0)1379 788959
Email   kathy@oakhousesuffolk.co.uk
Web   www.oakhousesuffolk.co.uk

Entry 120   Map 4

Newick Park Hotel & Country Estate

A heavenly country house that thrills at every turn. The setting – 255 acres of parkland, river, lake and gardens – is spectacular; come in winter and you may wake to find a ribbon of mist entangled in a distant ridge of trees. Inside, majestic interiors never fail to elate, be they colour-coded bookshelves in a panelled study, Doric columns in a glittering drawing room or roaring fires in a sofa-strewn hall. You get all the aristocratic fixtures and fittings – grand pianos, plaster mouldings, a bar that sits in an elegant alcove, views from the terrace that run down to a lake. Oils hang on walls, chandeliers dangle above. Country-house bedrooms are the stuff of dreams: lush linen, thick floral fabrics, marble bathrooms with robes and lotions, views to the front of nothing but country; some are the size of a London flat. A two-acre walled garden provides much for the table, so don't miss exceptional food, perhaps pan-fried Rye Bay scallops, pork belly with black pudding and sage, Earl Grey parfait and almond tuille. Peacocks roam outside, Ashdown Forest is close for pooh sticks. *Min. stay two nights at weekends during Glyndebourne.*

Price	£165–£285. Singles from £125.
Rooms	16 twins/doubles.
Meals	Lunch about £20. Dinner about £30.
Closed	New Year's Eve & New Year's Day.

 A chew toy for Sawday's dog guests

Michael & Virginia Childs
Newick, Lewes BN8 4SB
Tel   +44 (0)1825 723633
Email   bookings@newickpark.co.uk
Web   www.newickpark.co.uk

The Horsebox

Wilderness Woods is a labour of love in the hands of this second generation. The Yarrow family have dedicated themselves to making their 62 acres not only an award-winning sustainable slice of Sussex, but a place of fun, food and learning. The Horsebox adds a truckload of oddness to its corner of the wood. While perfect quiet cannot be guaranteed, it's away from all the main trails and other campers; you get your own gas oven, shower (in true rustic style) and compost loo; and dogs get water balls. Despite the red leather chesterfield and the reclaimed oak flooring, the Horsebox is for the hardier traveller; beds are raised and take some scrambling into and the shower stands in a spiral-fenced enclosure of birch branches, with water heated over a fire. It all adds up to an experience that combines the best of woodland fun with more than a hint of the unusual – and you can eat, catch up with a newspaper and toast your toes by the log stove of the nearby Barn Café. Activities range from Junior Ranger programmes to relaxed barbecue weekends; even, on occasion, celebrity guest speakers at candlelit outdoor dinners.

Price	From £80 per night.
Rooms	Horsebox for 4.
Meals	Self-catering.
Closed	Never.

  Biscuits while owners have coffee, plus ponds to jump into & woodland walks off the lead

Canopy & Stars
Hadlow Down, Uckfield TN22 4HJ
Tel +44 (0)1275 395447
Email enquiries@canopyandstars.co.uk
Web www.canopyandstars.co.uk

Entry 122   Map 4

Strand House

Strand House was built in 1425 and originally stood on Winchelsea harbour, though the sea was reclaimed long ago and marshland now runs off to the coast. You can walk down after breakfast, a great way to atone for your bacon and eggs. Back at the house, cosy interiors come with low ceilings, timber frames and ancient beams, all of which give an intimate feel. You'll find warm reds and yellows, sofas galore, a wood-burner in the sitting room and an honesty bar where you help yourself. It's a homespun affair: Hugh cooks breakfast, Mary conjures up delicious dinners... maybe grilled goat's cheese with red onion marmalade, Dover sole with a lemon butter, rhubarb and ginger crumble. Attractive bedrooms are warm and colourful and a couple are small; one has an ancient four-poster, some have wonky floors, all have beamed ceilings, good linen, comfy beds. Tall people are better off with ground-floor rooms as low ceilings are de rigueur on upper floors; all rooms have compact bathrooms. The house, once a workhouse, was painted by Turner and Millais. A short walk through the woods leads up to the village.

Price	£70-£135. Singles from £60.
Rooms	13: 8 doubles, 2 triples, 1 twin/double, 1 twin, 1 suite.
Meals	Dinner, 3 courses, £29.50.
Closed	4 January-12 February: Mon-Thurs.

 Hugh's hand-made dog biscuits

Mary Sullivan & Hugh Davie
Tanyards Lane, Winchelsea,
Rye TN36 4JT
Tel   +44 (0)1797 226276
Email   info@thestrandhouse.co.uk
Web   www.thestrandhouse.co.uk

Entry 123   Map 4

Wellington House

A stroll away from the gardens of Great Dixter is a warm, comfortable, charming B&B. Behind the Victorian red-brick façade the Brogdens have worked an informal magic, giving guests a cosy sitting room and two big peaceful bedrooms above. These are creamy-walled and carpeted, with comfy mattresses, antique bed linen, pristine shower rooms and good toiletries. Fanny is passionate about food, bakes her own bread, grows her own peaches – a treat; Vivian is a charmer. Visit Bodiam by river boat, comb Camber Sands, explore Rye, revel in Dixter… and return to tea and homemade cakes in the garden.

Linacre Lodge

On the edge of the small village of Rudgwick, and originally part of the Baynards Park Estate, this late Victorian lodge house is a relaxed and friendly home. The kitchen is full of historic, Italian James Bond posters and unusual little chairs are found throughout: Laura is a collector and loves having people to stay. Smart, pretty bedrooms include elderflower cordial, flowers, sweets and magazines; one has its own sitting room with children's books and games. There's a huge choice\at breakfast: full English or continental. Chris and Laura are keen walkers – borrow maps, order a packed lunch and set off from the door.

Price	£90. Singles £60.
Rooms	2 doubles.
Meals	Dinner, 3 courses, from £25 (min 4); 2 courses, £22. Pubs within 2 miles.
Closed	Christmas & New Year.

 Doggie chews & biscuits, & an enclosed garden for running around in

Price	From £85. Singles from £70. Child £10.
Rooms	2: 1 double; 1 double & sitting room.
Meals	Packed lunch £6.50. TV supper £12.50. Pub/restaurant 2 miles.
Closed	Christmas & New Year.

 Welcome letter, doggie pack, blanket, towel, water bowl & midnight snack

Fanny & Vivian Brogden
Dixter Road, Northiam,
Rye TN31 6LB

Tel	+44 (0)1797 253449
Mobile	+44 (0)7989 928236
Email	fanny@frances14.freeserve.co.uk
Web	www.wellingtonhousebandb.co.uk

Entry 124   Map 4

Laura Anstead
Baynards, Rudgwick,
Horsham RH12 3AD

Tel	+44 (0)1403 823522
Mobile	+44 (0)7980 003135
Email	chrisandlaura@linacrelodge.co.uk
Web	www.linacrelodge.co.uk

Entry 125   Map 3

The Red Lion

Dogs are welcome in this ancient warren of a pub and canine sketches adorn the walls. The pub's own Cocoa – 'The Landlady' – is often around. But that doesn't mean the whiff of wet canine… instead you get the mouthwatering aroma of excellent, imaginative cooking from Sarah Keightley, co-manager and chef. Crispy-battered cod and chips with caper berries and mushy peas are served here on *The Red Lion Times* while pork tenderloin comes wrapped in pancetta with apple purée, black pudding and Dijon mustard sauce. A meltingly warm pear and ginger pudding with toffee sauce will round it all off nicely. And you can stay, in five bedrooms that reflect the unfussy approach. With natural colours and crisp ginghams, their comfort and quality make up for their size; in a place that goes back 250 years, bedrooms are not likely to be huge. Downstairs is space for everyone, from the pool room to the restaurant to the beautiful flagged bar area warmed by a real fire and a wood-burning stove. A smart but sensitive refurb has not cost this village pub its character, nor its sense of community.

Price	£85-£185. Singles £55-£75.
Rooms	5: 2 doubles, 1 twin, 1 single, 1 family room.
Meals	Lunch & dinner £11.95-£18.95.
Closed	Never.

 Delicious home-cooked pigs' ears behind the bar

Lisa Phipps & Sarah Keightley
Main Street, Long Compton,
Shipston-on-Stour CV36 5JS
Tel   +44 (0)1608 684221
Email   info@redlion-longcompton.co.uk
Web   www.redlion-longcompton.co.uk

Entry 126   Map 3

Marston House

A generous feel pervades this lovely family home; Kim's big friendly kitchen is the hub of the house. She and John are easy-going and kind and there's no standing on ceremony. Feel welcomed with tea on arrival, delicious breakfasts, oodles of interesting facts about what to do in the area. The house, with solar electricity, is big and sunny; old rugs cover parquet floors, soft sofas tumble with cushions, sash windows look onto the smart garden packed with birds and borders. Bedrooms are roomy, traditional and supremely comfortable. A special, peaceful place with a big heart, great walks from the door and Silverstone a short hop.

Price	£85–£100. Singles from £60.
Rooms	2: 1 twin/double with separate bath; 1 twin/double with separate shower.
Meals	Supper, 3 courses, £29.50. Dinner £35 (min. 4). Pub 5-minute walk.
Closed	Rarely.

Dog-friendly walks, edible treats & lots of spoiling

Kim & John Mahon
Byfield Road, Priors Marston,
Southam CV47 7RP

Tel	+44 (0)1327 260297
Mobile	+44 (0)7813 831028
Email	kim@mahonand.co.uk
Web	www.ivabestbandb.co.uk

Entry 127   Map 3

The Bath Arms at Longleat

A 17th-century coaching inn on the Longleat estate in a gorgeous village lost in the country; geese swim in the river, cows laze in the fields and lush woodland wraps around you. At the front the 12 apostles – a dozen pollarded lime trees – shade a gravelled garden, while at the back two large stone terraces, separated by beds of lavender, soak up the sun (you can eat out here in good weather). Inside are the best of old and new: flagstones and boarded floors mix with a stainless steel bar and Farrow & Ball paints. The feel is smart and airy, with a skittle alley that doubles as a sitting room (they show movies here too) and shimmering Cole & Son wallpaper in the dining room. For lunch you can dig into a gamekeeper's ploughman's lunch, for dinner you can try pork reared by the hotel. Bedrooms are a real treat. Expect lots of colour, big wallpapers, beds dressed in Egyptian cotton, DVD and CD players; bathrooms come in black slate, some with free-standing baths, others with deluge showers. Longleat is at the bottom of the hill – the walk down is majestic.

Price	£95–£170. Singles from £85. Half-board from £75 p.p. Lodge £120 for 2–4. £20 per dog per night.
Rooms	15 + 1: 13 doubles, 2 twins. Self-catering lodge for 4.
Meals	Lunch from £5. Dinner, 2 courses, £25.
Closed	Never.

Scrumptious sausages at breakfast

Peter Stevens
Horningsham,
Warminster BA12 7LY

Tel +44 (0)1985 844308
Email enquiries@batharms.co.uk
Web www.batharms.co.uk

Entry 128   Map 2

The Compasses Inn

A 14th-century whitewashed inn, lost down Wiltshire's sleepy lanes. Little has changed in 600 years: flagged floors, stone walls and heavy beams are original, the beams salvaged from an ancient English naval fleet. Once the haunt of drovers and smugglers, now it's happy locals who jostle at the bar. Duck instinctively into the cosy darkness of this quirky inn to find low ceilings, a roaring fire and small booths divided by rustic cast-offs: a cartwheel here, a stable door there, an old piano at the end of the room. Lanterns glow, the odd pitchfork hangs on the wall and boarded menus entice you with super country cooking, perhaps potted crab, Gressingham duck, and brioche bread and butter pudding. Pretty bedrooms, all above, are a steal, with country rugs, wonky ceilings and well-dressed beds, flat-screen TVs and cool little bathrooms, a painted beam here, a window seat there, a French bed. There's also a quaint little self-catering cottage next door, with a cosy wood-burning stove. In summer, life spills onto the lawn, flowers tumble from stone troughs. Dogs and children are very welcome. Walks start from the door.

Price	£85. Singles from £65. Cottage £100-£130.
Rooms	4 + 1: 3 doubles, 1 twin/double. Self-catering cottage for 4.
Meals	Lunch from £5.50. Dinner from £15.
Closed	Christmas Day & Boxing Day.

 Professional dog training breaks for the beginner, improver or gun dog – at a discounted rate

Alan & Susie Stoneham
Lower Chicksgrove, Tisbury,
Salisbury SP3 6NB
Tel   +44 (0)1722 714318
Email   thecompasses@aol.com
Web   www.thecompassesinn.com

Entry 129   Map 3

The Ark

Welcome to woodworker James Noble's latest creation: the incredible Ark. Its curved, Gothic-inspired form sits by a river under an apple tree in a quiet corner of a Wiltshire farm, with views to the neighbouring village. This is for the more intrepid glamper, involving a bumpy tractor ride down to the site with all the gear and a few tricks and tips that James will explain. The site's solitude has been preserved by the ingenious construction of a trailer-mounted loo; this also transports the gas fridge and logs. The shower is a classic camping arrangement: heat your water in a large Kelly kettle, then hoist it into the trees. For cooking, a double hob has been hand-built into the structure, and there's a fire pit outside for campfire meals and songs. From the door, there are a couple of good dog walks to pretty villages, while the surrounding area is criss-crossed with biking and hiking routes. Note, you can ask to move alongside the Wagon if you're a bigger party! Further afield is plenty to explore – Stonehenge and Avebury and all those quintessentially English market towns. Lovely.

Price	From £90 per night.
Rooms	Ark for 3-4.
Meals	Self-catering.
Closed	Never.

Acres of space to run around & lakes to leap into

Canopy & Stars
Pewsey SN9 6HG
Tel   +44 (0)1275 395447
Email   enquiries@canopyandstars.co.uk
Web   www.canopyandstars.co.uk

Entry 130   Map 3

The Wagon

The approach to the owners' home is a country lane lined with oak, beech and ash trees. Using the natural forms of Sussex Oak, forester and furniture-maker James Noble conjures wonders out of wood. There's a chicken coop on stilts, gates of woven timber and, of course, The Wagon. The site was chosen not only to make use of natural features such as the lake but also to create perfect privacy. A charming living space encased in pale pine, it houses a comfy double bed, bunks for the children, a mini kitchen, and a seating area cleverly contrived with the help of a few well-placed hinges. Willow trees, planted to provide firewood for the clay pizza oven and the campfire, simultaneously form a habitat for wildlife. Complete seclusion means that you can swing in the hammock, laze by the lake and shower with just the trees for company. During the day, explore some of Britain's most famous pre-historic sites, take tea in old-fashioned market towns and walk across miles of rolling countryside. At night, light the barbecue, open the wine and give yourself up to the slow life.

Price	From £90 per night.
Rooms	Wagon for 2 + 2.
Meals	Self-catering.
Closed	October to April.

 Acres of space to run around & lakes to leap into

Canopy & Stars
Pewsey SN9 6HG

Tel	+44 (0)1275 395447
Email	enquiries@canopyandstars.co.uk
Web	www.canopyandstars.co.uk

Entry 131   Map 3

Fisherman's House

Ducks shoot the rapids of the Kennet river as it flows past the lawns of this exquisitely situated home – bliss to sit out here with binoculars on a warm day. Built in 1812 it looks every inch a doll's house, but charming Heather adds a deft human touch. Elegant breakfasts are served in the Edwardian style conservatory, there's a delightful guests' sitting room with an open fire and, upstairs, three sumptuously decorated bedrooms that face the garden and river; time slips by effortlessly here. Many people come to visit the crop and stone circles and Bath and Marlborough are a hop away. *Fly fishing can be arranged.*

Price	£85. Singles £40-£50.
Rooms	3: 1 double;
	1 twin, 1 single sharing bath.
Meals	Lunch/packed lunch from £5.
	Pub 500 yds.
Closed	Rarely.

 Biscuits & baskets for your pooch

Heather Coulter
Mildenhall, Marlborough SN8 2LZ
Tel   +44 (0)1672 515390
Mobile   +44 (0)7785 225363
Email   heathercoulter610@btinternet.com
Web   www.fishermanshouse.co.uk

Entry 132   Map 3

Long Cover Cottage

In a pocket of Worcestershire that overflows with hops and cider apple trees, stealing its name from the backdrop of ancient undisturbed woodland, the cottage and its surrounds make a natural family home – for both frazzled humans and local badgers. Winding your way up the track to this converted stable, you catch glorious glimpses of the Teme and Kyre valleys; on arrival, you're greeted by neighbour and owner, cheerful, thoughtful Ellie. Generous windows flood rooms with light, which bounces off polished elm floorboards; a wood-burner and Aga keep things cosy, the kitchen is handcrafted, the views are long and bucolic. Upstairs, bedrooms are brass-bedded and floral, tucked under the eaves in that cottagey way. You get a handy loo and basin up here, a sparkling bathroom with a roll top tub downstairs. Lucky dogs have seven acres to romp in, while children get a secret treehouse complete with hammocks and barbecue for midnight feasts. Resting on the borders of three counties, this is prime walking country, while bustling Ledbury and Ludlow, England's slow food capital, are just a drive away. *Also Studio for 2.*

Price	£500–£700 per week.
Rooms	Stable for 6.
Meals	Self-catering.
Closed	Never.

 Seven acres of specially fenced land for carefree scampers & no roads for miles

Ellie Van Straaten
Vine Lane, Kyre,
Tenbury Wells WR15 8RL
Tel   +44 (0)1885 410208
Email   ellie_vanstraaten@yahoo.co.uk
Web   www.a-country-break.co.uk

Entry 133   Map 2

The Coach House

Head for the hills… and the dancing daffodils. In the expansive grounds of a 16th-century timber-framed house, a perfect retreat for you and the dog. Way up a simple track, your stone-walled hideaway was built almost entirely from locally reclaimed materials. Inside it's open plan and easy. Settle onto the chesterfield, toes directed at a wood-burner stacked high with logs from the woods. The spacious kitchen, of hand-crafted oak, has a double Belfast sink and good wooden floorboards throughout. Exposed beams frame the bright bedroom; the shower room is a step away. It would be a treat to follow the babbling brook through the ancient orchid-dotted woodland, so rest awhile at the owner's little treehouse (with hammocks), then retire to your own private viewpoint with its lush views across open pastures to the Teme and Kyre valleys. Venture to Ludlow for gourmet shopping, Hay-on-Wye for vintage books and the grand industrial heritage that is Ironbridge. Take to the slow life on the steam railway, stride out on the Mortimer Trail. Buzzards soar overhead, rabbits scamper in the fields that surround you. *Also Stable for 6.*

Price	£300–£500 per week.
Rooms	Studio for 2.
Meals	Self-catering.
Closed	Never.

 Seven acres of specially fenced land for carefree scampers & no roads for miles

Ellie Van Straaten
Vine Lane, Kyre,
Tenbury Wells WR15 8RL
Tel   +44 (0)1885 410208
Email ellie_vanstraaten@yahoo.co.uk
Web   www.a-country-break.co.uk

Entry 134   Map 2

Skipwith Station, Derwent Flyer

Brilliant for families and walkers. In stunning contrast to the originals, these refurbished 1970s railway coaches are sleek and contemporary: wooden floors, Venetian blinds, snazzy cushions, snowy linen. Kitchens are well-equipped, showers are fabulous and there's a vintage rocking chair painted in shabby-chic fashion. The space is cosy but not cramped, well-designed but homely – the Southworths have done an excellent job. He was general manager at the Carriageworks in York, she is a garden designer. Looking for a project, they bought up the Station House, moved in, then bought and transformed two old carriages. As for Skipwith Common, it's the largest wetland heath in the North of England: cycle tracks, bridle routes, wildlife galore, and the lane leading to leafy Skipwith village is truly rural. Lizanne's creativity has extended to two landscaped acres... add several hens, the owners' own friendly dogs, and you'll soon feel at home. Books, games, DVDs, storage and air con – all yours, and if you stay for four nights there's a hamper as well. Lizanne is delightful and settles you in.

Price	£135–£495 per week.
Rooms	2 coaches: 1 for 4, 1 for 6.
Meals	Self-catering.
Closed	Rarely.

 Leaf through the dog-walk guide & pick your pooch's favourite route, then step out of your carriage into the country

Lizanne Southworth
North Duffield YO8 5DE
Tel   01757 282288
Email   lizanne@skipwithstation.com
Web   www.skipwithstation.com

The White Swan Inn

A dreamy old inn that stands on Market Place, where farmers set up shop on the first Thursday of the month. The exterior is 16th century and flower baskets hang from its mellow stone walls. Inside, discover a seriously pretty world: stripped floors, open fires, a tiny bar, beautiful windows. The restaurant is at the back – the heart and soul of the inn – with delicious food flying from the kitchen, perhaps Whitby fishcakes, rack of spring lamb, glazed lemon tart with blood-orange sorbet. Excellent bedrooms are scattered about. Those in the main house have padded bedheads, Osborne & Little fabrics and flat-screen TV/DVDs; bathrooms have robes and White Company oils. Rooms in the courtyard tend to be bigger and come in crisp contemporary style with black-and-white screen prints, mohair blankets and York stone bathrooms. You'll also find a cool little residents' sitting room here, with a huge open fire, an honesty bar, a purple pool table and cathedral ceilings. The moors are all around: fabulous walking, and Castle Howard and Whitby wait. Best of all, dog grooming is just around the corner!

Price	£150–£180. Suites £210–£260. Singles from £115.
Rooms	21: 14 doubles, 4 twins/doubles, 3 suites.
Meals	Lunch from £5.25. Dinner £25–£45. Sunday lunch £22.50.
Closed	Never.

 Advice on walks & dog-friendly places, & a dog-friendly bar & lounge

Victor & Marion Buchanan
Market Place,
Pickering YO18 7AA

Tel	+44 (0)1751 472288
Email	welcome@white-swan.co.uk
Web	www.white-swan.co.uk

Entry 136   Map 6

The Hayloft at Flamborough Rigg

On and on the road goes, deeper into the woods until the single track stops at a 1820s farmhouse surrounded by open fields. The gravelled drive crunches nicely under the tyres and the kitchen sports a hamper of local goodies (and, on occasion, home-brewed elderflower champagne!). Philip and Caroline love making guests feel at home and you may freely roam their super big garden with orchard, vegetable patch, loungers and barbecue. You can head off for a long walk over the rolling North Yorkshire Moors and come back to deep comfort. On your first floor: snuggle up with a book in front of the wood-burner, watch a DVD, play cards at the chunky table. There are quirky touches like old Singer sewing machines as table bases, a shelf of vintage china in the well-thought out kitchen/diner, and modern art on the walls. The bedrooms feel light and fresh with local oak furniture and cheerful cushions. Jump in the car for a trip to the coast or wander round the charming market town of Helmsley. The Hayloft feels as though it's in the middle of nowhere and yet moors, dales and the sea are wonderfully close.

Price	£250–£595 per week.
Rooms	Apartment for 4.
Meals	Self-catering.
Closed	Rarely.

 Every dog receives a guide to local dog-friendly pubs & beaches

Philip & Caroline Jackson
Flamborough Rigg Cottage,
Middlehead Road, Stape,
Pickering YO18 8HR
Tel   +44 (0)1751 475263
Email   enquiries@flamboroughriggcottage.co.uk
Web   www.thehayloftatflamboroughrigg.co.uk

Entry 137   Map 6

The Fox & Hounds

The 18th-century coaching inn sits handsomely on the main street in sweet Sinnington, on the edge of the North Yorkshire moors; the mounting block by the front door hints at its past. Somehow you feel embraced by the place the moment you walk in: Andrew and Catherine have been welcoming folk for many years and they have hospitality down to a fine art. The feel is utterly traditional, all oak settles, open fires, prints on dark green walls and hops hanging from beams; relax with a pint of Copper Dragon while choosing your lunch. Slow-roast pork belly with pickled walnuts and honey parsnip purée makes a mouthwatering starter; follow with trio of guinea fowl served with rösti; sausage with black pudding and apple; confit leg with spinach. If you can find room – portions are generous – the assiette of puddings is perfect for sharing: chocolate marquise, gooseberry fool and treacle sponge with custard should not to be missed. There are ten comfy, homely, spotless bedrooms, four of them on the ground floor, all with crisp linen, most with modern bathrooms. Lovely.

Price	£80–£130.
Rooms	10 doubles.
Meals	Lunch & dinner £9.95–£21.95.
	Bar meals (lunch only) £5.25–£7.95.
	Sunday lunch from £9.95.
Closed	Christmas Day & Boxing Day.

  Their very own exercise paddock: a large grassy area just for doggie guests

Andrew & Catherine Stephens
Main Street, Sinnington,
York YO62 6SQ

Tel	+44 (0)1751 431577
Email	fox.houndsinn@btconnect.com
Web	www.thefoxandhoundsinn.co.uk

Entry 138   Map 6

Little Garth

In the gentle foothills of the North York Moors, short miles from market towns, lies this ancient settlement with Norman church and trout stream. Tucked behind the hedge-fringed village street is a dear little house with a lavender-edged front lawn and cosy porch – drop your bags in the flagged hall and leave the world behind. Having swapped a holiday farmhouse in the Lakes for this listed stone cottage, Philippa has poured love and flair into Little Garth. All is light, warm and immaculate. Polished and flagged floors sport cheerful rugs, pots of fresh flowers glow on old pine tops, cotton-covered armchairs are deep and comfortable. A light-filled, contemporary kitchen, with all the kit, opens to the rose and honeysuckle back garden. Sweetly sprigged bedroom walls, gleaming white woodwork and comfortable, generously clad beds add a feminine air; lovely to come home to after trudging the sheep-speckled moors or battling with the Friday traffic. Light the candles, throw another log on the fire, pop the cork – or wander down the wide village street to the local pub. A great little hideaway for you and your dog.

Price	£260–£550 per week.
Rooms	House for 5.
Meals	Self-catering.
Closed	Never.

 Walks on the beach or the moors, scampers through National Park woods & strolls in the arboretum at Castle Howard

Pippa Galloway
Normanby, Sinnington,
York YO62 6RH
Tel   +44 (0)1904 431876
Email   p.galloway@talk21.com
Web   www.holidaycottage-normanby.co.uk

Entry 139   Map 6

Bewerley Hall Cottage

Once the home of Bewerley Hall's head gardener, this is a dreamy hideaway at the tail end of a terrace of stone cottages. The sitting room envelops you in cheering warmth: a wood-burner in the inglenook; one exposed stone wall, three in cream paint; two squishy red sofas dotted with smart cushions; a bookcase brimming with books; an iPod dock, guides and maps. For wellies there's a boot room; next to this, a light and cottagey kitchen. Upstairs is a four-poster king bed with lovely views over cherry trees and the village green, and a glam black-and-ivory bathroom, with a jacuzzi bath and Molton Brown soaps. Follow the sun from front to back, eat outside and soak up the views over Bewerley Park. Walks spider out from the door along the river Nidd or to the How Stean gorge; this is Nidderdale – very beautiful – and the Dales are a few miles away. Up to two well-behaved dogs are very welcome to stay, provided they live downstairs. For a more sedate ramble, stroll to charming Pateley Bridge and pick up your dinner: there's a deli, a butchers and, we're told, a rather good pub. Perfect!

Price	£295–£550 per week.
Rooms	Cottage for 2.
Meals	Self-catering.
Closed	Never.

 Pups are welcomed with a goodie pack of treats, the best local info on where to walk – & where to enjoy a friendly pub or two!

Sarah Manby
9 The Green, Bewerley,
Pateley Bridge HG3 5HU
Tel   +44 (0)1423 545787
Email   info@yorkshireboltholes.com
Web   www.cottageinbewerley.com

Entry 140   Map 6

The Tempest Arms

A 16th-century, award-winning ale house three miles west of Skipton with great prices, friendly staff and an easy style. Inside you find stone walls and open fires, six ales on tap at the bar and a smart beamed restaurant. An airy open-plan feel runs throughout with sofas and armchairs strategically placed in front of a fire that burns on both sides. Delicious traditional food is a big draw – the inn was packed for dinner on a Wednesday in April. Eat wherever you want, so grab a seat and dig into Yorkshire puddings with a rich onion gravy, cottage pie with a Wensleydale crust, treacle tart with pink grapefruit sorbet. Bedrooms are just as good – with one set aside for people with dogs. Crisp linen, neutral colours, slate bathrooms, flat-screen TVs… those in the main house are simpler, those next door in two newly built stone houses are rather indulging. Some have views of the fells, the suites are large and worth the money, a couple have decks with hot tubs. The Dales are on your doorstep – a great place for walkers. Skipton, a proper Yorkshire market town, is worth a look. Hard to fault for the price.

Price	£85. Suites £100–£140.
	Singles from £62.50.
Rooms	21: 9 twins/doubles, 12 suites.
Meals	Lunch & dinner £5–£25.
Closed	Never.

 Walks straight from the door – with a special leaflet to guide you on the best ones

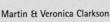

Martin & Veronica Clarkson
Elslack,
Skipton BD23 3AY
Tel   +44 (0)1282 842450
Email   info@tempestarms.co.uk
Web   www.tempestarms.co.uk

The Traddock

This family-run hotel is decidedly pretty and sits on southern fringes of the Yorkshire Dales; those looking for a friendly base will find it here. You enter through a wonderful drawing room – crackling fire, pretty art, the daily papers, cavernous sofas – but follow your nose and find polished wood in the dining room, panelled walls in the breakfast room and William Morris wallpaper in the sitting-room bar, where you can sip a pint of Skipton ale while indulging in a game of Scrabble. Bedrooms are just the ticket, some seriously swanky in contemporary style, others deliciously traditional with family antiques, quilted beds, perhaps a claw-foot bath. Those on the second floor have a cosy attic feel, all have fresh fruit, flat-screen TVs, homemade shortbread and Dales views. Elsewhere, a white-washed sitting room that opens onto the garden and fabulous local food in the rug-strewn restaurant, perhaps poached asparagus, fell-bred lamb, apple and butterscotch crumble. Three Peaks are at the door, so come to walk. Don't miss the caves at Ingleborough or Settle for antiques.

Price	£95–£185. Singles from £85. Half-board from £85 p.p.
Rooms	12: 8 doubles, 1 twin/double, 2 family rooms, 1 single.
Meals	Lunch from £9.50. Dinner, 3 courses, around £30.
Closed	Never.

Fun agility event in October! National Park walks from the door

Paul Reynolds
Austwick,
Settle LA2 8BY

Tel	+44 (0)15242 51224
Email	info@austwicktraddock.co.uk
Web	www.thetraddock.co.uk

Entry 142   Map 6

Old Cello Workshop

The former stringed instrument workshop, originally a farm byre, is a warm cosy bolthole for six. The setting is one of the most covetable in North Yorks: off charming Richmond's Green. Views are to the bottom of Marcia's garden (she lives just across the road) and up towards Culloden Tower; you're super-central. A wrought-iron gate opens to a front patio and a neat white front door, so step in to discover a three-storey space: kitchen/breakfast room and shared bathroom on the ground floor, a short flight of stairs to the living area above, and steps down to two doubles. A separate stair takes you to the twin room in the attic – sweet, secluded, perfect for older children. The fresh modern double (and double-glazed) bedrooms face the road, with feature wallpapers and comfy beds. The living room, lofty but cosy in spite of the rafter roof, sports matching sofas and armchairs, a gas-fired 'wood' stove, a bookcase stuffed with novels, jigsaws, games and DVDs. After a fabulous riverside walk to Easby Abbey, come home to your very own outside tap and bucket, and towels for muddy paws.

Price	£450–£655 per week.
Rooms	House for 6.
Meals	Self-catering.
Closed	Never.

 Every pooch gets a Lucky Dog Surprise Bag, & a folder filled with local trails – owners bring your walking boots!

Dennis & Marcia McLuckie
28 The Green,
Richmond DL10 4RG
Tel   +44 (0)1748 825525
Email   marcia.scorton@btconnect.com
Web   www.yorkshirecountryholidays.co.uk

Entry 143   Map 6

The Mollycroft

The Mollycroft is a gleamingly restored 1940s showman's living van, as eccentric as the people who once toured in it. A combination of dark wood and bright yellow and green décor creates a lively but homely feel, and there are interesting books and sofas in the living room and the bunk room – which doubles as the kitchen – so: plenty of space for lazy loafing in a tumbling, spacious wagon. Next to the Mollycroft is a fire pit complete with cooking gear and a barbecue down by the lake. The simple life is complemented by a few whizzy touches: gas hobs and fridge in the kitchen, mains power and WiFi. (Note: this is not ideal for toddlers, with a wooden deck three feet off the ground.) On the edge of the Yorkshire Dales National Park the scenery is stunning; Greville's modern art collection in the chapel should not be missed, nor the enormous Sunday market at Catterick racecourse. Swim in the lake, mess about on the river (there's a boat!) and keep the dogs on leads. Later you can roam miles across moors and valleys dropping into unspoiled pubs along the way; there's also a good food pub a mile and a half away.

Price	From £70 per night.
Rooms	Showman's van for 4.
Meals	Self-catering.
Closed	Never.

A swim in the lake at Mollycroft, from the jetty or the rowing boat

Canopy & Stars
Catterick Bridge,
Richmond DL10 7PE
Tel   +44 (0)1275 395447
Email   enquiries@canopyandstars.co.uk
Web   www.canopyandstars.co.uk

Entry 144   Map 6

Pubs-for-a-pint

When you're away on a break with your dog it's handy to have a list of dog-friendly pubs to visit for a pint or a snack. Here is a small selection of pubs in England that welcome dogs in at least one area of the pub – most likely to be by the fire, at the bar or in the garden. Most pubs, though – even the dog-friendly ones – draw the line at allowing dogs in dining rooms, but if you want to check the details beforehand just give them a call.

We've visited each of these pubs and written about them ourselves. They're here because we like them. (We've not inspected any bedrooms they may have.) They are all taken from our hugely popular *Pubs & Inns of England & Wales* guide. Now in its eighth edition, this guide brings you a huge variety of pubs from the charming to the rustic and the real-aled to the Michelin-starred. Visit www.sawdays.co.uk/bookshop to buy the guide.

Here is an explanation of the symbols you'll find at the foot of each pub's entry. They apply to bar areas.

  Wheelchair access to both bar and wcs.

  Children of all ages welcome in parts of pub (highchairs not necessarily available).

  Credit cards accepted, most commonly Visa and MasterCard.

  Pub serves four or more hand pumped ales.

  Pub serves eight or more wines by the glass.

  Wireless internet access available in the bar.

The Chimney House

The Victorian corner boozer in arty Seven Dials has become a gastropub of note and the Coggings are keeping it that way. Taking its stylish lead from the bistro pubs of London it has not lost its community feel – so settle in to leather armchairs, scrubbed tables and an open kitchen from which classic British dishes flow. As you might expect, the produce is local and well-sourced, the sort of place where the ketchup is homemade. From the daily menu, tuck into butternut squash soup, sea bass with creamy chorizo sauce, and a prune and pecan nut crumble. Or pop in at lunchtime for a hot beef and horseradish sandwich – or a bowl of hand-cut chips to soak up the very excellent Harveys ale. Tables are filled on a first come, first-served basis in the bar area – then head off with the dog to Brighton Beach!

The Preston Park Tavern

In a posh Victorian suburb of Brighton is a beautiful corner pub, Georgian, spruced up and perfect for a family lunch out. Under than same ownership as the nearby Chimney House, it attracts a mix of guests, so pop in for a glass of chilled pinot – there are 22 wines to choose from – or a morning cappuccino. More gastro than pub, the open kitchen serves dishes that merge Sussex and the Med, and change each day so you're guaranteed good produce. Test out the courgette and mint risotto or the pan-roasted cod with pepperonata, paprika potatoes and toasted almonds. Lunch on sophisticated sandwiches, a homemade burger or a Sunday roast. The fabulous pier is a 30-minute stroll if you feel the need for a stroll.

Meals	Lunch from £4.95. Dinner from £10.50. Sunday lunch £12.50.
Closed	3pm-5pm (Tues-Thurs) & Mon all day.

 Dog snacks at the bar (for a small donation to the local RSPCA), plus keep an eye out for the 'Scooby Snack' menu

Meals	Lunch from £4.95. Dinner from £11.
Closed	From 8pm Sun.

 Dog snacks at the bar (for a small donation to the local RSPCA), plus keep an eye out for the 'Scooby Snack' menu

Helen & Andrew Coggings
28 Upper Hamilton Road,
Brighton BN1 5DF
Tel   +44 (0)1273 556708
Email   info@chimneyhousebrighton.co.uk
Web   www.chimneyhousebrighton.co.uk

Entry 145   Map 3

Helen & Andrew Coggings
88 Havelock Road,
Brighton BN1 6GF
Tel   +44 (0)1273 542271
Email   info@prestonparktavern.co.uk
Web   www.prestonparktavern.co.uk

Entry 146   Map 3

The Black Horse

A hop from London, the Black Horse is the hub of Fulmer, a sleepy conservation village between Gerrards Cross and Slough. Made up of three 17th-century cottages that housed the craftsmen working on the church next door, the pub is a warren of tiny character-steeped rooms. It's warm, cosy, a charming mix of brocante finds, rich fabrics and heritage colours, while outside is a large garden and a peaceful terrace. Look forward to hand-pulled beers, European wines and robust 'British Colonial' cooking: try pork and lamb from Coleshill, game from around Marlow, wild garlic from the lanes. Dogs will love a stroll afterwards along Alderbourne Lane to the old-fashioned river ford, or a gambol on the heathland of Stoke Common, while those in search of proper walkies should head straight for Black Park – a mile away and 530 acres.

Meals	Lunch & dinner £4.75-£18.75.
Closed	Open all day.

 Walks for dog who like quiet country lanes, heath or woodland, plus tasty biscuits & fresh water to follow in bar or garden

  ♿ ⚇ ♟

David & Becky Salisbury
Windmill Road,
Fulmer SL3 6HD

Tel	+44 (0)1753 663183
Email	info@blackhorsefulmer.co.uk
Web	www.blackhorsefulmer.co.uk

Entry 147   Map 3

The Swan Inn

Swap the bland and everyday for the picture-book perfection of Denham village and the stylish Swan. Georgian, double-fronted, swathed in wisteria, the building has been transformed within by rug-strewn boards, chunky tables, cushioned settles, a log fire. Much-loved Patterdale Terrier Tucker loves to play with children and other dogs in the super big safe gardens out the back. There's a fabulous terrace for outdoor meals and the food is modern British. If pressed for time, choose from the 'small plates' list – devilled kidneys on rosemary focaccia toast with mustard and cream sauce, steamed mussels in cider. If you've nothing to rush for, linger over a rib-eye steak with Bloody Mary butter and hand-cut chips, with a pint of Courage Best or one of 20 wines by the glass. The owners have thought of everything.

Meals	Lunch, bar meals & dinner, all £11.75-£17.75.
Closed	Open all day.

 A happy welcome in garden & bar. Next door is Buckinghamshire Golf Club & Denham Country Park – great walks

David & Becky Salisbury
Village Road, Denham,
Uxbridge UB9 5BH

Tel	+44 (0)1895 832085
Email	info@swaninndenham.co.uk
Web	www.swaninndenham.co.uk

Entry 148   Map 3

The Jolly Cricketers

Watch out for dog shows here – they may become an annual event! When the Jolly Cricketers came on the market, village residents Chris Lillitou and Amanda Baker couldn't resist. What a transformation: now pretty plants clamber up the brickwork outside, and sweet shop jars of roasted nuts, olives and lollipops line up behind the bar – a picture of individuality that's matched by a freehouse ale selection showcasing the best of local breweries. Ornate fireplaces, oddment-cluttered shelves and quirky vegetable artwork create an unpretentious backdrop for cider-braised ham, crispy poached egg, pineapple chutney and triple-cooked chips; or beef rump, tongue and cheek with potato purée. Coffee mornings, book signings and pub quizzes contribute to a community spirit but do nothing to dilute this pub's new found dining status.

Old Queens Head

David and Becky Salisbury's mini-empire contains this pub by the green; it started life in 1666 and oozes character and charm. Old beams and timbers in the rambling bar and dining areas blend perfectly with the contemporary décor – rug-strewn flags, polished boards, classic fabrics, lovely old oak. Food follows the successful formula, imaginative seasonal menus and chalkboard specials mixing classic pub recipes with 'modern British' flair. Choices range from 'small plates' – harrisa spiced tempura squid with aubergine caviar – to big dishes of roast pumpkin and Jerusalem artichoke risotto with sorrel; great puddings too. There's a glorious garden for summer, and within a few minutes you can be in the middle of beautiful Common Wood, with its wide dog-friendly paths and abundance of history.

Meals	Lunch from £6. Bar meals from £8.50. Dinner from £12.50. Sunday lunch, 3 courses, £24.50. No food on Mon, except bank hols, or Sun eve.		Meals	Lunch, bar meals & dinner, all £11.75-£17.75.
Closed	Open all day.		Closed	Open all day.

 Homemade dog biscuits with proceeds to Stockenchurch Dog Rescue, & freshly topped up water bowls

 Plenty of fresh water & dog biscuits in the gated garden or bar & fun family walks in Common Wood

Amanda Baker & Chris Lillitou
24 Chalfont Road, Seer Green,
Beaconsfield HP9 2YG
Tel   +44 (0)1494 676308
Email   jacl.baker@virgin.net
Web   www.thejollycricketers.co.uk

David & Becky Salisbury
Hammersley Lane, Penn,
High Wycombe HP10 8EY
Tel   +44 (0)1494 813371
Email   info@oldqueensheadpenn.co.uk
Web   www.oldqueensheadpenn.co.uk

Entry 149   Map 3   Entry 150   Map 3

Buckinghamshire Pub

Royal Oak

The old whitewashed cottage stands in a peaceful hamlet on the edge of the common, one of a thriving small group of dining pubs we are delighted to promote. Beyond the terrace is a stylish, open-plan bar, cheerful with terracotta walls, rug-strewn boards, cushioned pews and crackling log fires. Order a pint of local Rebellion ale or one of the 20 wines available by the glass and take a look at the daily chalkboard or the printed menu. Fresh, innovative pub food comes in the form of 'small plates' (chicken liver and foie gras parfait) and of main meals, eg. glazed pork belly. The sprawling gardens are perfect for summer. There's a sweet little path up the hill from town that runs past the allotments into open dog country – and some of the best blackberries you'll ever find. Marlow Common is a mile away.

Meals	Lunch & dinner £11.75-£18.50.
Closed	Open all day.

 A couple of generous grassy acres, perfect to let off steam before a lazy lunch – dog biscuits are in the bar

   ♿ 🏃 📖 🍷 📶

David & Becky Salisbury
Frieth Road,
Marlow SL7 2JF
Tel   +44 (0)1628 488611
Email   info@royaloakmarlow.co.uk
Web   www.royaloakmarlow.co.uk

Entry 151   Map 3

Cambridgeshire Pub

The Eltisley

Lucky locals. The Eltisley – once a grubby old boozer – looks across the green of this deeply peaceful village but now the style is individual and quirky. The bar has an industrial late-Victorian feel with mock gas lamps, distressed paintwork and brick and flag floors; the restaurant has shimmering chandeliers, high backed leather chairs and pale walls. You will eat the freshest, most local produce: meat, poultry and eggs from nearby farms, freshly baked bread, fish from sustainable sources. Starters include mussels with vindaloo sauce and pan-fried mackerel fillet with fennel and orange salad; wild boar and local rabbit are braised slowly, and you can polish it all off with quince and almond tart. Sup a pint of the real stuff, or good wine by the glass; spill into the garden in summer, and listen to jazz on monthly Sundays.

Meals	Lunch & dinner £9.95-£20.
	Bar meals from £4.95 (lunch only).
Closed	3pm-6pm, Sun eves & Mon.

 Dogs are welcome in the bar & there's a nice garden behind

   ♿ 🏃 📖 🍷 📶

John Stean
2 The Green, Eltisley,
St Neots PE19 6TG
Tel   +44 (0)1480 880308
Email   theeltisley@btconnect.com
Web   www.theeltisley.co.uk

Entry 152   Map 3

Cheshire Pub

The Ship Inn

You're on the edge of the Peaks so the walks stretch in every direction; the pub provides a great little guide. Michael and Cathy are friendly and professional, know what makes a good pub tick and allow dogs in both the bar and the hikers' room – a winner all round. The little taprooms are pleasingly simple, one with an oak-topped bar, the other with stone flags and a cast-iron range. Tuck into a hot roast pork sandwich with apple sauce or a crusty ploughman's, or choose from a broad, daily-changing menu in the dining room extension; deep-fried squid, pheasant in red wine, chocolate truffle torte. Much of the produce is locally sourced, all is super fresh. There's a designated family room, too, and the pub is loved too for its beers – try a pint of J W Lees. The neat little beer garden is shaded by mature trees.

Meals	Lunch & dinner £9.45–£13.95. Not Sunday eve or Monday (except bank hols).
Closed	3pm-6pm & Mon (except bank hols).

 Water bowls & dog biscuits for your little tyke, plus an excellent pub walks book on sale

Michael Hazelton & Cathy Dean
Wincle,
Macclesfield SK11 0QE
Tel +44 (0)1260 227217
Email shipinnwincle@btconnect.com

Entry 153   Map 6

Cornwall Pub

Trengilly Wartha Inn

Well tucked down steep and twisting lanes, in the verdant heaven that is the Helford estuary, is this friendly Cornish inn. Grab a pint of Skinner's Trengilly Gold or St Austell HSD and enjoy a stroll in the six acres of old orchard with pond – and a gravelled pergola with ingenious underfloor heating. The main bar is a cracker with a wealth of mini-snugs formed by mid-height wooden settles, beer mats tacked to beams, cricketing memorabilia, local black and white photos, local paintings, and a display of some of the over 150 wines on offer; there are 40 malts too. Chef Nick Tyler has 20 years under his belt here and keeps it fresh, local and seasonal; a shame not to try the Falmouth River mussels with onion, white wine, cream and chips, or the crab thermidor that comes with homemade granary bread.

Rooms	8: 5 doubles, 1 twin, 2 family rooms.
Meals	Lunch from £4.80. Bar meals & dinner from £7.20. Sunday lunch, 3 courses, £20.
Closed	3pm-6pm.

Information on dog-friendly beaches.

Lisa & William Lea
Constantine,
Falmouth TR11 5RP
Tel +44 (0)1326 340332
Email reception@trengilly.co.uk
Web www.trengilly.co.uk

Entry 154   Map 1

White Hart Inn

The main counter drips with brass, hops and beer pumps; walls and shelves are strewn with clay pipes, sepia photos, taxidermy and tankards. It's a sleepy-snoozy village local, friendly too, where regulars cheerfully mingle with visitors over pints of Coniston and Hawkshead Bitter, decent wines and a delicious, no-nonsense menu: rare-breed meat from Aireys of Ayside; steak and Guinness pie; vegetarian chilli; and mallard and pheasant from the shooting parties that gather in the pub carpark on winter Saturdays. They source locally, and – yes! – do small portions for children. A sloping flagged floor reflects the light from the window; black leather sofas front stoves at each end, log-fuelled in cold weather. The whole of the National Park to explore – with woods aplenty. Marvellous.

The Grove Inn

This one is in the heart of old King's Nympton: a 'natural sacred grove'. A place of celebration for our pagan ancestors, so raise a glass to your good fortune in being here. There are paintings of the superb countryside by local artists, a picture gallery of faces past and present, beams hung with bookmarks, stone walls, a slate floor and a wood-burner; old and new combine with understated ease. Robert is the perfect host, Deborah his wife uses the freshest local produce to create her menus. Try roast rib of Lakehead Farm beef or Devon chicken breast for Sunday lunch, smoked trout with horseradish sauce, wild rabbit stew with mash, fish pie, white chocolate cheesecake with Patrick's blackcurrants. Ales are from local breweries, ciders are Sam's Dry and Poundhouse, wine and champagnes all come by the glass. A truly super local.

Meals	Lunch & dinner £10.75–£15.75.
Closed	Open all day.

 A whole woodland of new smells to discover – & the National Park on your doorstep

Nigel & Kath Barton
Bouth,
Ulverston LA12 8JB
Tel   +44 (0)1229 861229
Email   nigelwhitehart@aol.com
Web   www.whitehart-lakedistrict.co.uk

Entry 155   Map 5

Meals	Lunch & dinner £6–£19.50.
	Sunday lunch, 3 courses, £16.
	Not Sunday eves.
Closed	3pm–6pm & Mon lunch
	(except bank hols).

 Dog treats behind the bar for well-behaved dogs & a massive OS map on the wall for circular walks from the door

Deborah & Robert Smallbone
Kings Nympton,
Umberleigh EX37 9ST
Tel   +44 (0)1769 580406
Email   enquiry@thegroveinn.co.uk
Web   www.thegroveinn.co.uk

Entry 156   Map 2

The Harris Arms

You are welcomed on the way in and thanked on the way out. The passion Andy and Rowena have for food and wine is infectious and the awards they are gathering is proof of their commitment. Find a long bar, a wood-burner at one end, a patterned carpet, maroon walls and a big strawberry blond cat named Reg. Outside: a large decked area at the back with rich rolling views. The Whitemans are members of the Slow Food movement so real food is their thing: cheeses are the West Country's finest, fish, meat, vegetable and dairy produce come from exemplary local suppliers and wines are chosen from small growers. Flavoursome food is what the chefs deliver and whether it be roast belly pork with cider jus, fish and chips or Devon lamb steak with roasted vine tomatoes and balsamic jus, it is consistently good. Great value, too.

Meals	Lunch £8.95-£9.95.
	Dinner £14.95-£18.95.
	Sunday lunch, 3 courses, £17.
Closed	3pm-6.30pm, Sun eve &
	Mon all day.

Dogs are welcome guests in the bar & garden, with water bowls for the thirsty

Andy & Rowena Whiteman
Portgate,
Lewdown EX20 4PZ
Tel   +44 (0)1566 783331
Email   info@theharrisarms.co.uk
Web   www.theharrisarms.co.uk

Entry 157   Map 2

The Millbrook Inn

Arrive before the boats do. They drop anchor a step away and their first port of call is this gastro inn. Perfect ingredients are positively worshipped here, and in the best seasonal and local style. Feast on spotted Start bay crab, confit of duck leg with chorizo cassoulet and rhubarb and apple crumble – book for the lively guest chef nights. In winter, a log fire warms the immediate bar area while padded settles and wheelback chairs cluster comfortably around tables in several snugs. The stream-side terrace is tiny but guarantees entertainment in summer once the Aylesbury ducks are at play, so sit back and relax with a pint of West Country ale. The owners have ambition and integrity and succeed in delivering some of the best food and drink in the area.

Meals	Lunch from £5.50.
	Dinner from £10.
Closed	Open all day.

A paddling stream behind to cool down weary paws... & biscuits on tap

Ian Dent & Diana Hunt
South Pool,
Kingsbridge TQ7 2RW
Tel   +44 (0)1548 531581
Email   info@millbrookinnsouthpool.co.uk
Web   www.millbrookinnsouthpool.co.uk

Entry 158   Map 2

Devon

Normandy Arms

Allied troops were billeted here before the Normandy landings; the pub, formerly The Commercial, changed its name to honour the men who fell. It stands at the top of the high street looking down to the church, the village itself being rather pretty, decidedly lost in Devon's hills. Outside, the look is more auberge than village inn, but whatever it is, it's easy on the eye, with a garden three paces across the road, and views spreading south over the valley. Inside, a recent refurbishment has smartened things up. You get pale lemon walls and a sofa by a wood-burner, pretty art, low ceilings and a cosy feel. Blackawton ales are served at the bar, as are some very good wines. The food is rustic: venison pie, wild boar sausages, fish straight from the boats. And the walking is sublime.

Meals	Lunch & dinner £7.95-£16.95.
Closed	4pm-6pm
	(3.30pm-6.30pm in winter).

 Just what your little tyke is after: perfect dog-walking countryside

Nick Crosley
Blackawton,
Dartmouth TQ9 7BN
Tel   +44 (0)1803 712884
Email   info@normandyarms.co.uk
Web   www.normandyarms.co.uk

Entry 159   Map 2

Gloucestershire

The Ostrich Inn

In the village of Newland the Ostrich is where the beer drinkers go to sample eight changing ales. Across from All Saints Church, that 'Cathedral of the Forest', you'll mix with all sorts before a log fire. Huntsmen and trail bikers pile in for the massive portions of delicious food, from the Newland bread and cheese platter to rack of Welsh lamb with lashings of Masala sauce. The nicotine-brown ceiling that looks in danger of imminent collapse is supported by a massive oak pillar in front of the bar where the locals chatter and jazz CDs keep the place swinging. The weekly menu, served throughout the pub, takes a step up in class, and is excellent value. Energetic Kathryn and her team, including Alfie the pub dog, aide the buzzing atmosphere. To the back is a walled garden – and the loos, 'just by there', beyond the coal sacks.

Meals	Lunch & dinner £12.50-£18.50.
	Bar meals £5.50-£10.50.
Closed	3pm-6.30pm (6pm Sat).

 A warm welcome for dogs & a sausage for the well-behaved ones

Kathryn Horton
Newland,
Coleford GL16 8NP
Tel   +44 (0)1594 833260
Email   kathryn@theostrichinn.com
Web   www.theostrichinn.com

Entry 160   Map 2

The Bell at Sapperton

This elegant pub attracts wine-lovers, foodies, ramblers and riders. Inside is a spacious but intimate décor that spreads itself across several levels – stripped beams and wood-burners, modern art on stone walls, old settles and church chairs, fresh flowers and newspapers. Sup on local Uley Old Spot or Otter Amber Bitter, dine on fresh local produce and rare breed meats. Specials are chalked up above the fireplace and the food is generous in its range: pan-fried Madgetts Farm duck breast, lamb from Butts Farm, warm apple crumble crème brûlée with blackberry ice cream, a goat's cheese called Rachel. Not a typical family pub but Sunday roast lunches are popular and the wine list is expertly considered to match the clientele. Summer eating can be outside on the well-tended terrace and spills over into the sun-trapping 'Mediterranean' courtyard.

Meals	Lunch from £9.95. Bar meals from £4.95. Dinner from £10.95. Sunday lunch, 3 courses, £29.
Closed	2.30pm-6.30pm (3pm-7pm Sun). Open all day Sun (& Sat in summer).
	Customised dog walk can be followed by biscuits & water bowls to be found in the bar

♿ 📇 🍺 🍷

Paul Davidson & Pat Le Jeune
Sapperton,
Cirencester GL7 6LE
Tel   +44 (0)1285 760298
Email   thebell@sapperton66.freeserve.co.uk
Web   www.foodatthebell.co.uk

Entry 161   Map 3

Chestnut Horse

In the beautiful Itchen valley, a rather smart 16th-century dining pub where the standards of food and service are high, and there's grooming for your pooch while you dine! A decked terrace leads to a warren of snug rooms around a central bar warmed by log fires. At night it is cosy and candlelit. You can eat in the low beamed 'red' room, with its wood-burning stove, cushioned settles and mix of dining tables, or in the panelled and memorabilia-filled 'green' room. Try the two-course menu (smoked mackerel pâté, sea bream with pesto dressing, apple and walnut pie – good value – or tuck into beer-battered fish and chips, or lamb shank with broad bean risotto. Doggie dinners are on tap, too. There are great local ales, decent wines and champagne by the glass. A cracking food pub.

Meals	Lunch & dinner £10-£18; 2 courses, £12. Sunday lunch £12.
Closed	3pm-5.30pm. Open all day Fri-Sun.
	Great circular walks from the pub, through the National Park & along the River Itchen

🚶 📇 🍺 🍷 🕸

Karen Wells
Easton,
Winchester SO21 1EG
Tel   +44 (0)1962 779257
Email   info@thechestnuthorse.com
Web   www.thechestnuthorse.com

Entry 162   Map 3

Bush Inn

Down a meandering lane alongside the clear-running waters of the Itchen, a 17th-century jewel in Hampshire's crown. In winter the bar is dark and atmospheric: a roaring log fire, candles on tables, gas lamps lit. In summer, what better, in the words of a visitor, than to sit on the bridge with a pint, the evening sun pouring through the trees, the trout hiding in the reeds below. The setting and the cottagey garden are blissful in summer, and you can stroll along the river. Cottage furniture and high-backed pews fill a series of small rooms off the bar; walls are hung with fishing and country paraphernalia. City dwellers come for the atmosphere: cosy and peaceful – though busy in summer. The kitchen is driven by fresh local produce and presents a modern menu, and there are old favourites, too.

Meals	Lunch from £7.95.
	Bar meals & dinner £6.95-£10.50.
	Limited menu weekends.
Closed	3pm-6pm (7pm Sun).
	Open all day Jul & Aug.
	Tasty dog biscuits from dog-loving hosts

♿ 🚶 💳 🍷

Nick & Cathy Young
Ovington,
Alresford SO24 ORE
Tel +44 (0)1962 732764
Email thebushinn@wadworth.co.uk

Entry 163   Map 3

The Yew Tree

Tim Gray has revitalised a hard-to-find but worth-tracking-down inn. The re-worked, stone-flagged and beamed bar is immediately welcoming – a winter fire, a chiming clock, walls festooned with character prints, a happy mishmash of furniture – and a slightly more formal note to the dining area off to one side. As for Tim, he is "fuelled by passion and fun." On summer weekends it's especially buzzy as beer flows and the local cricket team play on the pitch opposite; if cricket's not your thing, bag a seat in the peaceful front garden, in the shade of the eponymous yew. Good fresh dishes are chalked up daily, so be cheered by a warm halloumi, chorizo, celery and red onion salad, fillet steak with a brandy, peppercorn and cream sauce, and maybe a Yew Tree white choc pot for pudding. It's a happy place.

Meals	Lunch & dinner £8.95-£17.95.
Closed	3pm-6pm & all day Mon.
	Open all day Sun.
	A welcome for people as well as dogs (including big hairy ones)

♿ 🚶 💳 🍷

Tim Gray
Lower Wield,
Alresford SO24 9RX
Tel +44 (0)1256 389224
Web www.the-yewtree.org.uk

Entry 164   Map 3

The Wellington Arms

Lost down a web of lanes, the 'Welly' draws foodies from miles around. Cosy, compact and decorated in style – wall benches, rustic pictures, terracotta floor – the single bar-dining room has just seven tables (do book!). Jason's modern British cooking is first-class and inventive, the boards are chalked up daily and the produce mainly home-grown or organic. Kick off with crispy fried pumpkin flowers stuffed with ricotta and parmesan, follow with a rack of saddleback pork with crackling and sticky red cabbage, finish with a sensational rhubarb, strawberry and elderflower jelly with 'fairy floss'! The mood is easy and there are local ales on tap. Migrate to the huge garden for summer meals and views of the pub's expanding small holding: bees, four pigs, Longwool sheep and 140 rarebreed chickens; eggs can be bought at the bar. *Small dogs welcome.*

Meals	Lunch & dinner £10.50–£19.50. Not Sunday eve.
Closed	3pm–6.30pm & Sun eve.

 Great for walks: public footpaths start straight outside the pub

Jason King & Simon Page
Baughurst Road,
Baughurst RG26 5LP
Tel   +44 (0)118 982 0110
Email   hello@thewellingtonarms.com
Web   www.thewellingtonarms.com

Entry 165   Map 3

The Stagg Inn

Surrounded by countryside is the first British pub to have been awarded a Michelin star. Gavroche-trained Steve Reynolds took it on and, defying all odds, ended up a Herefordshire food hero. As for provenance: the only thing you're not told is the name of the bird from which your pigeon breast (perfectly served on herb risotto) came. Most of the produce is very local, some is organic, with fresh fruit and vegetables from the kitchen garden or Titley Court next door. Seductive and restorative is the exceptional food: goat's cheese and fennel tart, saddle of venison with horseradish gnocchi and kummel, bread and butter pudding with clotted cream, a cheese trolley resplendent with 15 regional cheeses. The intimate bar is perfect and dog-friendly, there's beer from Hobsons, cider from Dunkerton's and some very classy wines.

Meals	Lunch & dinner £14.50–£20.50. Bar meals £8.90–£11.90. Sunday lunch, 3 courses, £18.50.
Closed	3pm–6.30pm, Sun eve & Mon all day.

 Walking opportunities galore

Steve & Nicola Reynolds
Titley,
Kington HR5 3RL
Tel   +44 (0)1544 230221
Email   reservations@thestagg.co.uk
Web   www.thestagg.co.uk

Entry 166   Map 2

The Oak Inn

Ten minutes from the Malvern Hills – and with a footpath on the doorstep – this freehouse that goes back to the 1600s has been sympathetically revived. The pretty garden is backed by apple orchards while inside, farmhouse tables and chairs jostle together on polished flagstones, hops hang from beams, wood-burners glow in exposed brick hearths – it's a country pub to the core. There are ales from Bathams and Wye Valley and good ciders like Robinson's Flagon and Weston's Perry. Traditional home-cooked food with modern twists are the order of the day; try slow-cooked pork belly with 'boozy' mustard mash or braised venison casserole with spiced red cabbage. There are also deli boards and sandwiches made with their own bread. As fires and candles glow in the bar, the two snugs and dining area are kept glowing by a bright and attentive team.

Price	£80-£140.
Rooms	4: 3 double, 1 family.
Meals	Lunch from £4.25. Dinner £11.50.
Closed	3pm-5.30pm (Mon-Sat), 3pm-7pm (Sun).

 Roast beef tidbits & other doggie treats. Dogs welcome throughout

Hylton Haylett & Julie Woollard
Staplow,
Ledbury HR8 1NP
Tel   +44 (0)1531 640954
Email   enquiries@oakinnstaplow.co.uk
Web   www.oakinnstaplow.co.uk

Entry 167   Map 2

The Alford Arms

It isn't easy to find, but this gastropub, in a hamlet enfolded by acres of National Trust beechwoods, is worth any number of missed turns. Inside, two interlinked rooms, bright, airy, with soft colours and scrubbed pine tables. The food is a treat, the ingredients as organic, free-range and delicious as can be. On a menu of 'small plates' and main meals, find roast fig tarte tatin with elderberry syrup, pollock fillet on chervil gnocchi with clam and smoked bacon broth, homemade spiced plum sorbet. Wine drinkers have the choice of 20 by the glass, and service is informed and friendly. Arrive early on a warm day to take your pick of the teak tables on the sun-trapping front terrace. There are walks to suit all physiques and dogs will be sorely tempted by the forest's wildlife! Don't miss the bluebells in spring.

Meals	Lunch, bar meals and dinner, all £11.75-£17.75.
Closed	Open all day.

 Fresh water & dog biscuits in the bar & the garden

David & Becky Salisbury
Frithsden,
Hemel Hempstead HP1 3DD
Tel   +44 (0)1442 864480
Email   info@alfordarmsfrithsden.co.uk
Web   www.alfordarmsfrithsden.co.uk

Entry 168   Map 3

The Fox

Cliff and James Nye's village pub has a fresh contemporary feel and a foodie menu that showcases British ingredients, including seafood from the Norfolk coast and local farm meats. It could beat many neighbourhood restaurants into a cocked hat but part of its charm is that it is still a place where beer drinkers are welcome – try a pint of James's Brancaster Best. A cool, formal dining room sits astride a relaxed bar where Brancaster oysters in sesame tempura add glamour to a menu that includes a beef and pork burger with sweet onion and chilli relish. The restaurant is a mix of French bistro and British pub: cod with spring onion and tiger prawn risotto, venison with braised red cabbage and blackberry jus, chocolate orange fondant. With a thriving fishmonger out back, this Fox is one you'd do well to hunt down. Dogs are very welcome in the bar.

Meals	Lunch & bar meals from £8.95. Dinner from £13.25. Sunday lunch, 3 courses, £24.20. Not Sunday eves.
Closed	Open all day.

 Man's best friend shouldn't be left in the doghouse so come to the pub with your owner, for a pat & a nice bowl of water

Cliff & James Nye
Willian,
Letchworth Garden City SG6 2AE
Tel   +44 (0)1462 480233
Email info@foxatwillian.co.uk
Web   www.foxatwillian.co.uk

Entry 169   Map 3

The Fox & Hounds

London chefs quitting fabulous establishments to transform country boozers are two a penny, but few have managed it with the aplomb of James Rix. Enter a comfy laid-back bar with a log fire, leather sofas, the daily papers, local ales on tap and a menu that changes twice daily. Tuck into something simple like a plate of Spanish charcuterie or tender calves' liver with mash with bacon – or a perfect ploughman's. Things step up a gear in the country-house-on-a-shoestring dining room that throws together polished old tables and a crystal chandelier, a funky backdrop to peppered venison steaks with beetroot and port sauce, and tagliolini with clams, garlic and chilli. Even the focaccia is homemade. It is a treat to see an old pub in the right hands, booking is recommended, and dogs are super-happy in enclosed gardens and bar.

Meals	Lunch & dinner £9-£22. Bar meals £4.95-£16.50. Sunday lunch, 3 courses, £27.50.
Closed	4pm-6pm, Sun eve & Mon all day (except bank hol lunches).

 Towels, blankets, treats, biscuits & water bowls. In the bar, a guide to all the best dog-friendly walks

James Rix
2 High Street,
Hunsdon, Ware SG12 8NH
Tel   +44 (0)1279 843999
Email info@foxandhounds-hunsdon.co.uk
Web   www.foxandhounds-hunsdon.co.uk

Entry 170   Map 4

London   Pub

The Duke of Cambridge

A dog-friendly pub in London! Thanks to Geetie Singh, 'organic' and 'sustainable' are the watchwords at Britain's first-ever organic pub, and British-rustic is the style. Wines, beers, spirits are certified organic and they buy as locally as they can to cut down on food miles. Most of the beers are brewed around London, meat comes from two farms, all fish is Marine Conservation Society-approved; impeccable produce and menus that change twice a day. It's a sprawling airy space with a comfortable, easy feel, whether you're in a party or on your own. Sit back and take your fill of lentil and pancetta soup, mussels with chorizo, fennel and chives, game pie with braised red cabbage, venison steak with redcurrant jus, crusty bread, fruity olive oil, quince crumble and cream – in here, or in the large restaurant. Justifiably rammed.

Meals	Lunch & dinner £9–£18.
Closed	Open all day.

 A friendly welcome & a water bowl for your pooch

Geetie Singh
30 St Peter's Street, Islington,
London N1 8JT
Tel   +44 (0)20 7359 3066
Email   duke@dukeorganic.co.uk
Web   www.dukeorganic.co.uk

Entry 171   Map 3

Norfolk   Pub

The Berney Arms

In an estate village in open country, by the village green, is a newly painted inn with candy-coloured tables out front. The sleek feel continues within, and there's much to love – from bar areas with beautiful fires and beams, settles, comfy leather chairs and cheeky Pirelli posters, to a bright sunshiney restaurant with linen clothed tables, bio-ethanol burner and stylish French-country feel. The menu is good-looking and tempting and attracts Norfolk foodies, and the two-course lunches are great value. Friendly staff under new landlords the Hirsts bustle efficiently, while the relaxed atmosphere – and the promise of afternoon tea – tempts many to linger. The garden flows round to the back – lovely for dogs and families in summer. Off the beaten track but well worth the drive, especially if visiting Oxburgh Hall.

Price	From £70.
Rooms	5: 4 doubles, 1 twin.
Meals	Lunch & dinner from £7.50. Bar meals from £4.95.
Closed	Open all day.

 In the middle of the country, with a generous garden & big rooms with paw-friendly wood effect flooring

Phil & Sue Hirst
Church Road, Barton Bendish,
King's Lynn PE33 9GF
Tel   +44 (0)1366 347995
Email   info@theberneyarms.co.uk
Web   www.theberneyarms.co.uk

Entry 172   Map 7

The Duck Inn

The Stanhoe Crown morphed into the Duck in 2010, the much extended and spruced up local surprising the residents of this sleepy backwater, close to trendy Burnham Market and the coastal saltmarshes. Enter from the car park a spanking new slate-floored bar, with barrels of Elgood's ale racked behind glass, and benches around a vast glass-topped table displaying local flints – something for strangers to get chatting about over pints of Black Dog. Cosy dining rooms beyond are rustic-smart with wood and slate floors, wood-burning stoves, candles on scrubbed tables and an antique dresser filled with collectables. Expect to find seasonal dishes and fresh fish on the short chalkboard menu, perhaps cockle and leek chowder, braised beef and venison stew, whole baked sea bass – and lovely local smoked salmon sandwiches. Don't miss Monday's music nights.

| Meals | Lunch & dinner £8-£15. Sunday lunch from £11. |
| Closed | 3pm-6pm. |

 A range of homemade gourmet treats for the discerning pooch

Julian Rivett
Burnham Road, Stanhoe,
King's Lynn PE31 8QD

Tel　+44 (0)1485 518330
Email　info@duckinn.co.uk
Web　www.duckinn.co.uk

Entry 173　Map 7

The Jolly Sailors

In 2009 Cliff and James Nye set about breathing new life into this 200-year-old village pub. 'Eat, Drink and be Jolly' says it all: not only is it a community boozer geared to local drinkers and families but it appeals to those who flock to Brancaster's glorious beach across the road. (It's quite different from Cliff's classy White Horse Inn down the road.) In the classic bar, replete with beams, tiled floor, old settles and a wood-burner pumping out the heat, grown-ups enjoy pints of home-brewed Brancaster Best while kids watch the pizzas being baked in the open-to-view oven. Hearty traditional pub dishes using fresh local produce include mussels cooked in wine, onion, garlic and cream; pork and cider pie; gammon, egg and chips; and good ol' fish and chips (it's delicious). A terrific pit-stop for families, beach bums and coastal walkers.

| Meals | Lunch, bar meals & dinner from £7.95. Sunday lunch, 3 courses, £17.95. |
| Closed | Open all day. |

 After your owner has had a drink demand you're taken to Brancaster beach, for a paddle or a race along the shore

Cliff & James Nye
Brancaster Staithe,
King's Lynn PE31 8BJ

Tel　+44 (0)1485 210314
Email　info@jollysailorsbrancaster.co.uk
Web　www.jollysailorsbrancaster.co.uk

Entry 174　Map 7

Red Lion

Tucked into the side of a hill, overlooking meadows where beef cattle graze, is a cosy inn that's a pleasure to step into: a warren of three small rooms with bare floorboards and 17th-century quarry tiles, 'clotted cream' walls, open log fires and a mix of stripped wooden settles, old pews and scrubbed tables. The pub attracts a loyal crowd for its fresh seafood – crab from Wells boats, mussels from Mark Randall in the village, beer battered cod. In season, roast partridge too, and first-rate ales from local brewers: Woodforde's and Yetmans. Locals rub shoulders with booted walkers and birdwatchers recovering from the rigours of the Peddars Way and Stiffkey's famous marshes. After a day on the beach the large and airy conservatory is popular with families – and, of course, dogs.

| Meals | Lunch, bar meals & dinner from £9.95. Sunday lunch, 3 courses, £20. |
| Closed | Open all day. |

 Treats at the bar

Stephen Franklin
44 Wells Road, Stiffkey,
Wells-next-the-Sea NR23 1AJ
Tel +44 (0)1328 830552
Email redlion@stiffkey.com
Web www.stiffkey.com

Entry 175   Map 7

Tarr Farm Inn

The garden views are sublime, and you can walk into fields from the door. Come for rare peace – no traffic, no mobile signals, not for miles. Tucked into the Barle valley, a short hop from the ancient clapper bridge at Tarr Steps, this well-established 16th-century inn is surrounded by beautiful woodland above the hauntingly high spaces of Exmoor National Park. The blue-carpeted, low-beamed main bar has comfy window seats and gleaming black leather sofas; Exmoor Ale and Mayner's cider flow as easily as the conversation. To fill the gap after a bracing walk the menu draws heavily on local game – hunting and shooting are big sports here. Dig into venison and rabbit casserole, pan-roasted partridge and a hundred French and New World wines.

| Meals | Lunch & dinner £12.95-£17.50. Bar meals £6.95-£12.50. |
| Closed | Open all day. |

 Miles & miles of river, woodland and moorland to roam, right from the door

Judy Carless & Richard Benn
Tarr Steps,
Dulverton TA22 9PY
Tel +44 (0)1643 851507
Email enquiries@tarrfarm.co.uk
Web www.tarrfarm.co.uk

Entry 176   Map 2

The Talbot Inn at Mells

Even in fog the village is lovely. Huge oak doors open to a cobbled courtyard and rough-boarded tithe barn bar on one side, and dining rooms on the other. Inside, a warren of passageways, low doorways, nooks, crannies and beams – all you'd hope for from a 15th-century inn. Butcombe Bitter flows from the cask and there are wines galore including five by the glass; it's a great drinking pub and, with a garden with views, a big draw for tourists in summer. Soak up any excess with battered cod and chips, chargrilled rib-eye steak with roasted red pepper and chilli butter, or local ham, eggs and chips, then head down to the brook and converse with the ducks. Dinner under the hop-strewn rafters highlights fresh Brixham fish such as brill fillets in nut-brown butter. The effortless hospitality is a further plus.

The White Horse

Built in 1640, with an 1800s addition, this rural beauty is worth more than a passing nod. For here Gary and Di Kingshott are continuing the modus operandi that made their previous pub, the Beehive at Horinger, a favourite with the local country-lifers. Stock in trade are: real ales from Adnams, a reasonably priced wine list, cosy fires, and a chatty, informal beamed bar. Fun, friendly and charismatic, it is hard to believe this grand cru of a pub was picked up in a distress sale. Comfortable dining areas come decorated with fresh, contemporary colours (one doubling as an art gallery with changing exhibits); so take a look at the blackboard menu. Fried duck egg on toast with a sauté of wild mushrooms, traditional beef bourguignon and treacle tart are unpretentious and strong on flavour. Wonderful walks radiate from the village.

Meals	Lunch & dinner £11.95-£17.95.
	Sunday lunch, 2 courses, £12.95.
Closed	2.30pm-6.30pm (3pm-7pm Sun).

 Wonderful walking country

Meals	Lunch & dinner from £9.95.
	Bar meals from £8.95.
	Sunday lunch, 3 courses, £24.45.
Closed	Sun eve.

 Best walking a dog could ever have!

	Rob Rowlands
	Selwood Street,
	Mells, Frome BA11 3PN
Tel	+44 (0)1373 812254
Email	enquiries@talbotinn.com
Web	www.talbotinn.com

Entry 177   Map 2

	Gary & Diane Kingshott
	Rede Road,
	Whepstead,
	Bury St Edmunds IP29 4SS
Tel	+44 (0)1284 735760
Web	www.whitehorsewhepstead.co.uk

Entry 178   Map 4

The Jolly Sportsman

Deep in Sussex, a little place with a passion for beers, food and wine. Brewery mats pinned above the bar demonstrate Bruce Wass's support of small breweries, while the food has been described as "robust, savoury, skilled and unpretentious". In the stylish restaurant, where oak tables are decorated with flowers and candles, plates are filled with mussel, prawn and herb risotto, marinated Ditchling lamb rump, peppered red deer fillet. In the bar, dogs doze, the fire glows and there are winter snifters from Bruce's impressive whisky collection to try, including rarities bought at auction. Outside, ancient trees give shade to rustic tables and the idyllic garden has a play area for children. A team of talented enthusiasts runs this pub; the Moroccan-tiled patio tables were even made by the pub's own 'washer-upper'.

The Chequers Inn

New life has been breathed into this north Cotswold pub by owners Kirstin and James – and how! A bold style of classic British meets country French thanks to rich tapestries, gilt mirrors, padded chairs, round tables and aged wooden flooring throughout. There is a proper glowing wood bar too with Old Hooky, Black Sheep and Betty Stoggs on tap; plus Stowford Press cider and several varieties of fizz for special occasions. The calm, elegant Provençal dining area at the back overlooks a well-planted and sheltered garden. Start with hot-smoked sea trout with pickled beetroot and horseradish cream, move on to grilled sea bream fillet, colcannon and crispy bacon and chive butter. The puds will also tempt, and then there's freshly ground coffee. Different, slightly decadent, and definitely worth a visit – with or without a dog in tow.

Meals	Lunch from £12.50. Bar meals from £9.75. Dinner from £16.50. Sunday lunch, 3 courses, £22.
Closed	Open all day.
	A jar of doggie biscuits on the bar, & every day a doggie special on the blackboard menu

Meals	Lunch & dinner £9.50-£16.95.
Closed	3pm-5pm, Sun eve & all day Mon.
	Dog chews, water & plenty of fuss provided. Nearby dog-friendly fields for a run around, too

    ♿ 🧍 🗐 🍷

Bruce Wass
Chapel Lane, East Chiltington,
Lewes BN7 3BA
Tel   +44 (0)1273 890400
Email   info@thejollysportsman.com
Web   www.thejollysportsman.com

James & Kirstin Viggers
91 Banbury Road, Ettington,
Stratford-upon-Avon CV37 7SR
Tel   +44 (0)1789 740387
Email   hello@the-chequers-ettington.co.uk
Web   www.the-chequers-ettington.co.uk

Entry 179   Map 4

Entry 180   Map 3

The Bluebell

Leigh and Duncan Taylor went to town updating a 500-year-old coaching inn, and created one of the most distinctive bistro-style pubs in the country. A clever combination of country casual and urban chic means atmosphere and style are delivered in spades: bold colours and striking furniture blend with ancient beams, flagstones and a big fireplace. Real ales, wines and an irresistible menu draw bon viveurs from near and far, ingredients are sourced with care and vegetables are grown on the owners' allotment. The menu combines colourful modern dishes – seared black pepper venison with rocket and parmesan, or open-style Scotch fillet steak Wellington with sautéed white truffle chard – with old favourites like steak and kidney pie, fishcakes, and battered haddock with chips. In summer, lunch on the decked area is sublime.

| Meals | Lunch & dinner £10.50–£17.95. Sunday lunch £12.75. |
| Closed | Mon lunch (except bank hols). |

 Dog bowls & biscuits on arrival

Duncan & Leigh Taylor
93 High Street,
Henley-in-Arden B95 5AT
Tel   +44 (0)1564 793049
Email   info@bluebellhenley.co.uk
Web   www.bluebellhenley.co.uk

Entry 181   Map 3

The Potting Shed Pub

The owners of the Rectory Hotel across the road have transformed the village inn. As well as the open fireplaces and the stylish kilim sofas, note door handles from trowels, hand pumps from fork handles and old butchers' block tables; the big airy dining room displays mix 'n' match antiques. And there may be a sleeping labrador in a windowseat, hoping for a generous passer-by. As for the food, it is exuberantly British, from the homemade pork scratchings and rabbit terrine to the battered hake and lamb hotpot. Two acres of lawns and an apple orchard at the back have been turned into an organic vegetable patch, while local ales, ploughman's lunches and vintage artwork (some of dogs) further reflect the laid-back focus. There's a good children's menu, and puds to warm your heart; try the spiced rice pudding. Brilliant walks; dog-pub heaven.

| Meals | Lunch from £3.95. Dinner from £11.95. |
| Closed | Open all day. |

 Assorted dog biscuits in a jar on the bar – alongside a jar of lollies for children!

Jonathan Barry &
Julian Muggridge
Crudwell, Malmesbury SN16 9EW
Tel   +44 (0)1666 577833
Email   bookings@thepottingshedpub.com
Web   www.thepottingshedpub.com

Entry 182   Map 3

The Vine Tree

With a fine store of ales and over 40 wines by the glass the old watermill is a watering hole in every sense. It may be hidden away but the faithful return, for the food and the beer. On Sundays, memorable roast sirloin of beef from the neighbour's farm is served with all the trimmings; just take your time. There's plenty of fresh fish, too, and local game in season, sautéed scallops with wild mushroom risotto, and rack of Cotswold lamb. Service is young and friendly and surroundings are inviting: deep red walls, candlelight and beams, a wood-burning stove; tables in the minuscule upstairs room are super-cosy. In summer, relax and gaze on the immaculate terrace – a delicious spot with urns of flowers and a fountain. This Vine Tree has a rich harvest for guests and their dogs to reap; no wonder Clementine the lab looks so content.

Meals	Lunch & dinner £11.90-£16.95. Bar meals £6.50-£9.50.
Closed	3pm-5.45pm. Open all day Sun in summer.

Stunning area with loads of walks around

Charles Walker & Tiggi Wood
Foxley Road, Norton,
Malmesbury SN16 0JP
Tel   +44 (0)1666 837654
Email   tiggi@thevinetree.co.uk
Web   www.thevinetree.co.uk

Entry 183   Map 3

The Red Lion

Unless you found yourself lost on Salisbury Plain, chances are you wouldn't stumble upon the Red Lion. You'd be missing much: this smart thatched village inn is both a local serving ale from Wiltshire microbreweries and a restaurant drawing food lovers from some distance. Owner-chefs Guy and Brittany Manning arrived with something of a star-spangled CV. Guy worked for three years at the Chez Bruce in London, both worked under Thomas Keller at the breathtaking Per Se in New York. The couple apply cutting-edge cookery techniques to simple rustic dishes and the results are special. The menu changes every day – sometimes twice – so expect the likes of pheasant and ham hock terrine, mushroom tortellini, roast pollock with olive oil mash and New England cheesecake with rhubarb. The Sunday roasts are superb.

Meals	Lunch & dinner £10-£18. Bar meals from £6.50. Sunday lunch, 2 courses, £15. Not Sunday eve.
Closed	3pm-6pm & Mon all day.

Slow-roasted beef marrow bones for a very tasty treat

Guy & Brittany Manning
East Chisenbury,
Pewsey SN9 6AQ
Tel   +44 (0)1980 671124
Email   enquiries@redlionfreehouse.com
Web   www.redlionfreehouse.com

Entry 184   Map 3

Fox & Hounds

If you love beech trees and high ridges, make time for a walk with views over the vale before you land at the 17th-century thatched pub on the green. Enter to discover two areas: one bright and conservatory-like, with a great view, the other older and cosier, its fireplace flanked by small red leather sofas. There are warming ales from Palmers and Butcombe, the inimitable Summer Lightning, and a well-presented wine card that tells you just what you get (which is what you'd expect from a no-nonsense landlord). Being a New Zealander, he cooks in an eclectic, untypical gastro style, so tuck into chorizo, bean and red pepper casserole in red wine with belly pork or sweet onion, ricotta and parmesan tart. Follow with vanilla cheesecake and stay till the pub closes – no hardship at all!

Meals	Lunch & dinner £8.50-£16.
Closed	3pm-6pm.

 A pub is man's best friend – & man's best friend is always welcome here

Murray Seator
The Green, East Knoyle,
Salisbury SP3 6BN
Tel   +44 (0)1747 830573
Email   pub@foxandhounds-eastknoyle.co.uk
Web   www.foxandhounds-eastknoyle.co.uk

Entry 185   Map 3

The Forester Inn

Tiny lanes frothing with cowparsley twist down to this fine little pub in Donhead St Andrew. The revitalised 600-year-old inn sports rustic walls, black beams, a log fire in the inglenook and planked floors; colours are muted, there's not an ounce of flounce and locals still prop up the bar of a late weekday lunchtime. Foodies come from far for chef Tom Shaw's cooking – rib-eye steak with béarnaise, 'a trio of lamb chops' with bubble-and-squeak, goat's cheese omelette, tomato tarte tatin – and fine puddings cooked to order, slowly. Tom uses local Rushmore venison, Old Spot pork and specialises in fresh Cornish seafood – brill with shellfish bisque and mussels, skate wing with brown butter and capers. Lucky dogs get delicious gravy bones, the garden terrace has views, there are three ales on tap, cider from Ashton Press and ten gorgeous wines by the glass.

Meals	Lunch & dinner £10-£25.
	Bar meals £7.50-£11.50.
	Sunday lunch £14.50.
Closed	3pm-6.30pm & Sun from 4pm.

 Gravy bones from the landlord

Chris & Lizzie Matthews
Lower Street,
Donhead St Andrew,
Shaftesbury SP7 9EE
Tel   +44 (0)1747 828038
Web   www.theforesterdonheadstandrew.co.uk

Entry 186   Map 3

The Chequers Inn

Fires glow, horse brasses gleam. This honey-stone village inn feels like it's in the Dales but you're a couple of miles from the A1! Panelled carpeted rooms radiating off the central bar are cosy with log fires and plush red upholstery; faded sepia photographs are a reminder of an earlier age. Rare hand-pumped ales from the Brown Cow Brewery at Selby do justice to good English food of Yorkshire proportions: steaming platefuls of shin of venison and red cabbage, roast corn-fed chicken breast on a lentil bed… just when you think you're replete, along comes a treacle sponge pudding. The pub has been welcoming travellers since the 18th century and still closes on Sundays; the tradition started in 1832 when the lady of Ledsham Hall, confronting a drunken farmer on her way to church, insisted they close on the Sabbath.

Meals	Lunch & dinner £4.95-£19.95.
Closed	Sun.

 Local walks, beer garden, dog chews & water bowls

Chris Wraith
Claypit Lane,
Ledsham, Leeds LS25 5LP
Tel   +44 (0)1977 683135
Email   cjwraith@btconnect.com
Web   www.thechequersinn.com

The Old Hill Inn

A proper, wild-country tavern with terrific beer and food. It used to be a farmhouse, then a doss-house for potholers; now it's a comfortable old inn, a warm, safe haven in a countryside of crags, waterfalls and moors. Enter the unpretentious bar – a large, comfortable room with open-stone walls, wood floors, old pine tables and big log fire. Six pumps deliver ales in top condition – Black Sheep Bitter, Dent Aviator – while food is served in the candlelit intimacy of the diminutive dining rooms. From a family of chefs comes butternut squash risotto, lamb shank with dauphinoise potatoes and a rich lamb gravy, duck with prune, port and orange sauce; from master confectioner Colin, warm chocolate pudding and lemon tart. His sugar sculptures alone are worth the trip, and the bread is deliciously homemade.

Meals	Lunch & dinner £10.95-£25.
	Bar meals £5.25-£10.
Closed	3.30pm-6.30pm (from 4pm Sun) & all day Mon (except bank hols). Open all day Sat.

 Marvellous walks straight outside the door

Sabena Martin
Chapel-le-Dale,
Carnforth LA6 3AR
Tel   +44 (0)1524 241256
Email   sabena.martin@btopenworld.com
Web   www.oldhillinn.co.uk

The Postgate Inn

This neck of the woods is best known for its 'Heartbeat' celebrity. Indeed, the Victorian stone pub sitting so handsomely at the bottom of the leafy Esk Valley – right by to the historic train line – is Heartbeat's 'Black Dog'. There's every reason to take the short trip inland from Whitby – for the big welcome, the homely feel (stone floors, beams, open fires) and the locally sourced ingredients brought together with such skill. Lamb noisettes with minted pea mash and a redcurrant and heather honey sauce are dense and toothsome; Whitby haddock and crab with gin crème sauce and white asparagus make the very best of the local catch. A terraced garden takes advantage of the views, making this a brilliant spot for you and your dog before stepping onto the steam train and rolling across the famous moors to Pickering.

Meals	Lunch & dinner £10.95–£18.95.
Closed	3.30pm–6.30pm (5.30pm in summer).

 Infinite walks – river ones too, & snoozes in front of an open fire

Mark & Shelley Powell
Egton Bridge,
Whitby YO21 1UX

Tel	+44 (0)1947 895241
Email	info@postgateinn.com
Web	www.postgateinn.com

Wales

Ty Mawr Country Hotel

Pretty rooms, attractive prices and delicious food make this super country house hard to resist. It's a very peaceful spot. You drive over the hills, drop into the village and wash up at this 16th-century stone house that glows in yellow. Outside, a sun-trapping terrace laps against a trim lawn, which in turn drops into a passing river. Gentle eccentricities abound: croquet hoops take the odd diversion, logs are piled high like giant beehives, a seat has been chiselled into a tree trunk. Inside, exposed stone walls, terracotta-tiled floors and low beamed ceilings give a warm country feel. There are fires everywhere – one in the sitting room, which overlooks the garden, another in the dining room that burns on both sides. Excellent bedrooms are all big. You get warm colours, big beds, crisp linen, good bathrooms. Some have sofas, all are dog-friendly, three overlook the garden. Back downstairs, the bar doubles as reception, and there's Welsh art on sale. Steve's cooking is the final treat: Cardigan Bay scallops, organic Welsh beef, calvados and cinnamon rice pudding.

Price	£113–£128. Singles from £70. Half-board from £77.50 p.p.
Rooms	5: 3 doubles, 2 twins/doubles.
Meals	Dinner £24–£29.
Closed	Rarely.

 A doggie pack with chews, details of pooch-friendly walks & poop bags on the house

Steve Thomas & Annabel Viney
Brechfa SA32 7RA

Tel	+44 (0)1267 202332
Email	info@wales-country-hotel.co.uk
Web	www.wales-country-hotel.co.uk

Entry 190   Map 2

The Hand at Llanarmon

Single-track lanes plunge you into the middle of nowhere. All around, lush valleys rise and fall, so pull on your boots and scale a mountain or find a river and jump into a canoe. Back at The Hand, a 16th-century drovers' inn, the pleasures of a traditional country local are hard to miss. A coal fire burns on the range in reception, a wood fire crackles under brass in the front bar and a wood-burner warms the lofty dining room. Expect exposed stone walls, low beamed ceilings, old pine settles and candles on the mantelpiece. There's a games room for darts and pool, a quiet sitting room for maps and books. Delicious food is popular with locals, so grab a table and enjoy seasonal menus – perhaps game broth, lamb casserole, then sticky toffee pudding. Bedrooms are just as they should be: not too fancy, cosy and warm, spotlessly clean with crisp white linen and good bathrooms. A very friendly place. Martin and Gaynor are full of quiet enthusiasm and have made their home warmly welcoming. John Ceiriog Hughes, who wrote "Bread of Heaven", lived in this valley. Special indeed.

Price	£90–£125. Singles from £52.50.
Rooms	13: 8 doubles, 4 twins, 1 suite.
Meals	Lunch from £6. Sunday lunch £20.
	Dinner £12–£20.
Closed	Rarely.

 Gravy bones in the bar, dog towels, & their own book for the very best walks

Gaynor & Martin De Luchi
Llanarmon Dyffryn Ceiriog,
Llangollen LL20 7LD
Tel   +44 (0)1691 600666
Email   reception@thehandhotel.co.uk
Web   www.thehandhotel.co.uk

Entry 191   Map 5

Pentre Mawr Country House

The setting is beautiful, 190 acres of deep country at the end of a lane. This is an old estate, in Graham's family for 400 years, and his to renovate; he's done a grand job. Outside, a lawn runs down to fields, and Doric columns flank the front door. Pentre Mawr is half B&B (informal, personal, very welcoming), half hotel (smart rooms, attentive service, a menu in the restaurant). Wander about and find a couple of sitting rooms, open fires, vast flagstones, a bust of Robert Napier. Bedrooms are scattered about. Big rooms in the main house have a country-house feel; stylish suites in the gardener's cottage have hot tubs on private terraces; super-cool safari lodges in the garden flaunt faux leopard-skin throws and great bathrooms. As for canine visitors, Graham and Bre's three beautifully behaved collies will make them most welcome – just as long as they remain on the lead around the farm, mind their manners and wipe their feet before they step in. There's a sun-trapping courtyard with a small pool, tennis on the grass, a kitchen garden that's being teased back to life. End the day with a fine dinner from Bre.

Price	£130. Suites £180. Lodges £160. Half-board £100–£130 p.p. (obligatory Friday & Saturday).
Rooms	8: 3 doubles. Gardener's Cottage: 2 suites. Garden: 3 canvas lodges.
Meals	Dinner, 5 courses, £35.
Closed	Christmas.

 Find chews, footballs, towels & snug blankets

Graham & Bre Carrington-Sykes
Llandyrnog,
Denbigh LL16 4LA
Tel   +44 (0)1824 790732
Email   info@pentremawrcountryhouse.co.uk
Web   www.pentremawrcountryhouse.co.uk

Entry 192   Map 5

Plas Penucha

Swing back in time with polished parquet, tidy beams, a huge Elizabethan panelled lounge with books, leather sofas and open fire – a cosy spot for tea in winter. Plas Penucha – 'the big house on the highest point in the parish' – has been in the family for 500 years. Airy, old-fashioned bedrooms have long views across the garden to Offa's Dyke and one has a shower in the corner. The L-shaped dining room has a genuine Arts & Crafts interior; outside, rhododendrons and a rock garden flourish. Beyond is open countryside and St Asaph, with the smallest medieval cathedral in the country.

Price	From £68. Singles from £35.
Rooms	2: 1 double, 1 twin.
Meals	Dinner £19. Packed lunch £5. Pub/restaurant 2-3 miles.
Closed	Rarely.

Cosy dog blankets, a roaring open fire for evening naps, & free dog biscuits

Nest Price
Peny Cefn Road, Caerwys,
Mold CH7 5BH

Tel	+44 (0)1352 720210
Email	info@plaspenucha.co.uk
Web	www.plaspenucha.co.uk

Entry 193 Map 5

The Bell at Skenfrith

The position here is magical: an ancient stone bridge, a much-ignored valley, glorious hills rising behind, cows grazing in lush fields. It's a perfect spot, not least because providence has blessed it with this sublime inn, where crisply designed interiors ooze country chic. In summer doors fly open and life spills onto a stone terrace, where views of wood and hill are interrupted only by the odd chef pottering off to a rather productive organic kitchen garden. Back inside you find slate floors, open fires and plump-cushioned armchairs in the locals' bar, but the emphasis here is firmly on the food with a very happy kitchen turning out exceptional cooking, perhaps wild garlic vichyssoise with Herefordshire snails, fabulous Welsh lamb with hazelnut couscous, a flawless raspberry soufflé with a champagne bellini. There's an imperious wine list to wash it down with and bedrooms that are as good as you'd expect: uncluttered and elegant, brimming with light, some beamed, others overlooking the river. Idyllic circular walks sweep you into blissful country.

Price	£110-£170. Four-posters £195-£220. Singles from £75.
Rooms	11: 6 doubles, 2 twins, 3 four-posters.
Meals	Lunch from £14. Sunday lunch £25. Dinner, 3 courses, around £33.
Closed	Last week Jan/first week Feb.

Lowdown on circular walks from two to six miles

William & Janet Hutchings
Skenfrith,
Abergavenny NP7 8UH
Tel   +44 (0)1600 750235
Email   enquiries@skenfrith.co.uk
Web   www.skenfrith.co.uk

Entry 194   Map 2

Slebech Park

An imperious position on the upper reaches of Daugleddau Estuary, part of a 600-acre estate that dates to 1760. You will probably think you've washed up at the main house, but incredibly, this crenellated building originally served as the mill and stables. It stands 30 paces from the water with views of river, wood and sky; the odd boat potters past, migrating birds come to bathe. Inside is the lap of luxury, the result of a total renovation. Each apartment comes with a super kitchen so you can look after yourself, but there's a rather good restaurant too (Welsh beef, fish from local waters, woodcock off the estate) and guests tend to do a bit of both. Apartments are sublime: grand yet contemporary, 21st-century country-house chic. You get vast sofas, padded window seats, beautiful colours and fabrics, huge beds wrapped in white linen, very fancy bathrooms. One on the ground floor has fine arched windows that open onto a terrace. Elsewhere, breathtaking gardens, the ruins of a 12th-century church and a sun-trapping courtyard where you can eat in summer. A perfect place. *Min. two nights at weekends.*

Price	£120-£185. Suites £210-£285.
Rooms	14 + 1: 10 twins/doubles, 3 studios, 1 suite. Self-catering cottage for 4.
Meals	Light lunches from £8.50. Dinner, 3 courses, £25-£40.
Closed	Never.

 Explore woodland, coastal paths & masses of dog-friendly beaches

	Geoffrey & Georgina Phillips Slebech, Haverfordwest SA62 4AX
Tel	+44 (0)1437 752000
Email	enquiries@slebech.co.uk
Web	www.slebech.co.uk

Llys Meddyg

This fabulous restaurant with rooms has a bit of everything: cool rooms that pack a designer punch, super food in a sparkling restaurant, a cellar bar for drinks before dinner, a fabulous garden for summer treats. It's a very friendly place with charming staff on hand to help, and it draws in a local crowd who come for the seriously good food, perhaps mussel and saffron soup, rib of Welsh beef with hand-cut chips, cherry soufflé with pistachio ice cream. You eat in style with a fire burning at one end of the restaurant and good art hanging on the walls. Excellent bedrooms are split between the main house (decidedly funky) and the mews behind (away from the road). All have the same fresh style: Farrow & Ball colours, good art, oak beds, fancy bathrooms with fluffy robes. Best of all is the back garden with a mountain-fed stream pouring past. In summer, a café/bistro opens up out here – coffee and cake or steak and chips – with doors that open onto the garden. Don't miss Pembrokeshire's fabulous coastal path for its windswept cliffs, sandy beaches and secluded coves.

Price	£100–£180. Singles from £85.
Rooms	9: 4 doubles, 4 twins/doubles, 1 suite.
Meals	Lunch from £7. Dinner £33.
Closed	Rarely.

 Newport Sands is dog-friendly all year with dunes & miles of sand – & cafés for exhausted owners

Louise & Edward Sykes
East Street,
Newport SA42 0SY
Tel   +44 (0)1239 820008
Email   info@llysmeddyg.com
Web   www.llysmeddyg.com

Entry 196   Map 1

The Felin Fach Griffin

This fabulous little inn goes from strength to strength. Its hallmarks are great staff, delicious food, a friendly bar and honest prices. It's a must for those in search of a welcoming billet close to the mountains and its quirky, homespun feel is utterly intoxicating. It thrives on a mix of relaxed informality and colourful style. The timber-framed bar resembles the sitting room of a small hip country house: sofas sit in front of a fire, backgammon waits to be played. Painted stone walls come in blocks of colour, and an open-plan feel sweeps you through to a restaurant where you can dig into wonderful country food, perhaps Portland crab, shin of Welsh beef, pink rhubarb trifle. Much of what you eat comes from a half-acre kitchen garden, while meat and game are from the hills around you. As for the bedrooms, expect comfy beds, Roberts radios, good books and framed photography (but no TVs unless you ask). Super tongue-and-groove bathrooms are being updated with cool limestone tiles. The Beacons are close, so walk, ride, bike, canoe – or head to Hay for books galore.

Price	£115–£155. Singles from £80. Half-board from £85 p.p.
Rooms	7: 2 doubles, 2 twins/doubles, 3 four-posters.
Meals	Lunch from £5. Dinner £21.50–£35.
Closed	Christmas & 4 days in Jan.

 Welcome dog biscuits on beds; dog towels & bowls; & reams of notes on good walks

Charles & Edmund Inkin
Felin Fach,
Brecon LD3 0UB
Tel   +44 (0)1874 620111
Email   enquiries@felinfachgriffin.co.uk
Web   www.felinfachgriffin.co.uk

Entry 197   Map 2

Hafod Y Garreg

A unique opportunity to stay in the oldest house in Wales – a fascinating, 1402 cruck-framed hall house, built for Henry IV as a hunting lodge. Informal Annie and John have filled it with a charming mix of Venetian mirrors, Indian rugs, pewter plates, gorgeous fabrics and oak furniture. Dine by candlelight in the fabulous dining room – maybe pheasant pie with chilli jam and hazelnut mash: delicious. Bedrooms are luxurious and comfortable with Egyptian cotton bed linen. Reach the Grade II*-listed house by a bumpy track across gated fields crowded with chickens, cats, goats... a special, secluded and relaxed place.

The Old Store House

Unbend here with agreeable books, chattering birds, and twinkling Peter, who asks only that you feel at home. Downstairs are a range-warmed kitchen, a conservatory for breakfast (scrambled eggs, local bacon and sausages, blistering coffee), tennis balls for dogs, and a charmingly ramshackle sitting room with a wood-burner, sofas and piano – no babbling TV. Bedrooms are large, light and spotless, with plump duvets, armchairs, bathrooms with views. The canal tow path at the bottom of the garden is fenced off from stock so dogs may run free. Bliss – but not for those who prefer the comfort of rules. *Self-catering available.*

Price	£82. Singles from £75.
Rooms	2 doubles.
Meals	Dinner, 3 courses, £24. BYO. Pubs/restaurants 2.5 miles.
Closed	Christmas.

 Gorgeous country walks straight from the door

Price	£80. Singles £40.
Rooms	4: 3 doubles, 1 twin.
Meals	Packed lunch £4. Pub/restaurant 0.75 miles.
Closed	Rarely.

Free dog-sitting for owners who fancy a night out on the town – or a supper down the pub

Annie & John McKay
Erwood, Builth Wells LD2 3TQ
Tel   +44 (0)1982 560400
Email   john-annie@hafod-y.wanadoo.co.uk
Web   www.hafodygarreg.co.uk

Peter Evans
Llanfrynach LD3 7LJ
Tel   +44 (0)1874 665499
Email   oldstorehouse@btconnect.com
Web   www.theoldstorehouse.co.uk

Ty'r Chanter

Warmth, colour, children and activity: this house is fun. Tiggy welcomes you like family; collect eggs, feed the lambs or the pony, drop your shoes by the fire. The farmhouse and barn are stylishly relaxed; deep sofas, tartan throws, heaps of books, views to the Brecon Beacons and Black Mountains. Bedrooms are soft, simple sanctuaries with Jo Malone bathroom treats. Children's rooms zing with murals; toys, kids' sitting room, sandpit – child heaven. Walk, fish, canoe, book-browse in Hay or stroll the estate. Homemade cakes, whisky to help yourself to: fine hospitality. Tip: bring dog jerseys for walks in the wild!

Price	£90. Singles £55.
Rooms	4: 1 double; 1 double with separate bath/shower; 2 children's rooms.
Meals	Packed lunch £8. Pub 1 mile.
Closed	Christmas.

 A banger for brekki! Dogs can snooze on the heated floor & enjoy a marshmallow in front of the fire

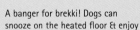

Tiggy Pettifer
Gliffaes, Crickhowell NP8 1RL
Tel   +44 (0)1874 731144
Mobile   +44 (0)7802 387004
Email   tiggy@tyrchanter.com
Web   www.tyrchanter.com

Entry 200   Map 2

Fairyhill Hotel

The Gower Peninsula has legions of fans who come for its glorious heathland, its rugged coastline and some of the best beaches in the country. Fairyhill is bang in the middle of it all, a sublime country house wrapped up in 24 acres of blissful silence. There's a terrace for lunch, a stream-fed lake, an ancient orchard, a walled garden with asparagus beds. Inside, country-house interiors come fully loaded with warmth and colour. You'll find an open fire in the bar, a grand piano in the sitting room and super local food in the restaurant, where as much as possible comes from Gower. So tuck into confit of duck and pistachio terrine, local sea bass with scallops and green beans, then apple and tarragon tart with ice cream. Most bedrooms are big and fancy, a couple are small, but sweet. Some have painted beams, others have golden wallpaper, all have robes in excellent bathrooms. Mattresses are Vi-Spring, but if that's not enough there's a treatment room, so book a massage. There's croquet on the lawn in summer, while duck eggs come courtesy of resident Muscovys.

Price	£180–£280. Singles from £160. Half-board from £125 p.p.
Rooms	8: 3 doubles, 5 twins/doubles.
Meals	Lunch from £15.95. Dinner £35–£45.
Closed	First 3 weeks in January.

24 acres of grounds to explore, & beautiful white-sand Gower beaches beyond

Andrew Hetherington
& Paul Davies
Reynoldston, Swansea SA3 1BS
Tel   +44 (0)1792 390139
Email   postbox@fairyhill.net
Web   www.fairyhill.net

Entry 201   Map 2

Pubs-for-a-pint

When you're away on a break with your dog it's handy to have a list of dog-friendly pubs to visit for a pint or a snack. Here is a small selection of pubs in Wales that welcome dogs in at least one area of the pub – most likely to be by the fire, at the bar or in the garden. Most pubs, though – even the dog-friendly ones – draw the line at allowing dogs in dining rooms, but if you want to check the details beforehand just give them a call.

We've visited each of these pubs and written about them ourselves. They're here because we like them. (We've not inspected any bedrooms they may have.) They are all taken from our hugely popular *Pubs & Inns of England & Wales* guide. Now in its eighth edition, this guide brings you a huge variety of pubs from the charming to the rustic and the real-aled to the Michelin-starred. Visit www.sawdays.co.uk/bookshop to buy the guide.

Here is an explanation of the symbols you'll find at the foot of each Pub's entry. They apply to bar areas.

   ♿ Wheelchair access to both bar and wcs.

   🏃 Children of all ages welcome in parts of pub (highchairs not necessarily available).

   💳 Credit cards accepted, most commonly Visa and MasterCard.

   🍺 Pub serves four or more hand pumped ales.

   🍷 Pub serves eight or more wines by the glass.

   📶 Wireless internet access available in the bar.

Denbighshire Pub

Pant-yr-Ochain

A long drive snakes through landscaped parkland to a magnificent multi-gabled country house sheltered by trees. To one side a huge conservatory opens up views across terraces to the estate lake; inside, a jigsaw of richly panelled rooms and drinking areas lures those who come to dine and others in search of the hop: note nine real ales. Below an eccentric ceiling line fine intimate corners, comfy alcoves and private snugs, open fires, quarry tiles and bare boards. Everywhere, a cornucopia of bric-a-brac: penny slots and cases of clay pipes, caricatures and prints. It sounds OTT but it fits here, while the ever-reliable Brunning & Price menus feature the likes of venison with sloe gin and cherry sauce, and smoked haddock and salmon fishcakes. Outside is a flower-filled, lakeside garden. Dogs will smile.

Meals	Lunch & dinner £5.75–£16.95.
Closed	Open all day.

 Beautiful big garden with lots of walks close by

 ♿ 🚶 💳 🍺 🍷

James Meakin
Old Wrexham Road, Gresford,
Wrexham LL12 8TY
Tel   +44 (0)1978 853525
Email pant.yr.ochain@brunningandprice.co.uk
Web   www.pantyrochain-gresford.co.uk

Monmouthshire Pub

Raglan Arms

An effortless combination of village local and convivial gastropub. In a bright spacious bar with slate underfoot, anticipation mounts as you scan the menu – from the comfort of leather sofas and roaring log fire. The landlord Giles prepares fairly priced dishes showcasing produce from the area, so try chicken liver and pistachio parfait, brill with linguini, local samphire, mussels and chilli or a posh open sandwich: slow-roasted shoulder of Gloucester Old Spot with apple sauce. To finish: pear and almond tart, a selection of cheeses. When the sun shines you (plus dog) can eat al fresco, on a raised deck area with planters and parasols. Butty Bach is the only real ale, but there are heaps of delicious wines. Roam Raglan castle – dogs are welcome on leads.

Meals	Lunch £6–£12. Dinner £10–£19.
	Sunday lunch, 3 courses, £22.
Closed	3pm–6pm, Sun eves & Mon.

 Dogs may doze in the bar & romp in the big garden at the back

 🚶 💳 🍷

Giles Cunliffe
Llandenny,
Usk NP15 1DL
Tel   +44 (0)1291 690800
Email theraglanarms@gmail.com

Hunter's Moon Inn

Haydn Jones and his partner Jana run this deep-country inn just off Offa's Dyke with passion. The original building, all low ceilings and 1217-flagged floors, was constructed by stonemasons establishing a place to stay before building the neighbouring church. Book ahead; the 'table for the evening' policy ensures much care is taken with the locally sourced food. Specials may include 28-day aged beef, shank of lamb, or pork cooked in a sage, cream and apple sauce. The local and guest ales are well-kept, the wine list well chosen, there's Leffe on draught and a range of bottled ciders. In summer you and dogs can go al fresco – under parasols overlooking the churchyard or in the beer garden; the famous Puskins (resident moggy) may make an appearance. There's a drying room for walkers, too.

| Meals | Lunch & dinner £8-£20. |
| Closed | Mon all day, Tues-Fri lunch, 3pm-6.30pm Sat (7pm Sun). |

 Offa's Dyke path 50 yards from the inn, with wonderful walks for dogs of all sizes

Haydn Jones
Llangattock Lingoed,
Abergavenny NP7 8RR
Tel   +44 (0)1873 821499
Email   huntersmooninn@btinternet.com
Web   www.hunters-moon-inn.co.uk

Entry 204   Map 2

Clytha Arms

The inn stands on the old coaching route into border country, in gorgeous surroundings. With two and a half acres of dog-happy garden, you can sit outside in fine weather and dive into cockles, crab sandwiches, tapas or a ploughman's with three local cheeses. Inside, two bars: one with button-back sofas and low tables, the other more rustic, with high ceiling, stripped floors and bar games; both have cheery fires. The restaurant is smart with marbled walls, new stone floor, white linen tablecloths. In the kitchen is Andrew Canning, host and chef, who rustles up grilled tuna Sicilian style, herb-crusted hake, and steak and oyster pie. The monthly set menu is full of temptations such as lamb mixed grill with garlic jus and seafood stew. The wine list (11 by the glass) and the range of beers and cider are impressive, and there's homemade perry for the bibulously curious.

| Meals | Lunch & dinner £14-£20. |
| Closed | 3pm-6pm & Mon lunch. Open all day Fri-Sun. |

 Acres of garden to explore, & exciting smells along a pretty river walk

Andrew & Beverley Canning
Clytha,
Abergavenny NP7 9BW
Tel   +44 (0)1873 840206
Email   theclythaarms@tiscali.co.uk
Web   www.clytha-arms.com

Entry 205   Map 2

Bear Hotel

Viewed from the square of this small market town, the 15th-century frontage of the old coaching inn appears modest. But behind the cobbles and the summer flowers, it is a warren of surprises and mild eccentricity – bars and brasserie at the front, nooks and crannies at the back – and a family- and dog-welcoming garden. The beamy lounge has parquet, plush seating and a mighty fire; settle in and savour their good beers, wines, whiskies and ports. There are two dining areas where at night you can feast on Welsh Black beef, Usk salmon, Brecon venison, locally grown seasonal vegetables and regional farmhouse cheeses. Homemade ice creams, mousses and puddings are equally sumptuous. We've never seen the place empty and Mrs Hindmarsh is still firmly in charge of an operation that rarely comes off the rails.

| Meals | Lunch & dinner £5.95-£20. |
| Closed | 3pm-6pm (7pm Sun). |

 Bowls of chicken on arrival!

♿ 🏃 💳 🍺 🍷

Judy Hindmarsh
High Street,
Crickhowell NP8 1BW
Tel   +44 (0)1873 810408
Email   bearhotel@aol.com
Web   www.bearhotel.co.uk

Entry 206   Map 2

Powys   Pub

Nantyffin Cider Mill Inn

Diners pour in here for menus that spotlight pork, lamb, duck, guinea fowl, beef – exuberantly casseroled in farmhouse cider. A network of small suppliers provides the rest, while autumn brings mushrooms and game from a nearby estate. It started life in the 15th century as a drovers' inn and an old cider press occupies one end of the impressive, high-raftered restaurant in the old mill room. You can also sit in one of two intimate bars and choose from a bar menu and a specials board that is chalked up daily. Expect country cooking concocted with minimum fuss and maximum flavour – lamb with colcannon mash and rosemary garlic sauce, fish casserole – plus ales and ciders on tap, delicious wines by the glass, hot punch in winter and luscious lemonade in summer.

| Meals | Lunch from £9.50. Bar meals from £6.95. Dinner from £10.95. Sunday lunch, 3 courses, £20.50. Not Sunday eve (October-March). |
| Closed | 3pm-6pm (7pm Sun), Sun eve in winter & all day Mon (except bank hols). |

 The lovely Brecon Beacons are perfect for doggie exploration & we have maps to help

♿ 🏃 💳 🍺 🍷

Vic, Ann & Sharon Williams
Brecon Road,
Crickhowell NP8 1SG
Tel   +44 (0)1873 810775
Email   info@cidermill.co.uk
Web   www.cidermill.co.uk

Entry 207   Map 2

The Harp

Chris Ireland and Angela Lyne have taken over this ancient Welsh longhouse tucked up a dead-end lane near the parish church and have no plans to change this deep-country gem. The wonderful interior is spick-and-span timeless: 14th-century slate flooring in the bar, tongue-and-groove in a tiny room that seats a dozen diners, crannies crammed with memorabilia, an ancient curved settle, an antique reader's chair, two fires and a happy crowd. Enjoy a pint of Wye Valley or Three Tuns bitter with a Welsh Black rump steak with chips and roasted root vegetables, or sea bass with salsa verde. Or take a ploughman's to a seat under the sycamore and gaze upon the spectacular Radnor Valley... total tranquillity. Life in this tiny village, like its glorious pub, remains unchanged.

| Meals | Lunch & dinner from £8.95. Bar meals from £4.25. Not Monday or Tuesday-Friday lunch. |
| Closed | Tues-Fri lunch, 3pm-6pm Sat & Sun & Mon all day. |

 Grand walks from the door (keeping an eye out for cattle & sheep), & a black lab to play with

Chris Ireland & Angela Lyne
Old Radnor,
Presteigne LD8 2RH
Tel   +44 (0)1544 350655
Email   mail@harpinnradnor.co.uk
Web   www.harpinnradnor.co.uk

Entry 208   Map 2

Wynnstay Hotel

In the quaint first capital of Wales, you'll be charmed to discover this rambling old coaching inn. It's rather more hotel than pub, but there's a cracking bar with traditional oak floors, low beams, scrubbed tables and candlelight. Bag a seat by the log fire in winter and peruse Gareth Johns's menus over a pint of fine Welsh ale. He applies his skills to fine local produce: Conwy mussels, Borth lobster, salmon and sewin from the river Dyfi, Welsh Black beef and lamb from the valley. Salt duck terrine with homemade chutney may precede hake with roasted vegetables and herb oil, or rib-eye of beef with chips; finish with Welsh cheeses. There are some wonderful wines from small producers and, surprisingly, a traditional pizzeria at the back. Walk off any excess with a glorious countryside stroll.

| Meals | Lunch £7.95-£15.95. Dinner from £11.95. Sunday lunch, 3 courses, £16.50. |
| Closed | 2.30pm-6pm (bar only). |

 Treats aplenty from bones to pigs' ears. Wonderful walks in farming country (some on the lead)

Gareth & Paul Johns
Heol Maengwyn,
Machynlleth SY20 8AE
Tel   +44 (0)1654 702941
Email   info@wynnstay-hotel.com
Web   www.wynnstay-hotel.com

Entry 209   Map 5

The Brigands Inn

The Cambrian Mountains loom like vast waves over the Dovey valley. This big old coaching inn on an ancient drovers' path has been offering sustenance to travellers for 500 years. The recent renovation has retained the integrity of the rambling building and as you step in to the big oak bar with its polished flagstones and waxed beams you feel that you've entered a well-run ship. Food is a mix of contemporary and classic Welsh cuisine. Best end of local Welsh lamb with baby veg, fondant potato and redcurrant jus stand alongside pan-fried fillet of bream with ratatouille, a sweet red pepper dressing and baby clams, so make your choice as you sip a pint of Clogwyn Gold. There's also a pretty view-filled garden and a field at the back, and a sofa'd snug in which to discover some rather tempting wines.

The Cross Foxes

It's set on a travellers' crossroads, as the highway crosses the waters of the Dee and both man and fish move in either direction, depending on the season. Rest on the terrace with a pint of Marston's Burton Bitter or Ringwood's Huffkin and soak up the views from a timeless spot. Inside, a log fire throws light on a well-carved bar front, polished wood tables and quarry tiles, and on the shelves glows one of the best whisky and armagnac collections for many a mile: cockle-warming stuff. The big blackboard at the end of the bar is scrawled with good things to eat, from Cumberland sausage with black pudding mash and onion gravy to venison and pheasant meat loaf with red cabbage and juniper sauce. Settle into the wood-panelled area, the fireside snug or the conservatory, and enjoy a genuine classic.

Meals	Lunch & dinner £8.50–£16.50.
Closed	Open all day.

 Parts of the dining room open to dogs so they can stay with their owners if they get lonely

Meals	Lunch & dinner £9.50–£16.95. Bar meals from £4.75.
Closed	Open all day.

 Dogs are very welcome in the tiled area of the bar – & dog bowls are provided

Dawn Davies
Mallwyd,
Machynlleth SY20 9HJ
Tel　+44 (0)1650 511999
Email　dawndavies8@hotmail.com
Web　www.brigandsinn.com

Entry 210　Map 5

Ian Pritchard-Jones
Erbistock,
Wrexham LL13 0DR
Tel　+44 (0)1978 780380
Email　cross.foxes@brunningandprice.co.uk
Web　www.crossfoxes-erbistock.co.uk

Entry 211　Map 5

Scotland

West Highland Terrier
Photo: www.istockphoto.com/
Sima_ha

Darroch Learg Hotel

The country here is glorious – river, forest, mountain, sky – so walk by Loch Muick, climb Lochnagar, fish the Dee or drop down to Braemar for the Highland Games. Swing back to Darroch and find nothing but good things. This is a smart family-run hotel firmly rooted in a graceful past, an old country house with roaring fires, polished brass, Zoffany wallpaper and ambrosial food in a much-admired restaurant. Ever-present Nigel and Fiona look after guests with great aplomb and many return year after year. Everything is just as it should be: tartan fabrics on the walls in the hall, Canadian pitch pine windows and doors, fabulous views sweeping south across Balmoral forest. Bedrooms upstairs come in different shapes and sizes; all have warmth and comfort in spades. Big grand rooms at the front thrill with padded window seats, wallpapered bathrooms, old oak furniture, perhaps a four-poster bed. Spotlessly cosy rooms in the eaves are equally lovely, just not quite as big. You get warm colours, pretty furniture, crisp white linen and bathrobes to pad about in. A perfect highland retreat.

Price	£140–£250. Half-board (obligatory at weekends) £95–£160 p.p.
Rooms	12: 10 twins/doubles, 2 four-posters.
Meals	Sunday lunch £24. Dinner £45; tasting menu, £55, on request.
Closed	Christmas & last 3 weeks in Jan.

Four acres of private woodland from the back door

Nigel & Fiona Franks
56 Braemar Road,
Ballater AB35 5UX
Tel +44 (0)1339 755443
Email enquiries@darrochlearg.co.uk
Web www.darrochlearg.co.uk

Entry 212 Map 9

The Old House

You drive for six miles along a leafy track that hugs the rushing river – or take the train to Bridge of Orchy and let the friendly owners collect you. The former Earl of Breadalbane's sporting lodge and has been renovated from top to toe with sensitivity and flair. The golden yellow sitting room has a wood-burning stove, the four-poster bedroom is on the ground floor – along with a Belfast sink for washing the day's catch and a 'wet room' in which the whole family can scrub up. Hikers are spoilt for choice: walk up the hill on the other side of the river to a clearing where the play of sunlight through woodland is magical, or climb 2,500 feet up Ben Udlaidh for views towards the islands. The pretty garden slopes towards the river: cluster round the table on the decking or dig up vegetables from the garden. In the bathrooms are lovely cosmetics from your hosts; their company harvests seaweed off the west coast islands. An extremely comfortable home for a family holiday – and if you need supplies from the local grocer's, the postman can be persuaded to deliver them to you with the morning mail.

Price	£425–£1,000 per week.
Rooms	House for 6.
Meals	Self-catering.
Closed	Rarely.

 Expert advice on wild, carefree walks – & a special welcome from terrier Boris the Arbuthnott

John & Erica Kerr
Arichastlich,
Glen Orchy PA33 1BD
Tel   +44 (0)1838 200399
Email   theoldhouse@glen-orchy.co.uk
Web   www.glen-orchy.co.uk

Entry 213   Map 8

Tiroran House

The setting is magnificent with 17 acres of lush gardens rolling down to Loch Scridian and the Ross of Mull rising beyond. Otters and dolphins pass by, as do red deer, who try to raid the garden. As for this 1850 shooting lodge, you'll be hard pressed to find a more hospitable island base. There are fires in the drawing rooms, fresh flowers everywhere, games to be played, books to be read, and owners who believe a house is not a home without a dog. Big country-house bedrooms hit the spot perfectly: crisp linen on pretty beds, beautiful fabrics and the odd chaise longue, watery views and silence guaranteed. You eat in a smart dining room, either at the front in the vine-shaded conservatory or at the back amid gilt mirrors. The food is exceptional with much from the island or waters around it: oak-smoked salmon, fillet of venison… You're bang in the middle of Mull with loads to do. Seek out Tobermory, the prettiest town in the Hebrides; Calgary for its dog-friendly, white-sand beach; day trips to Iona with its famous monastery; boat trips to Fingal's Cave. Come back for afternoon tea; it's as good as the Ritz.

Price	£165–£195.
Rooms	10: 5 doubles, 5 twins/doubles.
Meals	Dinner, 4 courses, £45.50.
Closed	November to mid-March.

Ideal dog walking territory & towels on supply from dog-loving hosts

Laurence & Katie Mackay
Isle of Mull PA69 6ES

Tel	+44 (0)1681 705232
Email	info@tiroran.com
Web	www.tiroran.com

Entry 214   Map 8

Ardanaiseig

You're lost to the world, ten miles down a track that winds past giant rhododendrons before petering out at this baronial mansion. Beyond, Loch Awe rules supreme, 30 miles of deep blue water on which to sail or fish. In one of the loveliest hotel drawing rooms you are ever likely to see – gold leaf panelling, cherubs in alcoves, Doric columns rising gleefully – an enormous window frames the view and a single sofa waits for those lucky enough to have it. Elsewhere, Wellington boots are on parade in the hall, fires roar wherever you go, eccentric art hangs on the dining room wall and a lawned terrace runs down to the loch. You're in hundreds of acres of private grounds; in May bluebells run riot. Country-house bedrooms are the real thing (old armoires, feather boa lamp shades, the odd four-poster), while the boat house has been converted into a funky suite with a wall of glass that opens onto a decked terrace. Dinner is a seven-course feast, as one might expect of this rather flamboyant hotel. Also, snooker, tennis and boats on which to row over to an island. Off-season breaks are a steal.

Price	£138–£298. Suite £280–£360. Singles from £99.
Rooms	18: 8 twins/doubles, 7 doubles, 2 four-posters, 1 boat house suite.
Meals	Light lunch from £4. Dinner, 7 courses, £50.
Closed	2 January–1 February.

 Set in 300 acres of perfect dog-walking land

Peter Webster
Kilchrenan, Taynuilt PA35 1HE
Tel   +44 (0)1866 833333
Email   info@ardanaiseig.com
Web   www.ardanaiseig.com

Inshriach Yurt

Inshriach House was built in 1906 as a shooting lodge, since when the estate has collected various interesting pieces of historic flotsam. Look out for the squash court from the 1930s, the Victorian dairy, the 18th-century steading – and the snooker table half buried in the garden. The terrain is as diverse as the history. The Cairngorm mountains give way to thick forest, and with the Spey running through below, the area is a wonderland for walkers, cyclists and anglers. As for the yurt, it's a warm wonderful space that sits in magnificent seclusion on the hillside. The owners tell us they are "a bit like The Wombles" – and when you see the recycled fence-post decking, the grand Victorian double bed, the tapestry tub chair and the old mahogany writing table, you gotta believe it! Kit drying room, shower and loo (shared with other guests on occasion) are at the farmhouse 700 metres up the hill, over some rough terrain. For civilisation, Aviemore is two miles up the road. Amazing!

Price	From £60 a night.
Rooms	Yurt for 2.
Meals	Self-catering.
Closed	Never.

 Fantastic walks through the national park all around

Canopy & Stars
Aviemore PH22 1QP
Tel   +44 (0)1275 395447
Email   enquiries@canopyandstars.co.uk
Web   www.canopyandstars.co.uk

Entry 216   Map 8

Kilcamb Lodge Hotel & Restaurant

A stupendous setting, with Loch Sunart at the end of the garden and Glas Bheinn rising beyond. As for Kilcamb, it has the ingredients of the perfect country house: a smart drawing room with a roaring fire; an elegant dining room for top-notch food; super-comfy bedrooms that don't shy from colour; views that feed the soul. The feel here is shipwreck-chic. There's a vast garden with half a mile of shore, so stroll up to the water's edge, look for dolphins, otters and seals, let your dog have a swim. Ducks and geese fly by, and if you're lucky you may see eagles. Back inside you'll find stained-glass windows on the landing, a ship's bell in the bar, dog treats in the bedrooms… Dress up smartly at eight for a three-course dinner and feast on scallops with cauliflower tempura, lamb with caramelised shallots, banana bavarois with rum and raisin ice cream. Bedrooms come in two styles: contemporary or traditional. Expect big beds, padded headboards, smart white towels and shiny bathrooms. Kind staff go the extra mile. Ardnamurchan Point – the most westerly point in mainland Britain – it at the end of the road.

Price	Half-board £110–£180 p.p.
Rooms	10: 7 doubles, 3 suites.
Meals	Lunch from £8.50.
	Dinner for non-residents £49.50.
Closed	January. Limited opening Nov & Feb.

 22 acres of loch side garden, safe for a gallop & a swim, with towels supplied for a good rub down

David & Sally Ruthven-Fox
Strontian, Acharacle PH36 4HY

Tel	+44 (0)1967 402257
Email	enquiries@kilcamblodge.co.uk
Web	www.kilcamblodge.co.uk

Arisaig House

Imposing Arisaig – a 19th-century industrialist's highland fantasy – sits in a walkers' paradise; the views to Skye are to die for. In former days it was a hotel; now Sarah, who has known Arisaig all her life, revels in returning house and gardens to their former glory. The sitting room is bright with Sanderson sofas, portraits and paintings and a huge open fire, and bedrooms are spacious and charming, with comfortable furniture and updated bathrooms. Lovely generous Sarah, passionate Slow Food member, serves breakfasts, high teas and dinners at the long oak table: don't miss the Stornoway black pudding!

Price	£100–£150. Singles £75.
Rooms	8 twins/doubles.
Meals	Dinner, 3 courses, from £25. Pub/restaurant 3 miles.
Closed	Rarely.

 Four friendly dogs for playmates, treats by the front door & splashing in the sea at the end of the garden

Sarah Winnington-Ingram
Arisaig PH39 4NR
Tel   +44 (0)1687 450730
Email sarahwi@arisaighouse.co.uk
Web   www.arisaighouse.co.uk

Entry 218   Map 8

Creagan House at Strathyre

Creagan is a delight – a small, traditional restaurant-with-rooms run with great passion by Gordon and Cherry. At its heart is Gordon's kitchen, from which flies ambrosial food to a baronial dining room: millefuille of veal sweetbreads, Isle of Gigha halibut with scallop, langoustine and crab pâté, bitter chocolate torte with mixed berry compote. Most of it is sourced locally – meat and game from Perthshire, seafood from west coast boats – and served on Skye pottery. There's a snug sitting room which doubles as a bar – find a good wine list and 50 malt whiskies, and if you like a dram you'll be in heaven: there's a guide to help you choose. Bedrooms fit the bill, the most peaceful away from the road: warm and comfortable with smart carpets, wood and florals, flat-screen TVs, a sofa if there's room. No airs and graces, just the sort of attention you only get in small owner-run places. Bag a munro, too; let the walking sticks at the front door help you and the dog up Beinn An T-Sidhein. A perfect wee retreat. *Donations in the Guide Dogs for the Blind tin welcome.*

Price	£130–£150. Singles £75–£95.
Rooms	5: 1 four-poster, 3 doubles, 1 twin.
Meals	Dinner, 3 courses, £31.50–£36.
Closed	Wednesdays & Thursdays. February.

 Reams of advice on local walks: hill, forest or riverside, all straight from the car park. Dog towels, bowls & balls on request

Gordon & Cherry Gunn
Callander FK18 8ND

Tel	+44 (0)1877 384638
Email	eatandstay@creaganhouse.co.uk
Web	www.creaganhouse.co.uk

Oldhamstocks Cottage

Next to the owners' house, at one end of a sleepy Scottish village is this immaculately restored, one-storey cottage. The sturdy pinkstone stable block has become a warm, cosy hideaway for four. You get a bright sunny sitting room (the cottage faces south), a well-equipped little kitchen with terracotta walls and a wooden dining table, two comfortable bedrooms sporting duvets and White Company linen, and a spotless white bathroom. There's also a large secure garage with room for storing bikes, fishing tackle, golf clubs and muddy boots. Thanks to the unspoilt sandy beaches, the rolling Lammermuir Hills and the 19 fabulous golf courses, walkers and sporty types will relish the position; the wonderful Southern Upland Way starts and finishes in the next village. And then there's Edinburgh, a 35-minute drive (though most people take the train from Dunbar). For winter there's a lovely coal fire for cosy nights in with games and DVDs, generously provided; for summer, a delightful enclosed garden with table and chairs, its door leading to the village and a small play park for children.

Price	£295–£595 per week.
Rooms	Cottage for 4.
Meals	Self-catering.
Closed	Never.

 A walled garden for safe doggie fun, walks from the back door to the beach, & chews & a basket on their return

Olivia Reynolds
Oldhamstocks, Dunbar TD13 5XN
Tel   +44 (0)1368 830233
Email   olivia@oldhamstockscottage.com
Web   www.oldhamstockscottage.com

The Bowtop & Cottage

In the woodland garden in front of Horseshoe Cottage stands a rare and authentic 1930s gypsy caravan. Rented as one space, cottage and caravan together sleep a party of four and up to two well-behaved dogs. How dreamy to sleep outdoors, separated from the night skies by a lovingly restored bowtop caravan, a stunning original from master painter Jim Berry (a distant relative of the owner). On chillier nights an original Queenie stove keeps you and the kettle warm. The rosy interior is beautifully decorated, while the bed, not quite a full double, is the type that's so cosy and comfy you won't want to get up in the morning! Horseshoe Cottage, converted from the old stables, sits a few yards away. Its pretty colours and style match those of the caravan and together they make a stylish pair. Inside the cottage: a bright roomy sitting room, a galley kitchen (no oven), a bathroom with a shower, and two bedrooms, a double and a twin. (Note, the total number of guests who may stay is four.) There's oil-fired central heating and a wood-burning stove, and a view of the legendary Eildon Hills. *Dogs welcome in the cottage only.*

Price	From £90 a night. £5 per dog per night.
Rooms	Cottage for 2. Bowtop caravan for 2.
Meals	Self-catering.
Closed	Never.

 You're spoiled for walks: by the river Tweed, up the Eildon Hills, along St Cuthbert's Way & around the local woods

Canopy & Stars
Bowden Mill House, Melrose TD6 0SU
Tel	+44 (0)1275 395447
Email	enquiries@canopyandstars.co.uk
Web	www.canopyandstars.co.uk

 Entry 221   Map 9

Ben Lomond

A fusion of Krgyk design and local materials, these lovely Mongolian style yurts have a homely, earthy feel, with thick rugs, rough tapestries and wood-burning stoves adding comfort. Ben Ledi and Ben Lomond yurts share the woodland just a little way on from Stuc a'Chroin yurt and the two together make a great family camp. In each is a double bed and a double futon, and a single futon which can be added so that they can sleep five. From the boardwalk leading to the well-equipped communal kitchen are impressive views across Flanders Moss National Nature Reserve. Arts and crafts courses aplenty too, including willow and felt crafting, spoon carving, paper making, Japanese block printing, batik dye work and mosaics… and yoga. There's also an abundance of very local produce, both from the revitalised kitchen garden and the cows that graze on the moss. With all this, the beauty of the lochs and the Arrochar Alps for the dog to explore, you won't be short of ways to create a memorable stay. And for those unhappy at having paws wiped, towels are provided at a modest price. *Ben Lomond yurt is dog-friendly.*

Price	From £75 per night.
Rooms	2 yurts for 4–5.
Meals	Self-catering.
Closed	Never.

 Great walks by Loch Lomond & in the Trossachs, then a cosy basket & food bowls for dogs with clean paws

Canopy & Stars
West Mossside Organic Farm
and Centre, Stirling FK8 3QJ
Tel   +44 (0)1275 395447
Email   enquiries@canopyandstars.co.uk
Web   www.canopyandstars.co.uk

Entry 222   Map 8

England

Berkshire

1   Dogs in need of some exercise can romp around the big field behind

2   A brimming biscuit jar for visiting canines & walking maps with routes straight from the door

Bristol

3   Private fields on the doorstep & tennis balls for fun

Buckinghamshire

4   Dog biscuits in the bedrooms & at the bar

5   Big village green to play on & treats galore – & a village wood teeming with smells & sounds

6   Both dog-friendly rooms have access to the garden

Cheshire

7   Mulsford mutt souvenir: a hymn sheet of 'How much is that Doggie in the Window' in Latin & Baskerville font

Cornwall

8   The South West Coastal Path is on the spot

9   A perfect place for mutts to stay, often frequented by 'Dodger', star of the TV programme Doc Martin

10   For dog walking there's the refreshing pooch-tastic coastal path, plus local pub & restaurant maps

11   A fleecy blanket to snuggle in perfect after a run to the lighthouse

12   Welcome biscuits, dog towels & bowls, & reams of notes on good walks

13   A ten-minute walk to the Cornish coastal path & our local sandy cove, where dogs may frolic all year round

14   A tasty sausage at breakfast

15   The coastal path is at the bottom of garden… & blankets, bowls & towels are provided for afterwards

16   Beautiful coastal walks from the door

17   Doggie guide to local walks & dog-friendly beaches. Tennis balls supplied for garden games

18   Toy cupboard filled with squeakies, balls & tug toys to take to the beach

19   Special mini dog cupcakes on arrival & food mats to guzzle them from

20   Teddy says, "If we have dogs to stay I will share my biscuits & sometimes an extra sausage too"

21   Friendly resident dogs to play with, & a free range field to run in

22   Garden access to the coastal path – & magnificent beaches in both directions

23   Runs around the exquisite wildflower meadow, safely fenced, specially for dogs

Cumbria

24   Drying facilities & free dog towels for soggy dogs, & a great garden with a river for swims

25 Iced water in the bar for visiting dogs
& bowls & towels in the bedrooms

26 Lots of lovely local walks

27 Lake District for excited hounds &
a tarn nearby to splash in

28 At the foot of the North Lakes Fells
& next to Greystoke Forest: endless
scope for owners to be dragged
around by their dogs

29 Suggestions for dog-friendly walks.
Water, food bowl & dog bed all provided

30 A welcome doggie treat for all hounds

31 A vast garden for dogs to explore full
of exciting whiffs, & ten acres of
private woodland

32 Juicy marrowbone from the on-farm
butchery & reams of fantastic walks
& tarns for swimming nearby

Derbyshire

33 Doggie treat walks with countryside
smells: rabbits, badgers, foxes.
Fresh spring water for thirsty pups
on their return

34 Toys & treats, bags & scoops, plus a
special doggie exercise area with a
tap & towels for muddy paws

35 Towels on offer for muddy paws &
tasty leftovers

36 A pooch-friendly walk across beautiful
countryside on the Chatsworth Estate,
straight from the inn

Devon

37 Dogs are allowed almost everywhere,
pigs' ears are always available &
there's fantastic walking from
the door

38 Fabulous farm walks, rivers to splash
in & a list of the best dog-friendly
pubs, gardens & beaches

39 Beautiful hiking country for you &
your dog

40 20 acres of woodland for wonderful
walks

41 A map for good dog walks & a Bonio
biscuit to keep tails wagging

42 Huge garden for romping in & all
manner of play things for your pooch

43 Doggie heaven! Great walks on the
moors & a boot room for after

44 Pigs' ears & assorted treats provided,
& well-behaved dogs on leads are
welcome throughout the pub

45 Tasty treats, five acres of garden,
plus beautiful walks in the Tamar
Valley & on Dartmoor

46 A Bonio in your room, dog biscuits at
reception... & towels, hose, spare leads,
emergency dog food & water bowls
just in case

47 Your hosts love dogs, beaches are right
outside & lovely countryside is
all around

48 Treats, bags & towels – & their own
dinner dish on the menu

49 Wonderful windy walks along the Jurassic Coast

50 3,000 acres: ample to please the most demanding hound

51 Afternoon tea for guests comes with a Bonio for the dogs... 15 acres of countryside, too

52 12 acres of land to roam & a swim in the river – let Archie & Cobble be your guides!

53 Lots of local, dog-friendly knowledge: wonderful walks from the front door along coastal paths & beaches

Dorset

54 Two daft Harlequin Great Danes to welcome you, & miles of footpaths through beautiful countryside

55 Lots of lovely walks & dogs are welcome in the bar

56 All doggie arrivals are given a treat & a guide to local paths & dog-friendly excursions

57 72 footpaths in & around the village, close to the old railway line for flat mud-free rambles

58 Right on the footpath to Hambledon Hill – fabulous for dogs. The river Stour is nearby for a splash, too

59 Dog treats behind the bar & VIP dog beds

60 Dogs staying two nights treated to a dog loofah frisbee

61 Walks straight from the garden gate into fields: maps & books of circular & waterside walks to borrow

62 Complimentary dog treats offered

Essex

63 Wonderful walking on the doorstep with field & woodland smells

64 A doggie bag filled with homemade biscuits, towels for muddy paws & a scrumptious sausage for breakfast

Gloucestershire

65 Four rooms open straight onto the garden – 55 acres. Spot-on for dogs to stretch their legs

66 Pups can motor about mown paths through fields & loll in grounds especially for dogs

67 Snug dog beds, water & food bowls in the room, & recommended walks

68 B&B for dogs too: scrumptious sausages to start the day

69 Dog bowls & a mystery treat provided

70 Delicious dog breakfasts of scrambled eggs, cosy dozes by a log fire – & dog-sitting!

71 Walks with our dogs in the day & friendly dog-sitting at night

72 Dog biscuits & treats at breakfast, good walks locally – just keep an eye out for sheep!

97 Snoopy the spaniel has whizzed up a welcome pack with lists of the best walks & beaches

98 A comfy bed, towel & biscuits on arrival for every pampered pooch

Northumberland

99 Heavenly forest & lakeside walks

100 Doggie 'welcome pack' with a Bonio biscuit & towel for muddy paws. And dogs may dine with their owners if they wish

Nottinghamshire

101 Guide to nearby walks

Oxfordshire

102 Scrumptious pigs' ears at the ready

103 Local walking guides, tennis balls for the garden, & a chew for every visiting dog!

104 Two walking routes for dogs, one including a swim in the river Thames

Rutland

105 Alfie the springer shares treats & walks. His top tip: sit by the youngest family member at meals (they may drop something!)

Shropshire

106 A private patio for pooches, the perfect spot for their sundowner after a hard day's walk

107 A tour of the grounds from resident lab Copper & a "proper bone" straight from the village butcher

108 A tour of the grounds from resident lab Copper, & a "proper bone" straight from the village butcher

109 A Bonio at bedtime

110 A jar of biscuits for every dog & details of local dog-friendly pubs & places to visit

111 Assorted dog chews, & towels on tap for muddy paws

Somerset

112 Perfect walks for dogs, starting right outside the door

113 Stride through the owners' fields to the dog-friendly village pub

114 Free meals, dogsitting, an orchard for romps with the resident dogs & lovely walks by the sea

115 Treats, towels and – if your dog needs one – a crate so you don't need to bring yours

116 Man's best friend is welcome on all West Somerset beaches all year round

Suffolk

117 Biscuits, bowls, blankets & brilliant walks on the doorstep

118 Fabulous walks on beaches, heaths & forest

119 Two Suffolk coastal footpath maps for all Sawday's guests with their dog

Highland

Perth & Kinross

Scottish Borders

Stirling

Treats from Pubs-for-a-pint England

Brighton & Hove

Buckinghamshire

Cambridgeshire

152 Dogs are welcome in the bar & there's a nice garden behind

Cheshire

153 Water bowls & dog biscuits for your little tyke, plus an excellent pub walks book on sale

Cornwall

154 Information on dog-friendly beaches.

Cumbria

155 A whole woodland of new smells to discover – & the National Park on your doorstep

Devon

156 Dog treats behind the bar for well-behaved dogs & a massive OS map on the wall for circular walks from the door

157 Dogs are welcome guests in the bar & garden, with water bowls for the thirsty

158 A paddling stream behind to cool down weary paws… & biscuits on tap

159 Just what your little tyke is after: perfect dog-walking countryside

Gloucestershire

160 A warm welcome for dogs & a sausage for the well-behaved ones

161 Customised dog walk can be followed by biscuits & water bowls to be found in the bar

Hampshire

162 Great circular walks from the pub, through the National Park & along the river Itchen

163 Tasty dog biscuits from dog-loving hosts

164 A welcome for people as well as dogs (including big hairy ones)

165 Great for walks: public footpaths start straight outside the pub

Herefordshire

166 Walking opportunities galore

167 Roast beef tidbits & other doggie treats. Dogs welcome throughout

Hertfordshire

168 Fresh water & dog biscuits in the bar & the garden

169 Man's best friend shouldn't be left in the doghouse so come to the pub with your owner, for a pat & a nice bowl of water

170 Towels, blankets, treats, biscuits & water bowls. In the bar, a guide to all the best dog-friendly walks

London

171 A friendly welcome & a water bowl for your pooch

Norfolk

172 In the middle of the country, with a generous garden & big rooms with paw-friendly wood effect flooring

173 A range of homemade gourmet treats for the discerning pooch

174 After your owner has had a drink demand you're taken to Brancaster beach, for a paddle or a race along the shore

175 Treats at the bar

Somerset

176 Miles & miles of river, woodland and moorland to roam, right from the door

177 Wonderful walking country

Suffolk

178 Best walking a dog could ever have!

Sussex

179 A jar of doggie biscuits on the bar, & every day a doggie special on the blackboard menu

Warwickshire

180 Dog chews, water & plenty of fuss provided. Nearby dog-friendly fields for a run around, too

181 Dog bowls & biscuits on arrival

Wiltshire

182 Assorted dog biscuits in a jar on the bar – alongside a jar of lollies for children!

183 Stunning area with loads of walks around

184 Slow-roasted beef marrow bones for a very tasty treat

185 A pub is man's best friend – & man's best friend is always welcome here

186 Gravy bones from the landlord

Yorkshire

187 Local walks, beer garden, dog chews & water bowls

188 Marvellous walks straight outside the door

189 Infinite walks – river ones too, & snoozes in front of an open fire

Wales

Denbighshire

202 Beautiful big garden with lots of walks close by

Monmouthshire

203 Dogs may doze in the bar & romp in the big garden at the back

204 Offa's Dyke path 50 yards from the inn, with wonderful walks for dogs of all sizes

205 Acres of garden to explore, & exciting smells along a pretty river walk

Powys

206 Bowls of chicken on arrival!

207 The lovely Brecon Beacons are perfect for doggie exploration & we have maps to help

208 Grand walks from the door (keeping an eye out for cattle & sheep), & a black lab to play with

209 Treats aplenty from bones to pigs' ears. Wonderful walks in farming country (some on the lead)

210 Parts of the dining room open to dogs so they can stay with their owners if they get lonely

Wrexham

211 Dogs are very welcome in the tiled area of the bar – & dog bowls are provided

Photo: The Potting Shed Pub, entry 182

Dog socks and dressing gowns, sunglasses and feather boas – is there no limit to a dog owner's obsession? It seems not now dog dottiness has gone virtual

Doggie-Dating.co.uk

Where lonely hearts can find love – or just someone to play with in the park. Take your pet for virtual 'walkies' through the online list of eligible dogs and bitches, or 'sit' them down and register them and let the other dogs come. Strictly no cats.

PetTube.com

YouTube for pets. Settle in to the 'funniest pet videos'; join the mailing list to receive a different video every day. You can upload videos of your own pets' antics – and try and make it into the Hall of Fame. Or take a turn at captioning the Photo of the Week. Fun fun fun.

Facebook

Poppy Larsen, 21st April 2011:
"Last night I was attacked by two dogs on the Hotwells Road, my neck is sore, my tail is missing but I am beginning to recover… Think I'd better stick to Clifton."
Friend of Poppy:
"OOOoh nooo… Poor Poppy. Get well soon! I guess on the bright side, you learned a good lesson of sticking to the safe zone :)"

Poppy is a dog, one of 439,000 on Facebook in the UK (according to doggyloot.com). Why? So that her cuteness is global. With 118 friends, she's ahead of the game (the average has a mere 83). Of dog owners who use social media websites, 14% have set up Facebook for their best friends, a further 6% are on Twitter, 6% on Flickr, and 27% have a YouTube account. Note that Sockington the cat (US not UK) has 1.5 million Twitter fans.

PetYourDog.com

Follow the Dog Blog and take a look at Hot Dog Topics (includes some exciting celeb gossip). There's an excellent dog breeder directory and an extensive database of dog names and breeds.

Wuffstuff.com

Online community for 'wuffsters' and 'wuffstresses' (that's you). Share your photos and films, tap into dog news stories with a serious slant, ask questions, make friends, and pray your pooch will be chosen as Dog of the Month.

MyDogSpace.com

You may be in the 'Dog House' but you won't be left out in the cold. 'Tweet' (er, 'bark') your latest newsfeed updates, create a MySpace page, chase fun and famous Pet Tails, or search over 50,000 global listings on 'Yap' – a dog-friendly 'Yelp'.

Dogster.com

Bringing you expert advice on everything from breeds, food and training to toys, treats and accessories. The Daily Tips email brings a sample directly to your inbox and you can ask questions of the vets online. Join the 'Community' to create an online profile for your dog; battle it out to be Dog of the Day.

DrivingWithDogs.com

Take advantage of Jem the Border Collie's exploration of the British motorways to find innumerable walks, beaches, pubs and motorway services to suit you and Fido's needs. A pretty amazing dog resource – with maps.

Puppy Tweets

May we draw your attention to an exciting new product that lets your dog use Twitter? The chunky tag (suitable for the bigger dog only) is attached to the collar, the dog's eating/barking/romping is sensed by the tag and is instantly transmitted to a USB receiver on your home computer – which selects one of 500 pre-recorded tweets. If you can handle being responsible for such gems as "I've finally caught that tail I've been chasing and… OOUUUCHH!" then this is for you. The verbally dextrous may prefer to create their own tweets.

Photo: www.istockphoto.com/iztok noc

For many years Alastair Sawday Publishing has been 'greening' the business in different ways. Our aim is to reduce our environmental footprint as far as possible and with almost everything we do we have environmental implications in mind. In recognition of our efforts we won a Business Commitment to the Environment Award in 2005, a Queen's Award for Enterprise in the Sustainable Development category in 2006, and the Independent Publishers Guild Environmental Award in 2008.

The buildings

Beautiful as they were, our old offices leaked heat, used electricity to heat water and rooms, flooded spaces with light to illuminate one person, and were not ours to alter.

So in 2005 we created our own eco offices by converting some old barns to create a low-emissions building. Heating and lighting the building, which houses over 30 employees, now produces only 0.28 tonnes of carbon dioxide per year – a reduction of 35%. Not bad when you compare this with the six tonnes emitted by the average UK household. We achieved this through a variety of innovative and energy-saving building techniques, some of which are described below.

Insulation By laying insulating board 90mm thick immediately under the roof tiles and on the floor, and lining the inside of the building with plastic sheeting, we are now insulated even for Arctic weather, and almost totally air-tight.

Heating We installed a wood pellet boiler from Austria in order to be largely fossil-fuel free. The heat is conveyed by water to all corners of the building via an underfloor system.

Water We installed a 6,000-litre tank to collect rainwater from the roofs. This is pumped back, via an ultra-violet filter, to lavatories, shower and basins. There are also two solar thermal panels on the roof providing heat to the one hot-water cylinder.

Lighting We have a mix of low-energy lighting – task lighting and up lighting – and have installed three sun pipes.

Electricity Our electricity has long come from the Good Energy Company and is 100% renewable.

Photo above: Tom Germain
Photo opposite: Jackie King

Materials Virtually all materials are non-toxic or natural, and our carpets are made from (80%) Herdwick sheep wool from National Trust farms in the Lake District.

Doors and windows Outside doors and new windows are wooden, double-glazed and beautifully constructed in Norway. Old windows have been double-glazed.

More greenery

Besides having a building we are proud of, and which is pretty impressive visually, too, we work in a number of other ways to reduce the company's overall environmental footprint.

- office travel is logged as part of a carbon sequestration programme, and money for compensatory tree planting donated to SCAD in India for a tree-planting and development project

- we avoid flying and take the train for business trips wherever possible
- car sharing and the use of a company pool car (LPG fuelled) are part of company policy
- organic and Fair Trade basic provisions are used in the staff kitchen and organic and/or local food is provided by the company at all in-house events
- green cleaning products are used throughout
- kitchen waste is composted on our allotment
- the allotment is part of a community garden – alongside which we keep a small family of pigs and hens

However, becoming 'green' is a journey and, although we began long before most companies, we realise we still have a long way to go.

Many of you may want to stay in particularly environmentally friendly places. You may be passionate about local, organic or home-grown food. Or perhaps you want to know that the place you are staying in contributes to the community? To help you we have launched our Ethical Collection, so you can find the right place to stay and also discover how each owner is addressing these issues.

The Collection is made up of places going the extra mile, and taking the steps that most people have not yet taken, in one or more of the following areas:

Environment

Those making great efforts to reduce the environmental impact of their Special Place. We expect more than energy-saving light bulbs and recycling; here you will

find owners who make their own natural cleaning products, properties with solar hot water and biomass boilers, the odd green roof and a good measure of green elbow grease.

Community

Given to owners who use their property to play a positive role in their local and wider community. For example, by making a contribution from every guest's bill to a local fund, or running pond-dipping courses for local school children on their farm.

Food

Awarded to owners who make a real effort to source local or organic food, or to grow their own. We look for those who have gone out of their way to strike up relationships with local producers or to seek out organic suppliers. It is easier for an owner on a farm to produce their own eggs than for someone in the middle of a city, so we take this into account.

How it works

There is stacks more information on our website, www.sawdays.co.uk. You can read the answers each owner has given to our Ethical Collection questionnaire and get a more detailed idea of what they are doing in each area. We review each questionnaire carefully before deciding whether or not to give the award(s). The final decision is subjective; it is based not only on whether an owner ticks 'yes' to a question but also on the detailed explanation that accompanies each 'yes' or 'no' answer. For example, an owner who has tried as hard as possible to install solar water-heating panels, but has failed because of strict conservation planning laws, will be given some credit for their effort (as long as they are doing other things in this area).

We have tried to be as rigorous as possible and have made sure the questions are demanding. We have not checked out the claims of owners before making our decisions, but we do trust them to be honest. We are only human, as are they, so please let us know if you think we have made any mistakes.

The Ethical Collection is a new initiative for us, and we'd love to know what you think about it — email us at ethicalcollection@sawdays.co.uk or write to us. And remember that because this is a new scheme some owners have not yet completed their questionnaires — we're sure other places in the guide are working just as hard in these areas, but we don't yet know the full details.

Ethical Collection in this book
On the entry page of all places in the Collection we show which awards have been given.

A list of the places in our Ethical Collection is shown below, by entry number.

Environment
23 • 54 • 73 • 110 • 127 • 213

Community
5 • 24 • 54 • 105 • 108 • 127 • 142

Food
5 • 23 • 24 • 54 • 73 • 105 • 108 • 110 • 127 • 142 • 213

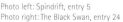

Photo left: Spindrift, entry 5
Photo right: The Black Swan, entry 24

THE BECKFORD ARMS

SPECIAL PLACES TO EAT & DRINK

Alastair
Sawday's

Pubs

Find handpicked pubs with passion on our dedicated website and iPhone app.

Alastair
Sawday's
Special Places to Eat & Drink

Pubs

"*Sawday's has never once let us down - invaluable.*"
Simon Hoggart, The Guardian

Alastair Sawday has been publishing books since 1994 finding Special Places to Stay in Britain and abroad. All our properties are inspected by us and are chosen for their charm and individuality and now with 25 titles to choose from there are plenty of places to explore. You can buy any of our books direct at a reader discount of 25%* on the RRP.

 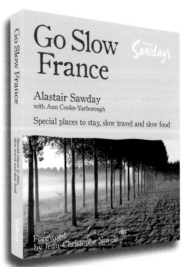

www.sawdays.co.uk/bookshop

List of titles:	RRP	Discount price
British Bed & Breakfast	£15.99	£11.99
Special Places to Stay in Britain for Garden Lovers	£19.99	£14.99
British Hotels and Inns	£15.99	£11.99
Pubs & Inns of England & Wales	£15.99	£11.99
Venues	£11.99	£8.99
Cotswolds	£9.99	£7.49
Wales	£9.99	£7.49
Dog-friendly Breaks in Britain	£14.99	£11.24
French Bed & Breakfast	£15.99	£11.99
French Self-Catering	£14.99	£9.74
French Châteaux & Hotels	£15.99	£11.99
Italy	£15.99	£11.99
Portugal	£12.99	£9.74
Spain	£15.99	£11.99
India	£11.99	£8.99
Go Slow England & Wales	£19.99	£14.99
Go Slow France	£19.99	£14.99

*postage and packaging is added to each order

How to order:
You can order online at: www.sawdays.co.uk/bookshop/
or call: +44(0)1275 395431

Sawday's CANOPY &STARS

A beautiful collection
of treehouses, yurts, cabins,
Gypsy caravans, wagons
and more - across Britain,
France, Spain and Portugal...

Everything you love about
Sawday's, but outdoors.

UNDER
CANVAS

OUT IN THE
WILDERNESS

UP IN THE
TREES

Wheelchair-accessible

At least one bedroom and bathroom accessible for wheelchair users. Phone for details.

Pets live here

Owners' pets live at the property.

Licensed

These places are licensed to sell alcohol.

Bikes

Bikes on the premises to hire or borrow.

Quick reference indices

Alastair Sawday's

'More than a bed for the night...'

Britain
France
Ireland
Italy
Portugal
Spain

www.sawdays.co.uk

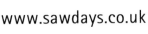

Self-Catering | B&B | Hotel | Pub | Canopy & Stars

Photo: The Wellington Arms, entry 165

Hotel & Self-catering   Norfolk

The Hoste Arms

Nelson was a local, but now it's farmers, fishermen and film stars who jostle at the bar and roast away on winter evenings in front of a roaring fire. In its 300-year history The Hoste has been a court house, a livestock market, a gallery and a brothel. These days it's more pleasure dome than inn and even on a grey February morning it was buzzing with life. The place has a genius of its own with warm bold colours, armchairs to sink into, panelled walls, a conservatory, its own art gallery. Fabulous food can be eaten anywhere and anytime, so dig into Brancaster mussels, Holkham venison, sticky toffee pudding. In summer life spills out onto tables at the front or you can dine on the terrace in the garden at the back. Rooms are all different: a tartan four-poster, an oak half-tester, leather sleigh beds in the Zulu wing, country-house elegance across the road in the Vine House; bathrooms are all predictably over the top (note the ladies' loo). Burnham Market is gorgeous, the north Norfolk coast is on your doorstep, there are vast sandy beaches for running off any excess – and don't miss afternoon tea!

Price	£122-£312. Half-board from £76.50 p.p. Dogs £10 per stay.	
Rooms	49 + 3: 34 twins/doubles & suites. Vine House: 7 doubles. Railway Inn: 7 doubles, 1 carriage. 3 railway cottages.	
Meals	Lunch from £6. Dinner, £25-£30.	
Closed	Never.	
	Christmas stockings & Easter Eggs...	

Emma Tagg
Market Place, Burnham Market,
King's Lynn PE31 8HD
Tel   +44 (0)1328 738777
Email   reception@hostearms.co.uk
Web   www.hostearms.co.uk

Entry 92   Map 7

stars. Tents, bell tents, treehouses, yurts, gypsy caravans and romantic log cabins – the choice is inspiring.

Bedrooms

We tell you if a room is a single, double, twin/double (with zip and link beds), suite (a room with space for seating), family (a double bed + single beds), or triple (three single beds) – and whether they are in the main building or in apartments, suites or cottages.

Bathrooms

The vast majority of bedrooms in this book are en suite. Only if a bedroom has a shared or a private-but-separate bathroom do we say so.

Sitting rooms

Most hotels have one or two communal areas, while most B&Bs offer guests the family sitting room to share, or provide a sitting room just for guests.

Self-catering places

Perfect independence for couples – and families – with dogs. Cottages, farmhouses, coach houses, studios, mills, barns – each and every one has been visited by us and found to be special. We don't include places we wouldn't stay in ourselves.

Canopy & Stars

For those who love to be at one with nature, welcome to our collection of beautiful, simple, quirky (and sometimes luxurious) places to sleep under the

Meals

Unless we say otherwise, breakfast is included, simple or extravagant. Some owners are fairly unbending about breakfast times, others are happy just to wait until you want it, or even bring it to you in your room.

Many B&Bs offer their guests dinner, usually an opportunity to get to know your hosts and to make new friends among the other guests. Note that meal prices are per person. Always book in advance.

Photo: Bridget Bishop (Boss)

11

Prices

Self-catering prices are mostly quoted per week. Each other entry gives a price PER ROOM per night for two. The price range covers a night in the cheapest room in low season to the most expensive in high season. Some owners charge more at certain times (during regattas and festivals, for example) and some owners ask for a minimum two nights at weekends. Others offer special deals for three-night stays. Prices quoted are those given to us for 2011–2013 but are not guaranteed. Double-check when booking.

At most of these places dogs go free, at others where there's a charge, we say so.

Bookings and cancellations

Sometimes you will be asked to pay a deposit. Some are non-refundable; some people may charge you for the whole of the booked stay in advance; and some cancellation policies are more stringent than others. It is also worth noting that some owners will take the money directly from your credit/debit card without contacting you to discuss it. So ask them to explain their cancellation policy clearly before booking to avoid a surprise. Always make sure you have written confirmation of all you have discussed.

Payment

All our owners take cash and UK cheques with a cheque card, and those who take credit cards have our credit card symbol. Check that your particular credit card is acceptable.

Photo: www.lucypopecom.

Tipping

Owners do not expect tips – but if you have been treated with extraordinary kindness, drop your hosts a line. If you are on Facebook or Twitter, your can sing their praises from our website www.sawdays.co.uk. Find their Special Place, then 'share' or 'tweet.'

Arrivals and departures

Say roughly what time you will arrive (normally after 4pm; for inns, after 6pm), as most hosts like to welcome you personally. Be on time if you have booked dinner. If, despite best efforts, you are delayed, phone to give warning.

12

Closed

When given in months this means the whole of the month stated. In our 'Pubs-for-a-pint' section Closed means the days or times of day the pub is not open.

Feedback

The accuracy of our books depends on what you, as well as our inspectors, tell us. Your feedback is invaluable and we always act upon comments. Tell us whether your stay has been a joy or not, if the atmosphere was great or stuffy, the owners cheery or bored. Importantly,

Photo above: Hornacott, entry 20
Photo opposite: Chris Banks (Daisy)

a lot of new places come to us via our readers, so keep telling us about new places you've discovered. Just visit our sites:

www.sawdays.co.uk/recommend
for hotels, inns, B&Bs and self-catering properties
www.canopyandstars.co.uk
for glamping/camping retreats.

Complaints

Please do not tell us if the bedside light was inadequate, the hairdryer was broken or the bedroom was cold. Tell the owner instead, and ask them to do something about it. Most owners are more than happy to correct problems and will bend over backwards to help. If you think things have gone seriously awry, do tell us.

Symbols

There is an explanation of the symbols used for our Special Places to Stay on the inside back cover of the book. Use them as a guide, not as a statement of fact. However, things do change: bikes may be under repair or a new pool may have been put in. If an owner does not have the symbol that you're looking for, it's worth discussing your needs.

Note that the symbol shows places that are happy to accept children of all ages; it does not mean that they will have cots and high chairs. Many who say no to children do so not because they don't like them but because they may have a steep

stair, an unfenced pond or they find balancing the needs of mixed age groups too challenging.

The  symbol is given when the owners have their own pet on the premises. It may not be a cat! But it is there to warn you that you may be greeted by a dog, serenaded by a parrot, or indeed sat upon by a cat.

Quick reference indices

At the back of the book we list properties that are licensed, have pets of their own, are wheelchair-friendly or that have bikes to hire or borrow.

Pubs-for-a-pint sections

Entries 145-189 and 202-211 are pubs to visit during your stays in our Special Places. These are dog-friendly pubs that we've visited and like; we have not inspected the bedrooms in these pubs.

The symbols used at the foot of these entries apply to the bar and not (should the pub have them) to its bedrooms.

Sawday's Travel Club

At the back of the book we list those Special Places that offer something extra to Club members. It may be money off your room price, a bottle of wine or a basket of home-grown produce.

Treats

Dog treats provided by owners are shown on each entry and listed at the back of the book for a bit of fun. How about a poached egg on wholemeal dog biscuits garnished with crispy bacon rind, or a coastal walk straight from the door? Or a tour of the grounds from the resident lab, and a bone from the village butcher? Many dogs like to share their favourite treats and walks, and some owners are willing dog

Photo above: The Bath Arms at Longleat, entry 128
Photo opposite: www.istockphoto.com/Caitlin Cahill